TIMELY
TEACHINGS *Gold Mountain Monastery in the early 1970s*

VENERABLE MASTER **HSUAN HUA**

**Buddhist Text
Translation Society**
CALIFORNIA

Timely Teachings
Gold Mountain Monastery in the early 1970s
Venerable Master Hsuan Hua

Library of Congress Cataloging-in-Publication Data
Hsüan Hua, 1908-1995.
   Timely teachings : Gold Mountain Monastery in
the early 1970s / Hsuan Hua.
      p. cm.
   ISBN 978-0-88139-938-7
   1. Religious life—Buddhism. 2. Buddhism—
Doctrines. I. Title.

   BQ5410.H785 2008
   294.3'444—dc22

2007027743

Primary Translation:
Bhikshunis Heng Hsien, Heng Yin 恆賢, 恆音
Reviewed by: Bhikshuni Heng Yi 恆異
Edited by: Upasaka David Rounds 果舟
Certified by: Bhikshuni Heng Ch'ih 恆持

Published by
Buddhist Text Translation Society

1777 Murchison Drive, Burlingame CA 94010-4504
www.drba.org
Printed in Taiwan

TIMELY TEACHINGS

Gold Mountain Monastery in the early 1970s

VENERABLE MASTER HSUAN HUA

TABLE OF CONTENTS

I MASTER-DISCIPLE RELATIONSHIP

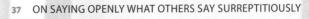

II TEACHING & TRANSFORMING

TABLE of CONTENTS

III MONASTIC LIFE

IV THE FOUR ASSEMBLIES

V LAYPEOPLE

TABLE OF CONTENTS

VI KARMIC CONDITIONS

VII AFFLICTIONS

VIII CULTIVATION

TABLE of CONTENTS

IX STUDY HABITS

X LECTURING ON THE SUTRAS

TABLE OF CONTENTS

APPENDIX

The Venerable Master with disciples in Taiwan, 1974

PREFACE

This book opens a window onto the daily life of Gold Mountain Monastery in San Francisco during the early years of the Venerable Master Hsüan Hua's ministry in America. In the summer of 1968, the Venerable Master began a series of lectures on the great scriptures of the Mahayana, completing first the *Śūraṅgama Sutra*, then the *Lotus Sutra*, and finally the *Avataṃsaka [Flower Adornment] Sutra* in 1979, and he continued lecturing regularly until his gradual retirement in the late 1980's. These incomparable lectures were the first of their kind to be heard in any Western country. In the early years his audience consisted largely of young Americans like myself, each of us drawn to him by some lucky and inexplicable circumstance, and his lectures were one of his many means of molding Buddhist practitioners out of our unpromising American clay. We were the fortunate ones who had the opportunity, and the desire born of a deep intuition, to return again and again into the presence of this extraordinary being. Once there, he instructed us, cajoled us, entertained us, scolded us, comforted us, fed and housed us, always leading us in our commitment to a pure life, always urging us forward in our spiritual practice—in short, teaching us, as he would put it, how to be human beings.

All this required time, both his and ours, and the prime time was 7:30 every evening, when, after a formal request in the traditional manner, he would come downstairs to lecture on the sutras. But the sutras were not his only topic. Any problem among us, any event that had surprised or distressed us, any visitor welcome or otherwise, any antic of a wayward disciple, any plan, any temple business, any news concerning one of us, any report from someone who had

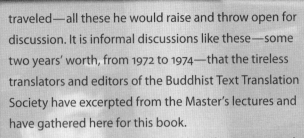

traveled—all these he would raise and throw open for
discussion. It is informal discussions like these—some
two years' worth, from 1972 to 1974—that the tireless
translators and editors of the Buddhist Text Translation
Society have excerpted from the Master's lectures and
have gathered here for this book.

In his informal teachings, such as these presented
in the pages that follow, one hears the voice of the
Master perhaps more clearly than in his formal lectures. His brilliant intelligence, his transcendent play-
fulness, his simple kindness, his deep common sense,
his unmatchable wit and effortless eloquence—all
these were present in discussions of the most ordinary
matters. For the Master, nothing was permitted to be
ordinary; everything was an occasion to try once again
to move a disciple another inch towards wisdom. One
can see, too, in the excerpts that follow, how insistent
the Master was in involving his disciples, both lay and
monastic, in the public discussion and resolution of
whatever issue lay at hand. His goal was not primarily
to solve problems but to turn every difficulty into an
opportunity to teach compassion and wisdom and to
build a spiritual community. He was loath to impose
his will and had no interest in blind obedience. What
he required of us was that we be open, straightforward, truthful, unselfish, and vigorous—that, in
his words, we try our best. In return he gave us the
greatest of his gifts: simply that, despite our many fail-
ures and the many opportunities given him to move
on, he stuck with us.

David Rounds (Guo Zhou 果舟)
February 24, 2005

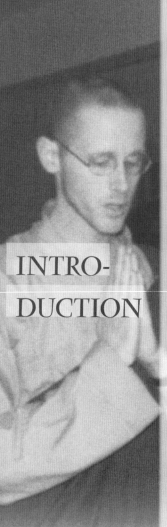

INTRO-DUCTION

The first Gold Mountain Monastery on 15th Street in the Mission District of San Francisco was ready to move into and renovate sometime during the 98-day winter *chan* session that was being held at the Buddhist Lecture Hall on Waverly Place in Chinatown, San Francisco from November 15, 1970 to February 20, 1971. Thus some of the participants who had skills and/or brawn that would be needed for the renovation project volunteered to pack up and move to the new site on 15th street. Other participants who had dedicated themselves to the fourteen-week *chan* session remained in the Buddhist Lecture Hall and maintained the rigorous schedule to its completion. Both groups, each heroic in its own way, received the Master's blessing and support.

The Master, who kept his multitasking unobtrusive, expanded the scope of his duties accordingly. From his role at the Buddhist Lecture Hall of guiding our meditation and telling us inspiring accounts of eminent monastics in the history of Buddhism, he added the role of guiding the reconstruction of Gold Mountain and began instructing us in how monastic life works, what discipline and deportment is essential for monastics to embody, what roles laypeople should fulfill, how to be thrifty with and protect the property of the Triple Jewel, and so forth.

By 1972, Gold Mountain Monastery was up and running and housed the monks and laymen, while the nuns and laywomen moved eventually to the Washington Street women's monastery, located in Pacific Heights overlooking the western Bay and Golden Gate Bridge. The Master named this facility the International Institute for the Translation of Buddhist Texts and indeed many of the early publications of the

Buddhist Text Translation Society were prepared at this location.

The Master started the *Avataṃsaka* [*Flower Adornment*] lectures at Gold Mountain by speaking full commentaries to the Preface and Prologue by National Master Qing Liang and by 1972 had begun the commentary on the sutra text. But he continued to sprinkle instructions for daily life and practice in his lectures, not only in the *Avataṃsaka* (*Flower Adornment*) *Sutra*, but throughout his decades of commentating on the sutras. For instance, during this 1972-1974 period, when two of his monastic disciples decided to conduct a bowing pilgrimage from San Francisco, California, to Marblemount, Washington, the Master often spoke about their practice and progress during evening lectures and added his insights so that we who were not bowing gained benefit in learning from their experiences.

The Buddhist Text Translation Society members working on the Master's commentary on the *Avataṃsaka Sutra* decided to compile these special instructions into an ongoing series of Timely Teachings, with this first volume covering the years 1972-1974. These Timely Teachings have been collected and edited with the aim of providing a user-friendly manual detailing many aspects of life and practice within Mahayana Buddhism and emphasizing the traditions established by Master Hua as he brought Buddhism into the West. Those readers who spend some time absorbing these instructions will reap the rewards of this gentle guidance backed by astute wisdom.

Bhikshuni Heng Chih
August 2006

THE EIGHT GUIDELINES OF THE BUDDHIST TEXT TRANSLATION SOCIETY

I.   A volunteer must free him/herself from the motives of personal fame and profit.

II. A volunteer must cultivate a respectful and sincere attitude free from arrogance and conceit.

III. A volunteer must refrain from aggrandizing his/her work and denigrating that of others.

IV. A volunteer must not establish him/herself as the standard of correctness and suppress the work of others with his or her fault-finding.

V.   A volunteer must take the Buddha-mind as his/her own mind.

VI. A volunteer must use the wisdom of Dharma-Selecting Vision to determine true principles.

VII. A volunteer must request Virtuous Elders in the ten directions to certify his/her translations.

VIII. A volunteer must endeavor to propagate the teachings by printing sutras, *śāstra* texts, and *vinaya* texts when the translations are certified as being correct.

HOW TO
USE
THIS
BOOK

This book can be considered a companion volume to the series titled *Flower Adornment Sutra: A Commentary by Venerable Master Hsuan Hua*. When the Venerable Master lectured on the *Flower Adornment Sutra*, he often interspersed instructions to his disciples in the commentary of the sutra text itself. This is a compilation of those instructions given during the sutra lectures that are not directly relevant to the sutra text but shed light on how the Venerable Master taught and transformed his disciples or provide interesting historical background.

These instructions have been grouped under twelve different topics. To provide historical context, each entry is labeled with the date and day it was given, as well as the chapter, page, and paragraph where they were extracted from in the multi-volume series *Flower Adornment Sutra: A Commentary by Venerable Master Hsuan Hua* (shown in the header of each page).

Chapter One Part Two | page 62 | following paragraph 1

I. Master-Disciple Relationship

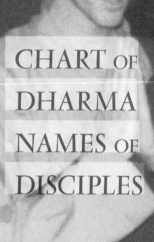

The religious names of many of the Venerable Master Hsuan Hua's disciples appear in this book. Lay disciples receive a Dharma name beginning with "Guo" when they take refuge. Ordained monastics have two names, an ordination name beginning with "Heng" by which they are addressed in general, and a Dharma name beginning with "Guo" that only the Master uses. For the sake of clarity the "Guo" and "Heng" names are matched in the chart below and the disciples are classified as ordained monks (Bhikshus), ordained nuns (Bhikshunis), novice nuns (Shramanerikas), laymen (Upāsakas) and laywomen (Upāsikās). Note that a person addressed as "Guo So-and-so" by the Master could either be a monastic or a layperson, so this chart can be used to identify them. The romanized Chinese names of disciples are spelled using *pinyin*, unless they currently use another spelling.

CHART OF DHARMA NAMES OF DISCIPLES

Ordained Monks	Dharma Name	Ordination Name
	Guo Qian	Heng Qian
	Guo Su	Heng Chao
	Guo Ning	Heng Jing
	Guo Xian	Heng Shou
	Guo Yi	Heng Ding
	Guo Hu	Heng Shoou
Bhikshu	Guo Meng	Heng Bai
	Guo Yu	Heng Ju
	Guo Zhan	Heng Guan
	Guo Dao	Heng Yo
	Guo Yi	Heng Lu
	Guo Hang	Heng Kong
	Guo Hui	Heng Lai

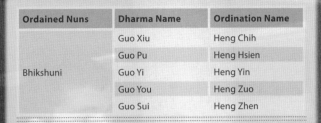

Ordained Nuns	Dharma Name	Ordination Name
	Guo Xiu	Heng Chih
	Guo Pu	Heng Hsien
Bhikshuni	Guo Yi	Heng Yin
	Guo You	Heng Zuo
	Guo Sui	Heng Zhen

Novice Nuns	Dharma Name
Shramanerika	Guo Man
	Guo Mo

Laymen	Dharma Name
	Guo Gui
	Guo Tong
	Guo Zhou
Upāsaka	Guo Rong
	Guo Xian
	Guo Yang

Laywomen	Dharma Name
	Guo Jin
	Guo Tong
	Guo Wu
Upāsikā	Guo Ming
	Guo Yao
	Guo Zhao
	Guo Fang

The Venerable Master having lunch with disciples,
including Bhikshus Heng Ju and Heng Yo during their Three Steps One Bow pilgrimage in 1973

I | Master-Disciple Relationship

NOVEMBER 8, 1972 | WEDNESDAY EVENING

On Cultivating Blessings & Wisdom

Cultivation of blessings brings about the adornment of the fine hallmarks and characteristics. Cultivation of wisdom gets rid of delusion. Why are we deluded? Because we haven't cultivated blessings and wisdom. Why are we poor? Because we haven't cultivated blessings and wisdom. I am using my true mind to speak true Dharma for you. If you can accept the true Dharma, you will truly be able to cultivate. Therefore, you must be sincere. Don't engage in fault-finding. It is extremely foolish to always be finding faults in others.

Cultivators must be courageous and vigorous. Be true cultivators. Every day you should work harder and be more vigorous. Don't engage in gossiping about rights and wrongs, so that day after day you grow more and more lax and retreat. That would be very dangerous.

I speak on this topic today because I perceive these causes and circumstances. Right now, none of you has these problems. But I see that these problems could develop in the future, and so I have brought them up today to prevent their arising in the future. ⊣

DECEMBER 7, 1972 | THURSDAY EVENING

On Training Tigers with Horns

In this country, I advocate reciting the Buddha's name as well as investigating *chan*. Why? Because I want to train "tigers with horns." When people see those tigers, they will be scared. Tigers are fierce to begin with, but with horns on their heads, they are even fiercer! In the future, all of you have to be horned tigers. That doesn't mean you should go out and gobble people up. It means that you should go everywhere to propagate the Buddhadharma, and that when the demon kings see you, they will behave themselves. You must subdue the celestial demons and people who follow wrong paths.

This is an analogy. Don't think that tigers will really grow horns on their heads and prowl up and down the mountain. There is a saying, "To practice *chan* and the Pure Land is to be like a tiger with horns." Someone who investigates *chan* and also recites the Buddha's name is like a horned tiger. That is what the analogy stands for. ⊣

DECEMBER 31, 1972 | SUNDAY EVENING

On a Teacher's Aspirations for his Disciples

Now that you are studying German, you should put in real effort. Don't think, "Well, the teacher is a nun, and I am a monk. How can I study under her?" If you have that kind of an attitude, you are finished; nothing can be made of you. You are like "rotten wood which cannot be carved, or a wall of dung and earth which cannot be painted." Rotten wood is decayed and full of holes made by insects. No matter how many ornate flowers you try to carve in this wood, it won't look good. If you are the first to go bad, you are a piece of rotten wood.

Guo Meng is basically very diligent and loves to learn. But after his trip to New York, he said he didn't want to study Sanskrit any more and only wanted to study Chinese. Wouldn't you say this was foolish? When you eat, you take bread, butter, peanut butter, and other things. Why is it that you stick to one subject and refuse to study others? In eating, you want to eat some oil cakes, or Italian food, or Mexican cooking, or French cuisine. You think of all sorts of ways to make different dishes. Why don't you do the same when it comes to studying? Such a stance is extremely foolish. You only know how to eat, not how to study. Don't imitate pigs; they have no opportunity to study like you do. When you try to teach them something, they don't get it. They don't know how to do much of anything except eat. Having eaten, they sleep.

I. Master-Disciple Relationship

All of you are talented people — dragons and elephants within the Dharma. Why do I encourage you to study different languages? It's because I don't know many languages, and so everywhere I go I am at a disadvantage. I have to take flak from others. Even here in America, I have to take it from you young Americans. When I went to Australia, I had to take it from Australian kids. Everywhere I went, people bullied me because I didn't understand their language. I look upon this with great regret. And therefore, although I myself do not have much talent, I want my disciples to be talented. As the saying goes, "Azure comes from blue, but surpasses blue." There's another saying, "Most top-ranking scholarly disciples did not have top-ranking scholarly teachers." Students may become top scholars, even though their teacher isn't one.

By the same token, you are studying the Buddhadharma now, although your teacher is a ghost ridden with karmic obstacles. Why am I bringing this up? Because the topic under discussion is "living beings' faculties." My faculties may be such that I'm a karmic-obstacle ghost; however, with your faculties, you may become Bodhisattvas. But for now, you must undergo a period of training before you reach that level of accomplishment.

MARCH 18, 1973 | SUNDAY NOON

On Obvious and Subtle
Instructions to Disciples

Next week, it's not known which day, I will be going to Brazil. However, the lecture series will go on as usual. Guo Ning [See Editor's note on page 8] can lecture in the evening; the other monastics can rotate in lecturing during the daytime. Save one evening for the laypeople to take turns lecturing. Probably Saturday or Sunday evening would be best, since most of the laypeople will have time on those evenings.

So, that's how it will be: Guo Ning will lecture on the *Śūraṅgama Sutra* in the evenings; the other monastic disciples can lecture during the day. Since many people have not heard the *Śūraṅgama Sutra*, they can come and listen to it being explained. And Guo Ning can talk on Sunday at noon as well.

Whoever you are, you should listen to instructions given by Guo Ning and Guo Zhan. These two people should not fall asleep at the same time. If one person goes to sleep, the other person should stay awake. You should work things out among yourselves and take turns in sleeping. Watch over the monastery and do not lose track of it.

Although I am going to Brazil, I hope that I can come back soon, since I'm not through entertaining you young Americans. So I will come back quickly. Little Guo Fang [Editor's note: a toddler at the time.] in particular is a lot of fun. If I try to say goodbye without giving her candy, she says, "No, No." However, if I hand her a piece of candy, she willingly says, "Bye-bye!"

No matter what happens, work things out among yourselves; do not develop an attitude of dependence. Guo Ning is very bright. The other day he asked me about a principle in the *Śūraṅgama Sutra* but I ignored him. All I would say in reply was, "You ask me when I am here, but whom will you ask when I am not around?" All of you must learn to stand on your own. However, do not put on special airs. Don't claim, "Above in heaven and below, I alone am honored. Nobody can watch over me." If people cannot watch over you, they will ignore you and not pay attention to you. That's the way to deal with evil-natured monks: silently ignore them. Since there are two such evil-natured monks in our midst, you should show your disapproval of them by ignoring them.

Originally Guo Su made the decision to become a monk quite quickly, but he has become foolish and is now doing confused things. Yesterday, he ended the session prematurely. He started out all right, but did not bring the session to a complete close. He goofed off. Thereupon I told him, "A monk as lazy as you should quickly go off to rebirth. That would be the best, since you are of no use to the world."

[Editor's Note:

A Send-off for Dhyāna Cultivator Heng Jing ("Tranquil") [Guo Ning] as He Sets Out to Propagate the Dharma in Taiwan and Hong Kong

> In the great void the Proper Dharma
> ought to rise and flourish.

For the Teaching's sake, do not fear suffering.
East and West are not beyond a single
　　transformed source.
North and South do not transcend divisions
　　of the sixth consciousness.
The mind, Buddhas, and living beings
　　fundamentally are not different;
Yet the extent of awakening in all creatures
　　may range from deep to shallow.
Use patience, apply vigor, develop *prajñā pāramitā*.
Precepts and *samādhi* must also be
　　practiced with diligence.

Today the fields of science, technology, and communications have expanded, making great progress. Most people think that this is extraordinary; I consider it quite commonplace. These developments are but a portion of what is found in the Buddha's teachings. It is unfortunate that people who do not know the full extent of those wonderful principles become fascinated with just one aspect.

Now you should do what is difficult to do; endure what is hard to endure. Base yourself on the heroic vigor that great vows inspire; forget yourself for the sake of the Dharma. Rescue the many beings with whom you have affinities. I urge you to be at peace and exhort you to remain tranquil!

] 日

JULY 29, 1973 | SUNDAY NOON

On Everything Being a Test

[Upon the Master's return from a trip to South America] Good and wise teachers! All of you have received the aid of the Buddha's light. Therefore, upon my return from South America, I see that you are still very sincerely coming to Gold Mountain Monastery to study Buddhism.

In studying Buddhism, do not have an attitude of dependence. If you have an attitude of dependence, you will never be able to stand on your own. Therefore, my trip to South America was also a real test for all of you. I spoke a verse for you some years ago. Although the verse contains only twenty characters, you should never forget it. Remember it every day, every hour, every minute and every second. What does the verse says?

> Everything's a test
>   to see what you will do.
> Mistaking what's before your face,
>   you'll have to start anew.

Do you want to start anew? Ask yourselves. Your teacher cannot end your birth and death for you. The Sangha, the Dharma, the Buddha—they cannot end your birth and death on your behalf. You yourself have to end your own birth and death. Stand on your own. Do not have an attitude of dependence. Do not be like young children always demanding milk or candy, expecting your parents to spoon-feed you.

This time, when I went to South America for an extended period of time, you were being weaned. That was a test to see if you could still survive. It's been over four months, but you haven't starved to death. Many of you have developed a little skill in standing on your own. However, some of you have sizably increased your skill in being lazy, as well. You should increase your skill of independence, but you should decrease your skill of being lazy. Then you will accord with the Middle Way. ◁

I. Master-Disciple Relationship

On Dharma Spoken Upon Belated Request

During lunch, I asked you: Did you want me to speak Dharma today, or did you want to pick a representative from your midst to speak Buddhadharma? You all turned mute at that time. No one spoke up. You didn't say you wanted me to speak, and you didn't select someone from your group to speak. Therefore, I thought you had agreed by silent consent that a high American Sangha member would speak, and so I did not prepare to speak.

But after you finished reciting sutras and bowing to the Buddhas, some of you "dug a well at the last minute since you were thirsty," and so a few of you came upstairs and invited me to speak. That was too late! I had not made any preparations to talk. But you almost forced me into speaking, and that was very unnatural. I don't like to do things when they are forced upon me. Nor do I like to do things in too spontaneous a manner, since that is the theory of a heterodox sect. Neither forced nor spontaneous—skill should be applied between these two extremes.

The dozen or so of you saw that your teacher has come back, so you are determined to give him some work to do, not allowing him any leisure time. You must have gotten together and reasoned: "How can we allow him to rest? That's impossible." Therefore, right after my return I have to slave like a horse or ox, and speak some meaningless words for you.

Although the words are meaningless, if you understand them, they will have some meaning. If you don't understood, then they will have no meaning. But, if you are enlightened, "General discussions and detailed descriptions all express the ultimate truth." As for those who are not yet enlightened, no matter what I say, you will react with, "Huh, what did he say? Did you hear what was said? I don't think I fell asleep, how is it that I didn't hear the Master speak?" Then my words will be meaningless for you.

And so, forced by circumstances, I am speaking a few words for you. My message is: Stand up on your own. Do not develop an attitude of dependence on your teacher. If you always like to rely on others, you are not a hero! You are not a true disciple of Śākyamuni Buddha. Śākyamuni Buddha was a great hero, the teacher of gods and humans. Why do we want to be Buddhist disciples who lack gumption? We should model ourselves after our original teacher, Śākyamuni Buddha, and his heroic spirit and magnanimous actions that made him the teacher of gods and humans.

Therefore, all of you should work hard on your own. Do not be overly dependent on your teacher. Get rid of your greed, anger, and delusion. Diligently cultivate precepts, *samādhi* and wisdom; put to rest greed, anger, and delusion. The bottom line is: *Cut off your desire*! Do not allow even a hair's worth to remain! ⊣

I. Master-Disciple Relationship

On Issuing Test Results

It's been a long time since I had the opportunity to investigate the teachings of the sutras with you. Today we have a good opportunity to look into the sutras and the Buddha's teachings together. My trip to South America was a test. That is why when I talked to you right upon coming back I spoke the following verse:

> Everything's a test
> To see what you will do.
> Mistaking what's before your face,
> You'll have to start anew.

Who among you should start anew, or not start anew, you should know yourselves. During my absence from San Francisco, some people behaved in a confused way, while others practiced according to the teachings. As for some of you, not only did you not practice according to the teachings, you did away with the teachings totally and did not rely on them to practice. You revealed your delusion—your real nature revealed itself, from which I have come to recognize your true features. When I was gone, those who were prone to laziness gave in to laziness; those who were prone to indulgence gave in to indulgence. Those who wanted to be *gandharva* kings became *gandharva* kings. Those who wanted to be *gandharva* citizens became *gandharva* citizens. Whatever your aspirations were, they are now fully revealed. Your true features are exposed. Now let us see what you will do. ⊣

AUGUST 15, 1973 | WEDNESDAY EVENING

On Correcting One's Own Mistakes

Since I am reciting the text from memory, sometimes I make mistakes. You should tell me when I do. Since none of you spoke up, I have corrected my own mistake. ◁

SEPTEMBER 2, 1973 | SUNDAY NOON

On Welcoming Varying Viewpoints

All people love their stinking skin-bags. [Editor's note: their physical bodies]; they simply can't bear to give them up. Does anyone have on opinion about that statement? You can bring up your opinion and we'll discuss it together. Nobody has an opinion? Well, I've got one: whenever I speak incorrectly, you can object and bring it up for discussion. Anyone is welcome to bring up his or her own viewpoint. We can use it as we would a mirror — as a point of reference. ◁

SEPTEMBER 2, 1973 | SUNDAY NOON

On Encouraging New Students

Guo Xian, an American, began his study here at this year's summer session. And he is already able to write the Ten Powers and recite them from memory in Chinese. I examined him impromptu this morning when I passed him on the stairs. "What are the Ten Powers?" I asked. He was not taken off-guard in the least—he just stood there and recited them for me in Chinese!

You think it over. Some of you have been studying here for several years and still cannot remember that list. Isn't that curious? ◁

I. Master-Disciple Relationship

SEPTEMBER 2, 1973 | SUNDAY NOON

On Learning from Disciples

I heard Guo Xian recite the Ten Powers this morning, but I don't know if he can explain them. So now I will be quiet and let him explain all ten — from the first one: the wisdom of understanding what is and is not true, all the way to the last one: the wisdom of severing habits that started *kalpas* ago. Now I will listen and learn from you. I really do learn from you disciples; don't assume that I know everything. ◁

SEPTEMBER 4, 1973 | TUESDAY EVENING

On Searching for Number One

Right now at Gold Mountain Monastery we are looking for someone to be number one. But this isn't easy. Someone who has no temper, doesn't get angry, and is not ignorant can be number one. Anyone who is without afflictions can be number one. Someone who is afflicted all day long cannot be number one. People who get afflicted have ghosts in their minds. People who are happy have Bodhisattvas in their minds.

Moreover, you all ought to talk less. Don't talk so much. Those who practice the Path do not casually open their mouths to say even one sentence, unless they are lecturing on the sutras. Talk less, and recite the Buddha's name more.

Do not have a temper. Then you can be number one. Whoever wants to be number one should quickly turn afflictions and ignorance around. I'm not the one who is looking for number one. Don't think that your teacher is looking for a number one disciple. That's not the case. Rather, the Buddhas and Bodhisattvas of the three periods of time and the ten directions are looking for a number one right within this *bodhimaṇḍa*—someone who will become enlightened first. ⊣

I. Master-Disciple Relationship

OCTOBER 5, 1973 | FRIDAY EVENING, AT WASHINGTON STREET

On Being Blessed with Good Food

Tomorrow two Dharma Masters are coming to Gold Mountain Monastery for lunch, and we will have an extremely fine vegetarian meal. Just the thought of it makes my mouth water. When you taste it tomorrow, it will be such that you wouldn't even feel the pain if someone sliced your ears off. That's how delicious it will be. If you don't believe it, just invite your family and friends to come and sample the flavors. The more people who come, the better. Each of you is welcome to bring a hundred friends. If each person brings a hundred, then there will be "a hundred blessings assembling together." Do you understand? Someone comments: "Our Teacher is always joking." When I joke, I am speaking the truth. And when I speak the truth, sometimes I express it in a joke. ⊣

OCTOBER 12, 1973 | FRIDAY EVENING

On Pointing out Mistakes

If there are errors in what I have said, please do not be polite — tell me about them. But if I haven't lectured incorrectly, there's no need to be hypercritical and deliberately find fault, which would also be a mistake. We should investigate in accord with the Middle Way. Tonight we also include our guest Dharma Master, who has just arrived. If I have made errors in lecturing, please do not begrudge your pearls and jade — that is, your precious opinions — but point my mistakes out to me. ◁

On Analyzing a Dilemma

Master: Do you understand?

Disciple: No.

Master: Then why didn't you speak up?

Disciple: I was waiting for the Master to speak.

Master: Since you were waiting for me, I'm asking you. None of them were waiting for me, so I'm not asking them. And by the way, since you wanted to get married, you got married. Isn't your wish fulfilled? Tell me.

Disciple: I want to be married but I also want to become a monk. I don't know what to do.

Master: Aren't these your own wishes and desires? Why don't you do whichever you want to do more? What is it you want to do most? Become a monk?

Disciple: I want to become a Buddha.

Master: To become a Buddha you have to cultivate. If you don't cultivate, and you can't give up your wife, how can the Buddha fulfill your wish? Tell me. Ah, the fish looks good to eat, but so does the bear paw, so you put the fish in your mouth and also the bear paw. Yet your mouth doesn't have that much room. How can you stuff so much in there? Bear paws and fish are both culinary delicacies, but they can't be savored together. You would like to have a wife, and also to become a Buddha. If your wish for a wife far outweighs your wish to be a Buddha, you can figure out for yourself why you don't reach Buddhahood! ◁

OCTOBER 15, 1973 | MONDAY EVENING

On Vows

Two of the monks at Gold Mountain Monastery want to make a strange vow to go on a pilgrimage bowing once every three steps as a prayer for world peace. They want to bow all the way to Seattle, more than a thousand miles from here. When Guo Yu wanted to make this vow, I didn't want him to. When Guo Dao asked to go along as a Dharma protector, I didn't grant him permission either to start with. However, I myself have a vow which says, "Everything's O.K." If I didn't allow them to go, that would not be "O.K." And for it not to be O.K. would mean I did not fulfill my vow. Hence, the objection could be made, "You say everything's O.K., but only the 'K' is left, and you've dropped the 'O'." Due to that consideration, I had to say, "O.K., O.K., go ahead. If Bhikshus want to go, that's fine, and it's fine for laymen to go too. Go ahead and go."

But Guo Zhan was very upset. Why? He's going to lose an assistant. He had trained Guo Dao in all the various jobs connected with *Vajra Bodhi Sea* [Editor's note: a monthly journal begun in 1970 and still being published to date] including developing photographs, and now Guo Dao wants to leave the monastery to go on this pilgrimage. Well, Guo Zhan has been inventing all kinds of ways to keep Guo Dao from leaving, so today I thought of a method to retain him. I asked Guo Hui if he would go instead. But, the method didn't work. There was no way to prevent Guo Dao [Editor's note: Dao means "Path"] from walking his Path.

The Path must be walked; if it's not walked, it's not the Path. Therefore, there was nothing I could do.

[Editor's note:

The following exhortations were written by the Venerable Master Hua, Abbot of Gold Mountain Monastery, on the occasion of sending Bhikshu Heng Ju and Bhikshu Heng Yo off on their journey to complete their vows (October 16, 1973).

A Send-off for Dhyāna Cultivator Heng Ju, Who Has Vowed to Bow Every Three Steps Seeking for World Peace

At Gold Mountain Dhyāna Monastery, in the United States of America, the Sangha is young and numerous. They concentrate on safeguarding the proper Dharma, and each one has his particular good points. Now you have made a vow never made before, and will practice the conduct of Sages, which has never before been practiced, bowing every three steps to the Jewels of the Buddha, Dharma, and Sangha throughout the ten directions.

Because your sincerity and earnestness in seeking for world peace is genuine, you will certainly evoke a magnificent response. Although your initial resolve came easily, it may be difficult to fulfill your vows. Don't give up; remain firm, sincere, and constant. The thousand miles over which you will pass is only one small step within the Dharma Realm. Be resolved not to cease until you have reached your goal. Raise up your spirits!

I leave you this verse of parting

> Practicing what is difficult to practice
> is the conduct of the Sage;

Enduring what is hard to endure is
    the genuine patience.
All Buddhas throughout the ten directions
    have walked down this road,
And the eighty thousand Bodhisattvas
    have followed right along.
Blow the magnificent Dharma conch,
    and raise up your cry;
Shake your precious tin staff; transform stingy greed.
Your work complete, the result full,
    return midst songs of triumph.
Then I'll give my disciple a meal of berry pie.

Instructions to Dhyāna Cultivator Heng Yo, Who Protects and Aids Cultivator Guo Yu as He Fulfills His Resolve to Bow to the Buddhas, Seeking for World Peace for All Living Beings:

From start to finish, don't waver; when faced with difficulties, don't change. Acting as his protector, help him to realize the power of his vows. The ancient worthy ones most esteemed the ability to forget oneself and safeguard others. In the present day, worthy ones are rare. Among the practices of a Bodhisattva, this is one practice. Among the passages into liberation, this is one passage. Never, even for an instant, forget your initial intent; always maintain it single-mindedly right to the end. Be heroic and diligent, and defeat the demonic hordes. If gods or dragons come to pay their respects, don't be pleased. If you meet with obstructions, even less should you become angry. Be without knowing and without attainment, and the wonderful function will be difficult to exhaust. When your studies are put into practice, you will have the translucence of fine jade. Remember these instructions, and don't turn your back on my heart.

> I leave you with this verse of parting:
> In every step fiercely progress on to victory.
> Guo Dao, Heng Yo, act as his guardian and aid!
> As Guo Yu passes over three thousand
>   li [Chinese miles],
> He will cross, as would a car, eighty thousand steps.
> Here in the scientific age, you are practicing as of old.
> The evoked response from the Buddha's teaching
>   will shake beings from their confusion.
> Strive forward! Strive forward! Ever strive forward!
> Don't stop! Don't stop! Don't ever stop!

]日

Three Steps One Bow pilgrimage, August 4, 1974 in Everett, Washington

OCTOBER 24, 1973 | WEDNESDAY EVENING

On Not Disturbing Those Who Want to Sleep

Let us consider our own situation. As we listen to the sutra, we start to feel tired and doze off. Be careful or your head may hit the table and end up with a bleeding wound. Yesterday evening I stood in front of Guo Hang and watched how he was listening to the sutra on the one hand, and falling asleep on the other. I considered boxing his ears to get him to wake up, but I was afraid it might scare him to death. If I let him continue to sleep, at least he wouldn't die of fright. However, if I boxed his ears he might say to himself, "This world is truly rotten. I'd better go to rebirth in the Land of Ultimate Bliss as soon as possible!" If he left too quickly, no one would be able to bring him back, so I decided not to wake him. Tonight, if any of you want to sleep, I won't bother you. If you want to sleep, please go right ahead. Get as much sleep as you want—it's no problem. You can listen to the sutra all the same in your dreams. ⊣

OCTOBER 26, 1973 | FRIDAY EVENING

On Disciples Learning What They Should Learn

In the master-disciple relationship, emphasis is on top-ranking disciples, not a top-ranking teacher. You disciples will become Buddhas in the future, but your teacher will perhaps go back to being a ghost, returning to suffer in the path of hungry ghosts! So you should not imitate your teacher, but instead should learn what you ought to learn. ⊣

OCTOBER 27, 1973 | SATURDAY EVENING

On Doing What One Is Supposed to Do

All of you should realize that the present threat [Editor's note: the Comet Kahoutek, which was headed for Earth] is billions of times greater than that of atomic or nuclear explosions. The pending disaster is incredibly formidable. We'll have to see if our two monks can turn it aside or not. That's why I told them when they left, "If you're not sincere, don't come back to see me."

That's my standard method. When you went to Taiwan, I told you that if you didn't maintain my rules, you should not come back to see me. And if Heng Qian doesn't translate the *Wonderful Dharma Lotus Flower Sutra* while he's in Hong Kong, then he doesn't need to come back to see me either. Ultimately what use is there in seeing me? It's useless. That's why I may prevent people from seeing me. Does anyone have any opinions? ⊣

OCTOBER 29, 1973 | MONDAY EVENING

On a Vow to Give Away Wisdom

I also remember something else that happened to me. I realized that each person wants to be better than everyone else, smarter and wiser. At that time I made a peculiar vow. What was it? None of you knows. I vowed that I wanted to be more stupid than anybody else, to give away all the wisdom that I was supposed to have as a gift to all people. I wanted to be dumber than any person, more stupid than any living being. After I made that vow, I did in fact become stupid. Stupid to what point? If I had money, I wanted to give it away so others could use it. I did the same with any other possessions I had. Not only did I give away dictionaries, I even gave away my body, mind, and life. That was what I did in the past, and now I don't know whether it was in a dream, or while eating or sleeping, that I seemed to recall such a thing taking place. This is true, actual, and not false. ⊣

I. Master-Disciple Relationship

NOVEMBER 3, 1973 | SATURDAY EVENING

On Expelling Poisons

Guo Hui, you returned! Come up in front and tell us what's going on with them [Editor's note: referring to the two monks who were making a pilgrimage of Three Steps One Bow from San Francisco to Washington State].

Guo Hui: They're over at Bodega Bay now, and they're ready to start in the morning, again, from where they left off a couple of days ago. They had to stop for a while, because Heng Ju was hurting pretty bad. [Editor's note: He had a bad case of poison oak from using poison oak leaves for toilet paper.] He's looking pretty good now, and they're going to try it some more. They have all the right equipment now.

Master: Where are they?

Guo Hui: They're at the other side of Bodega Bay. They're camping…

Master: Not having a barbeque?

Guo Hui: They might have a little fire…

Master: Did Guo Yu eat the licorice root I gave him?

Guo Hui: Yes, he's begun eating it.

Master: How is he eating it?

Guo Hui: I told him to put it in the tea, or just eat it. I'm not sure how he's doing it. I thought I saw some tea he made.

Master: It doesn't have to be brewed into a tea. The root itself can be eaten. It's not as potent taken as a brew. When I gave it to you to take to them before, I didn't expect them to be staying in people's houses. My idea was that he could just chew on it. It can dispel poison. Honey is very good for that too. What else is going on?

Guo Hui: Guo Zhou is going to bring food to them tomorrow. They said the best time to find them on the road, if anyone goes looking for them, is at noon. They get on the road at daybreak, as soon as the cars can see them. And they start looking for a place to stay around 4 P.M., sometimes later. They stay on the road; they don't go on the beach.

I. Master-Disciple Relationship

NOVEMBER 4, 1973 | SUNDAY EVENING

On Responding to Questions

From now on, all of you should answer during the question and answer period. If someone asks a question, don't wait for me to respond. It's true the person's question is directed at me, but even so, I'll wait to see if one of you can answer first. I don't want to push you out of the picture, using my rank as teacher to keep you down, preventing you from developing your wisdom and eloquence. Do you agree to this new process?

Now all of you have your own inherent wisdom and eloquence and can answer people's questions. I am here at present, so if you answer incorrectly, or if the person asking doesn't accept what you say, he or she can reopen the matter for investigation by saying, "That's not right," or "I am not satisfied with that answer." We'll use whether the person is satisfied or not as the criterion. If he or she isn't satisfied with your reply, then we'll find someone else. Should that answer also prove unsatisfactory, we'll get another person. If none of you can answer, I will speak at the end. We'll see how it goes if you reply; then I won't have to exert my brain, and can take a little nap. ⊣

NOVEMBER 17, 1973 | SATURDAY EVENING

On Developing One's Own Wisdom

When you lecture on the sutras, you shouldn't just recite the commentary. I have noticed that when you lecture on the sutras, you simply read the English version of what I have lectured. That's not right. You should develop your own wisdom. I have not completely explained everything fully in my lecture, and you should use your wisdom to expand upon certain points more. Look at the meaning, and then, based upon what you discern through your own wisdom, give your own lecture. Don't simply read what I have said. That doesn't count as your own lecture—it's still my lecture, except that you are reading it aloud.

I'll tell you something: When I lecture on sutras, I don't just reiterate material from the commentaries. I might look through them, but I don't strive to remember them in the way that Guo Hu does. When he heard we would be lecturing the *Śastra on Awakening of Faith in the Great Vehicle*, he first looked at the *Explanation of the Śastra on Awakening of Faith in the Great Vehicle*. Of course, that is permissible. But if all you do is look at the works of others, they will never be your own, and eventually you will lose them. You will forget them.

When I tell you to develop your own wisdom, that doesn't mean taking an opposing stance, or protesting against what your teacher has lectured, pointing out ways in which your teacher's explanation was incorrect. If you are that correct, you don't

I. Master-Disciple Relationship

need to study with a teacher. You can withdraw and set out on your own!

In short, if you do look at commentaries, you should also add some of your own interpretation. ⊣

JANUARY 26, 1974 | SATURDAY EVENING

On Being 'Just This Way'

I'm going to say some things none of you want to hear. First let me make it clear: if anyone wants to oppose his teacher, he is most welcome to do so. I do not care more for those who don't oppose their teacher. I do not necessarily regard people who follow my instructions as being good disciples or consider anyone who doesn't follow instructions as necessarily bad.

I'm not afraid of people opposing me. Why? It's because I don't have any sense of self. Whether you oppose me or follow my instructions, I'm just the same. What you do is your business, not mine. Why? It was aptly stated by Great Master Yongjia, who said:

> Let others slander me;
> I bear their condemnation.
> Those who try to burn the sky only exhaust themselves.
> When I hear it, it's just like drinking sweet dew.
> Having accepted it, suddenly one
>   enters the inconceivable.

If you slander me, it doesn't matter. If you criticize me, it's okay. If you raise a torch in an attempt to burn the sky, you will only wear yourself out, since the sky is beyond your reach. When others slander or insult me, their words are like sweet dew. "Having accepted it, suddenly one enters the inconceivable." A person who really has this kind of attitude will have tasted the true flavor. ⊣

JUNE 21, 1974 | FRIDAY EVENING

On Saying Openly What Others Say Surreptitiously

If you have no questions, I have something to tell you. Having been to Gold Mountain Monastery, when you go out, you should do your best to tell people how terrible this place is. Don't praise Gold Mountain Monastery. What disadvantages does it have? First of all, it's as cold as an icebox here. Second, no one is allowed to be lazy here. Any lazy individual feels ashamed here. Third, this place is like a concentration camp. Everyone here is a criminal. No one is innocent. That's what you should tell people, so they will be scared to come here. ⊣

JUNE 23, 1974 | SUNDAY EVENING

On the Master's Hope for All Beings

Gold Mountain Monastery and Sino-American Buddhist Association were formerly known as the Buddhist Lecture Hall. At that time, the Buddhist Lecture Hall was a small place on the fourth floor of a building. It was opened at the beginning of the summer session in 1968. Many people came from Seattle to attend the 96-day summer session. We maintained a busy schedule. There was no time to rest during the day. There was only a half-day break on Saturdays for people to do laundry or take care of personal business.

At first there was one lecture on the *Śūraṅgama Sutra* each day. After a while, thinking that there was not enough time, we scheduled two daily lectures. Still thinking that was not enough, we began to hold three lectures a day. Finally, near the end, we had four lectures per day, and we managed to finish lecturing the *Śūraṅgama Sutra* in 96 days.

At that point, five people asked to leave the home life. Three became Bhikshus, and two Bhikshunis.

These were the first Americans to officially enter Buddhist monastic life and receive full ordination. Sessions were held every summer after that, and people came to study.

The number of students has been neither too many nor too few. Why do I say it's not too many? There could never be too many people in this country truly studying Buddhism. Why do I say

38

I. Master-Disciple Relationship

it's not too few? Gold Mountain Monastery values quality, not quantity. As long as the participants genuinely investigate the Buddhadharma and earnestly resolve to cultivate, then even one is plenty, not to mention more than one.

Gold Mountain Monastery publishes a Buddhist monthly journal, *Vajra Bodhi Sea*. We at Gold Mountain Monastery are panning for gold in the sand. Some people who come to Gold Mountain Monastery feel as if they are coming home. They think everything is perfect here. Although it gets a bit cold, they find the coolness refreshing. Although there is little conversation, they find it easy to read a book without being interrupted. One can investigate the Buddhadharma every day.

Among the massive population of the United States, those who truly study the Buddhadharma are extremely few. People become Buddhas one by one, not in hordes. In the world, whatever is rare is valued. Therefore, the few of you who have come to study the Buddhadharma at Gold Mountain Monastery have also become invaluable. Each of you, once you master the Buddhadharma, will be able to propagate the Dharma in all places, teach and transform sentient beings, and quickly bring them to Buddhahood. This is my hope for all of you.

Each participant in the summer session should be mindful of the time. Don't let the time go by in vain. It's important not to waste precious time. You must learn some true principles. ◁

JULY 25, 1974 | THURSDAY EVENING

On Being Considerate of Others

Today is the eleventh day of the fast undertaken by two cultivators at Gold Mountain Monastery. For the duration of the fast, everyone should help them out with their work since they don't have that much energy. Everyone should be compassionate. Don't think this way:

> Even Mahāsattvas pay no attention to others.
> Amitābha Buddha looks after himself.

Since they have made such a resolution to follow the path to *bodhi*, we should help them to achieve their goal. Starting tomorrow I will come downstairs before the lecture, so they won't have to expend the effort to walk upstairs to request the Dharma. All of you should also take up more responsibilities on their behalf. ⊣

I. Master-Disciple Relationship

SEPTEMBER 29, 1974 | SUNDAY NOON

On Mentioning Disciples' Unspoken Criticisms

Some people are thinking, "Oh, the Master read the text wrong again. He read *shi xian* as *xi xian*." Several nights ago when I referred to Devadatta as Bodhidatta, many people were thinking, "How can he forget Devadatta's name and get it as wrong as Bodhidatta? The Master says his memory is good, but sometimes it's worse than anyone's, even worse than mine. Even I can remember Devadatta's name." ⊣

SEPTEMBER 30, 1974 | MONDAY EVENING

On One Being Enough

So now you blame the mouth for not listening to the mind? That's nothing strange. No wonder sons and daughters don't listen to their parents. No wonder they do all sorts of things away from home that you don't know about. If the mind can't even control what the mouth says, how can an incapable teacher make his talented disciples listen to him? It's hardly possible, but he has to try. Maybe one in ten thousand, a hundred thousand, a million, or ten million will become an excellent Good Advisor. But one is enough. So I don't set my hopes too high. Since I don't harbor high expectations, everything is okay to me. ⊣

II | Teaching & Transforming

The Venerable Master blessing Bhikshus Heng Ju and Heng Yo on their Three Steps One Bow pilgrimage, October 14, 1973

OCTOBER 31, 1972 | TUESDAY EVENING

On Responding to Conditions

Tomorrow Guo Pu is bringing some of her students to learn meditation. [Editor's note: a class from UC Berkeley, where this nun was a Ph.D. candidate] For that reason, our Chinese lesson will be changed to a meditation class. After meditation, we can give them an instructional talk, and then have our sutra lecture. ⊨

NOVEMBER 1, 1972 | WEDNESDAY EVENING

On Teaching Techniques

Master addresses class: Everybody must take notes. You can give them to the instructor of this class.

Master addresses instructor: Next time if they take good notes, give them more points. If they don't remember, give them fewer points.

Someone is thinking, "This Dharma Master must have studied psychology. Otherwise, how could he know what I'm thinking?" That's right, I've studied psychology. If any of you have psychological ailments, they will disappear after you come here. ⧠

NOVEMBER 3, 1972 | FRIDAY EVENING

On Neutralizing Poisons

I am in the process of creating new blood for Buddhism. I won't allow any poison in the new blood. Not only that, we must neutralize the poison in other people. "Poison" refers to the three poisons of greed, anger, and delusion. To neutralize other people's poison means to change their greed, anger, and delusion around. An editor of a respected Buddhist periodical [who was visiting from Taiwan] was surprised when he heard those comments. He had never heard anything like that before. He said, "I must remember this. I must put your words here," and he put his hand over his heart. ⊣

II. Teaching and Transforming

DECEMBER 31, 1972 | SUNDAY NOON

On the Wordless Sutra

In the twinkling of an eye, two recitation sessions and one
chan session have passed. Now we will continue lecturing on
the sutra, and in another twinkling, we will finish lecturing the
entire *Flower Adornment Sutra*. After we complete this lecture
series, we will go on to explain the "wordless sutra." [Editor's
note: The "wordless sutra" refers to the true teaching, which is
beyond words.] ⊣

TIMELY TEACHINGS

JANUARY 16, 1973 | TUESDAY EVENING

On Not Believing an Earthquake Won't Happen

People are strange creatures. Some time ago, when a rumor was going around that there would be an earthquake here, most people believed it and many left San Francisco. At that time there was a very wealthy Chinese man, probably a millionaire, who lived in Oakland. Thinking that Oakland would be damaged by the earthquake, he and his wife decided to move to Reno to avoid death. However, halfway to Reno, the couple died in an auto accident. If they hadn't run away, they might not have died. But since they were fleeing, they met their death on the highway. They were survived by several children.

Although I have made the claim that there won't be an earthquake, to this day people refuse to believe it. They say, "There wasn't going to be an earthquake to start with. It wasn't because you said there wouldn't be one that there hasn't been an earthquake." They don't believe it. If someone says there will be an earthquake, people will believe it. But if you tell them there won't be an earthquake, they don't believe it. Even though no earthquake occurred either on the 13th or the 14th [Editor's note: as was predicted], they still refuse to believe. They insist that it was a coincidence.

There have been predictions that an earthquake would hit San Francisco in 1968, 1969, 1970, 1971, and 1972. To this day there hasn't been an earthquake. But if we state that there won't be

II. Teaching and Transforming

an earthquake, nobody believes it. "Well, I believe it," someone says. But for one person alone to believe is still useless. ◁

FEBRUARY 4, 1973 | SUNDAY NOON

On Using Modern-Day Analogies

[Editor's note: The following entry refers to an earlier part of the Master's lecture, as follows:

An ancient poet [Su Dongpo] once said:

> The sounds from the gurgling brooks
>   are the vast, long tongue.
> The colors of the mountains are none
>   other than the pure, clear body.

The sounds of the flowing streams are the Buddha's vast, long tongue speaking Dharma. And the colors of the mountains are the Buddha's pure Dharma body. The poet Su Dongpo said those lines. Not only are the sounds of the gurgling brooks part of the vast, long tongue, in fact, all the sounds in the world are part of the Buddha's vast, long tongue.]

When you attend the evening lectures, I can speak to you with a vast, long tongue. What is a vast, long tongue? It's the telephone. A radio is also a vast, long tongue. And how about displaying a pure body? Images that you can see on television in or movies can be likened to displaying a pure body. Some of you are thinking, "Let's display pure bodies!" Well, that would be possible. You're welcome to appear on TV. ⊣

II. Teaching and Transforming

AUGUST 17, 1973 | FRIDAY EVENING

On Serious Shortcomings

Don't think you can simply get angry if people treat you badly. That is the ugliest, the lowest, the most spineless thing to do. Once you get angry, all the effort you put into cultivation is lost. Cultivation means being patient with what others cannot be patient with, yielding to what others cannot yield.

[Editor's note: Master addresses a certain disciple] You, on the other hand, are especially impatient and unyielding. You are the first to eat, but the last to work. Should someone say a few words to you, you blow up in anger and get all upset. You have those serious shortcomings.

People who have cultivation and virtue never really get angry. If a virtuous person makes a show of anger, people find it very easy to take. If a person lacking virtue blows up, however, it won't work. Don't think, "Now that I have virtue, I can get mad at others." That will not do. Any indication of anger is a sign of your own stupidity. You may not get mad at anyone. You must not get angry even at people who are one or two levels junior to you, or who are lower than you in position, much less your Dharma peers. Just because you have your own afflictions and ignorance does not mean you may attack others. ◁

AUGUST 24, 1973 | FRIDAY EVENING

On How the Specifics May Change, but Principle Remains

The other day a visiting Dharma Master came and talked about "stinking pickled vegetables," which is a colloquial term for sitting in meditation. Basically, we've been discussing principles of meditation here for a long time. But after his talk, he asked one of my disciples whether she had ever heard what he discussed before, she said, "No."

Well, if you hadn't heard about meditation, what have you been doing all along? All he did was use a different term for meditation, that's all. He called it "stinking pickled vegetables" and you said that you had never heard anything about it before? We look into questions about meditation every day. But since you said you hadn't heard of it before, the Dharma Master thought you were not at all well-informed.

Basically, what we investigate every day is connected to the practice of meditation. How could you fail to see that, just because he used the expression "stinking pickled vegetables"? He was merely using a different phrase. Take your own names, for instance. Originally you were known by your lay name and now you are known by your Dharma-name. Now, if someone, who knew you by your lay name, heard your Dharma-name, they would probably say, "Who's that?" The same idea works here. Because your experience is limited, you are easily swayed by something new. So when someone brings up a term like "stinking pickled vegetables," you say, "I've never heard of it." Basically, "stinking

II. Teaching and Transforming

pickled vegetables" is a specific term for a principle that you
know very well. ⊢

SEPTEMBER 3, 1973 | MONDAY EVENING

On Dreaming of Flying

[Master to one of his disciples:] So, you had a dream that you were flying. But when you woke up you found that you couldn't fly. Were you aspiring to be an astronaut? Were you out training in space for a trip to the moon? I'll tell you something: once you truly know how to fly, you won't want to fly. It's just now, when you don't know how to fly, that you wish you could. ◁

II. Teaching and Transforming

SEPTEMBER 4, 1973 | TUESDAY EVENING

On the Importance of One Word

I remember that before Guo Xiu [full Dharma-name: Guo Xiu ("result of cultivation"), Heng Chih ("ever upholding")] went to be ordained and receive the precepts, she wrote a four-line verse:

> The result cannot be attained.
> Cultivate blessings and virtue.
> Ever mindful of *samādhi* and wisdom,
> Upholding the precepts, we can become Buddhas.

I changed one word of her verse. She said, "The result cannot be attained." I changed that to read, "The result **must** be attained." One must attain the result. If one cannot attain the result, one is finished. Well, how does one attain the result? By cultivating blessings and virtue, and by always being mindful of *samādhi* and wisdom and upholding the precepts. That's now people can become Buddhas. At the time she wrote this verse in Chinese, she knew hardly any Chinese and she did not know how to translate. This proves she has deep affinities with the Chinese language. ⊣

SEPTEMBER 16, 1973 | SUNDAY NOON

On the Esoteric School

This afternoon, following the sutra lecture, there will be a Chinese class on an essay I wrote about the Esoteric School [Editor's note: also known as Tantric Buddhism]. Most people consider the Esoteric School fantastic—truly wonderful because it's secret Dharma! Almost everyone who studies the Esoteric School is selfish, due to that attitude of wanting to keep the Dharma hidden and not let others know it. You should know this principle—that the majority of Esoteric School adherents are selfish and only a handful are public-spirited.

First of all, most followers of the Esoteric School eat meat and drink liquor. They like the idea of being able to become a Buddha without the inconvenience of having to be vegetarian. In other words, they like having their cake and eating it too, as the saying goes.

However, Mencius pointed out, "One cannot have both fish and bear's paws." Such "convenient" practice of the Esoteric School can be dangerous, for it may lead to a fall into the path of *asuras*. Don't underestimate that danger! ☐

On Exploring Collective Wisdom

Let us look into the matter of Guo Yu's vow to make a Three Steps One Bow pilgrimage of 800 to 1,000 miles. You should all investigate whether he can make it. Anyone who has an opinion should express it. The collective wisdom of a multitude of people is equivalent to that of a sage. The wisdom of a single person is limited, but the wisdom of everybody put together is infinite. Let's consider the feasibility of the matter. [Editor's note: Some opinions are expressed.]

[Editor's note: Master responds to one person's opinion.] This is his own vow. Why should you delve so much into his personal affairs? I'm asking the others to evaluate the feasibility of his vow, because they understand him well, whereas I don't know him that well. [Editor's note: In response to another opinion.] His vow is not that immense in itself, but no one else in this country has ever done such a thing. He wants to be the first one. ◁

OCTOBER 7, 1973 | SUNDAY NOON

On Using Children as an Alibi

This Night-ruling Spirit [mentioned in the text of the *Flower Adornment Sutra*] uses boundless kindness to gather in all children, and to cherish and protect them. She is not like some of our laypeople who get upset as soon as they see children come to attend the lectures. They say they don't attend the sutra lectures because of those kids. Not only do they themselves not attend sutra lectures, they tell everyone else not to come either. They say they dislike the kids.

Actually, even if there were no kids, they wouldn't come to the sutra lectures or come and investigate the Buddhadharma. They spend their time and energy investigating other things instead. They watch movies, go dancing, and listen to music. They devote their time to that. They like entertainment; that's what they are engaged in.

Several disciples and laypeople who don't come to listen to sutra lectures or investigate the Buddhadharma themselves are jealous of other people coming. So they tell other people not to come. Some whom they tell that to don't have any better sense than to follow their advice. They hear those people say, "The kids go there and cry and scream and squabble. You can't hear the Master's lecture clearly." Actually, that's just an excuse. They use that as an alibi, a rationale for their not attending. In reality, it's totally contradictory: they don't want to study but they are jealous when others want to.

II. Teaching and Transforming

They are leading others down the wrong road. So, all of you should be wary of such people who try to make you retreat from your resolve to follow the Path.

If people were sincerely seeking the Dharma, they would still want to come investigate the Buddhadharma even if there were man-eating tigers here, not to speak of children. So you see, even though we have many tigers here, nonetheless so many people have come; and they haven't been eaten by the tigers.

OCTOBER 7, 1973 | SUNDAY EVENING, AT WASHINGTON STREET

On Giving People a Chance

When I went to Los Angeles, one person who saw me didn't bow, but when his little dog saw me, it bowed and bowed. Everyone thought that it was very amusing. I said, "This dog understands the Buddhadharma. But all of you must be understanding toward people who don't know how to be respectful to the Triple Jewel, since they haven't seen the Triple Jewel before." ⊣

OCTOBER 15, 1973 | MONDAY EVENING

On Transcending Dualities

Master: Who else is going to speak? [Editor's note: Silence ensues.] There's a ghost who wants to speak but doesn't dare.

Young Layman (Guo I): I don't understand, but I try hard to see what I don't understand, and just give myself a big headache trying to figure out what I don't understand. So I guess I'll just stop trying to figure out what I don't understand.

Master: If you don't investigate what you don't understand, do you want to investigate what you do understand?

Young Layman: Yes.

Master: Either way will give you a headache. If you don't want headaches then you shouldn't want to understand or not want to understand. Not to understand is "bad" and understanding is "good". You should apply yourself to not thinking of good and not thinking of bad, and then your head won't ache. ◁

OCTOBER 17, 1973 | WEDNESDAY EVENING

On a Play on Words

Master to disciple Bhikshu Heng Jing: [Editor's note: This is Guo Ning's ordained name] Tall monk! [Editor's note: This term *gao seng* is usually translated High Sanghan, and is reserved for monks who, through the course of time, reached high levels in their practice.] What about you? What's your opinion? Speak up.

Bhikshu Heng Jing: The word for "practice" (行) can be a noun or a verb in Chinese. As a noun, it's usually pronounced *heng*. As a verb, it's pronounced *xing*. This may seem like a small matter from the Chinese perspective, but when translating into English, nouns and verbs have different forms and functions. Chinese can allow both interpretations in some contexts. When that is the case, then which part of speech should we choose in English? A case in point is the term in this sutra passage that can be read *guang heng* or *guang xing*.

Master: First give your explanation. How should it be interpreted? Should it be pronounced *heng* or *xing*?

Bhikshu Heng Jing: I think probably both explanations make sense. The difference is not great in Chinese, but sometimes small differences in Chinese become large ones in English; and sometimes big differences in English become small ones in Chinese.

Master: That's right. I absolutely accept your opinion. Who else has an opinion? How do you think it should be interpreted?

II. Teaching and Transforming

Should it be *guang heng* or *guang xing*? How should *guang heng* be translated into English? And what should be the English translation of *guang xing*? Since you claim there is a distinction in English, let's consider the meaning of the English. What is the translation of *guang heng*?

Bhikshu Heng Jing: "Light conduct," or "brilliant conduct." In the context of the four characters here, the final two characters being *zhuang yan* (莊嚴), if it is pronounced *guang heng zhuang yan*, it would mean something like "adorned by brilliant conduct." But if the character is pronounced *xing*, making it a verb, we have to look at what the object of the verb "practice" would be. Maybe something like, "he practices adorned conduct." Then, explaining by extension what adorned conduct would be: it has light, or it uses light as adornment. The two ways of translating are not widely different, so it doesn't matter much in this particular example. But sometimes the discrepancy is large. Even if both interpretations make sense in Chinese, the English language only allows one, because of its rules of grammar.

Master: The meaning is about the same in Chinese. It's pronounced *heng* when that sounds better in the context. For example, in the line, "while practicing the profound *prajñā pāramitā*," the character is pronounced *xing*, not *heng*. However, some people pronounce it *heng* even so. The meaning is not very different. If the character is pronounced *heng*, one should add a circle to indicate it's in the "entering" tone; but if it's pronounced *xing*, there is no need to draw a circle. That's the distinction in Chinese.

In English you need to consider the context. For example, there is the Chinese expression "cultivating ascetic practice," where the pronunciation is *heng*, not *xing*. One could talk about being "adorned with ascetic practice," that is using ascetic practice to adorn the Dharma-body. Here it is "adorned with luminous practice," which is why I pronounced the character *heng* instead of *xing*. That's because the speed of light is very fast. When light is emitted, it arrives immediately, without traveling. [Editor's note: pun on Chinese homonym — traveling is another meaning of *xing*.] It reaches any place however far. Light travels faster than sound. So it's read *guang heng*. In English *heng* is a noun, isn't it?

Bhikshu Heng Jing: Yes.

Master: It's a noun in Chinese, too. Do you think I'm wrong or right to pronounce it *heng*?

Bhikshu Heng Jing: Either pronunciation — I don't think this is a very big problem here. Either *heng* or *xing* will work. Probably it should be pronounced *heng*. In this passage, if I hadn't heard it before, but had to translate it, I would translate it as *heng*. Sometimes it can be a problem, but sometimes not.

Master: No, this isn't a problem. Just use whichever translation you think works best. Use whichever one fits the overall context and is most appropriate and meaningful. Don't use one that doesn't make sense. You asked about *heng* "conduct" — is there anyone asking about *wu heng* "lack of conduct"? Who doesn't vote for *heng*? ◁

OCTOBER 20, 1973 | SATURDAY EVENING

On Doing What Shouldn't Be Done

Twenty-two years ago, when I was in Hong Kong, at a place called Daofeng Mountain, there was a Christian pastor named Ai. I forget where he came from. That place specialized in getting monks to return to lay life. That pastor enticed them with money and lust. Once a monk moved in there, he stayed on and on. He would drift, get entangled, forget to return, become wild, and finally be lost. What is meant by drifting, getting entangled, forgetting to return, becoming wild and being lost?

> Going along with the current and forgetting
> to return starts one drifting.
> Going against the current and failing
> to return gets one entangled.
> Hunting pleasures without restraint makes one wild.
> Drinking intoxicants without satiation
> causes one to get lost.

These describe the faults and failings of certain emperors throughout history.

So, at that time "imperial" Dharma Masters were going there, drifting, getting entangled, becoming wild, forgetting to return, and ending up lost. How did that happen? Well, first of all, the place provided money, and second of all, it provided women. I also went there to see what that place was like. [Editor's note: This place became established during the influx of Buddhists from China in the 1940's. Many monks and nuns arrived in Hong Kong with no place to stay and no means of support.] But once I got there and looked around, I saw it had no affinities with me.

Instead, I debated with Pastor Ai. I told him, "What you are doing here goes against Jesus' intentions. You are not a Christian, and do not qualify as a Christian. Jesus helped people to be successful and didn't undermine them. But you undermine people and do not help them to succeed. You get ordained monks to stop being monks. You undermine their pure conduct."

I said more than that: "I'm not a Buddhist either. If I were a Buddhist, I should be as kind and compassionate as the Buddha and save you. Unfortunately, I am unable to save you. I don't have the power to rescue you, and so I am not a Buddhist."

All he could do was stare at me — there was nothing he could say. Afterwards he asked me to be in a photograph with him, to which I replied, "We shouldn't have it taken. Any photo of the dregs of Christianity like you and the dregs of Buddhism like me would only detract from Christianity and detract from Buddhism." In the end, we didn't have the photograph taken. This is to investigate a problem that we shouldn't investigate. ◁

OCTOBER 29, 1973 | MONDAY EVENING

On Gently Bringing Someone to an Understanding

[Editor's note: The young woman in the dialogue that follows was visiting Gold Mountain Monastery in San Francisco for the first time. She had been living in Africa. Because the Venerable Master spoke in Chinese and the young woman spoke in English, the exchange took place with a translator as intermediary. Later, the Master allowed her to enter monastic life and gave her the name Guo Mo.]

Master: [To the translator:] Ask that young woman whether she is a man or a woman.

Young woman: I'm female.

Master: Why did you shave your head?

Young woman: Because I'm a Buddhist.

Master: Are you a layperson or ordained?

Young woman: I'm a layperson.

Master: Since laypeople generally have hair, why did you shave yours off? Who told you to shave it off?

Young woman: I did.

Master: Have you realized enlightenment?

Young woman: I don't know what that is.

Master: To realize enlightenment is to have control over your own birth and death. You can be born or die at will, but you don't die by committing suicide. [Editor's note: The young woman remains silent.] Why aren't you answering?

Young woman: Because I'm trying to think of what to say. If I say yes, then you will tell me to die.

Master: This dying is not a case of me telling you to do so, but something one just does on one's own. If I told you to die and you did, then I would have broken the law, and the police would come to take me to jail. Have you seen other Buddhist laypeople shave their heads, especially women?

Young woman: No.

Master: Then why do you want to be the first?

Young woman: It's an offering to the Buddha.

Master: Where is the Buddha?

Young woman: Everywhere.

Master: If the Buddha is everywhere, then which one are you making an offering to?

Young woman: The one where I am.

Master: How long is your hair now?

Young woman: It's no length.

Master: Śākyamuni Buddha in a previous life spread out his hair to cover the mud, enabling Dīpaṅkara Buddha to walk on his hair. He used that to make an offering to the Buddha. If you were to encounter such a situation now, what would you use as an offering to the Buddha?

Young woman: Oh, I would lie down.

Master: What if he crushed you to death?

Young woman: That would be all right.

Master: This is not just intellectualizing.

Young woman: I'm not.

Master: Where do you live now?

Young woman: I'm going to be living in an apartment.

Master: I'm not asking about tomorrow. I'm asking about yesterday and today.

Young woman: Yesterday I stayed with a friend who is a Zen student. Before, I had a room in an apartment.

Master: Have you been living with hippies?

Young woman: No.

Master: What was the point of shaving your head yourself?

Young woman: Like I said, it was an offering to Buddha.

Master: Where is the hair you shaved off now?

Young woman: I don't know.

Master: If you don't know, then what are you using as an offering to the Buddha?

Young woman: That's not the offering. The offering is not having hair.

Master: Hmm. Not having hair as an offering? What is the difference between having hair and not having hair?

Young woman: None.

Master: Then why did you want to shave off your hair as an offering to the Buddha?

Young woman: Why not?

Master: Because in Buddhism it is important to have the appropriate style. It would be all right if you were a monastic. But you yourself admit that you are still a layperson. Since you are a layperson, and all the laypeople, especially women, have hair, why do you want to be different? Are you trying to be unusual, not like other people?

Young woman: No.

Master: Do you want to be a lay Bhikshuni?

Young woman: I don't mind.

Master: You can't be a lay Bhikshuni, but you can still be a lay Buddhist. However, it would be better for you to let your hair grow out. Okay?

Young woman: Okay. ◁

II. Teaching and Transforming

OCTOBER 29, 1973 | MONDAY EVENING

On Not Believing
One's Own Mind

Master to the young woman: Don't believe your own mind. Because you have not become a sage, you cannot believe your own ideas. That's from the Buddha. The Buddha said, "Be careful not to believe your own mind. Your mind is not trustworthy. It is only after you become an Arhat at the fourth stage that you can trust your own mind." Once you have achieved that level of sage-hood, which means you will have ended birth and death, then you can believe your own ideas and trust your own opinions and understandings. ◁

OCTOBER 29, 1973 | MONDAY EVENING

On Effortlessness

Master: Anyone who is willing to cultivate can gain this ability [of appearing everywhere in all worlds without moving from one's original place]. One goes from the small to the great, from what is near to what is far, and from one's own self to identity with others. Let me give a simple illustration of what not moving from one's original place means. It's as when you do a lot of work, yet in your mind you don't feel that it is exhausting. It's not the case that you do some work and then experience mental fatigue, "Ah! I am tired." Your feeling of fatigue is nullification of your original place. If you don't feel tired, then you experience that you are doing things as if nothing were going on, that it's very good to be doing them, that it's good exercise for your body. For example, today Guo Hu went to haul lumber. When he couldn't lift it, he wanted to cry as he exclaimed, "Ai! It's too heavy!" Did you actually shed tears?

Bhikshu Heng Shoou [Guo Hu]: No, but the work was really too hard.

Master: Ah! The Path of effortlessness is to be working but to feel that no work is being done. That is not to move from your original place. If your mind does not move, then you have not moved from your original location, which is your mind. ⊣

NOVEMBER 1, 1973 | THURSDAY EVENING

On Avoiding Arrogance

The investigation of truth should not take status into account. All of us are equal. It is a matter of your own wisdom. If your wisdom surpasses that of all other teachers, then you are the best teacher. I myself also wish to learn from the teacher who is out in front. I will be delighted if one of you wants to be the number one teacher. Don't be like me, always wanting to be last. You should be first; don't be the last one. I like to be last in everything, and so I don't amount to much. You ought to be a lot better than I am.

On the other hand, you shouldn't develop an arrogant attitude and proclaim, "Now I'm Number One. I surpass everyone. I can beat my teacher, how much the more anyone else." If you look down on everyone in that way, you make the mistake of being conceited. You will end up having wrong views and calling what is wrong right and what is right, wrong. You need to possess an accurate eye for distinguishing dharmas. You can't just go around stirring up trouble when there is none, nitpicking for nonexistent faults. That's not right. The right way is to maintain a proper understanding and outlook and develop genuine wisdom, authentic prajñā light that dispels all darkness.

You shouldn't have the attitude that no monk is as good as you, much less the nuns, or that laymen are of even less use, not to mention laywomen. If you have an attitude that you alone are honored in the universe, there will be no hope for you in the

73

future. Once you have blasted space apart at the seams, there will be no place to hold you. This is something important which you need to know. ◻

II. Teaching and Transforming

On Etiquette Concerning Questions

You should not answer questions asked by any Dharma Master who comes here, unless it is during a formal lecture or class. As soon as you answer, you are wrong. There is no way to be right. Why? The purpose of most monastic visitors' questions will to expose your faults. Even if you answer correctly, the Dharma Master will maintain that you are wrong, thereby showing that he is better than you. Basically, any well-educated person knows not to ask questions when visiting other places. He is not supposed to test others to see what they understand and what they don't. If people put on their robes and sashes, hold their sitting cloth, kneel down and put their palms together to seek your instruction, then you may answer. If they ask you to explain a point without putting on their robes and sashes and holding their sitting cloth, then you should not respond, nor should you ask them to explain it. To ask them shows your own lack of knowledge, and to answer them also reveals your ignorance. All of you should know this.

If anyone starts asking you questions, regardless of whether it is a layperson or a monk or nun, you can tell the person that the time for asking questions is during lectures and classes, and that everyone has work to do at other times.

Why, when this Dharma Master questioned you about non-self, did you recklessly blurt out an explanation? Actually, the nonexistence of the ego can be explained in a million different ways.

There is no one right way or wrong way. Since the self doesn't even exist, what is there to talk about? How can there be a small self, a great self, or a divine self? None of these exist. To even speak of the non-self is already wrong. If you haven't even understood the true character and the original meaning of dharmas, how can you answer him? You have made a mistake just by saying something. Each individual has his or her own interpretation and theory. How can there be a 'right' or a 'wrong'? You explain it your way, and I explain it my way. Even if I consider your interpretation wrong, I don't have any basis to criticize it. Since there is no basis, what's the point of debating the issue at all?

You foolishly answered him, because you thought that to not answer would have been wrong. Actually, not answering would have been the right thing to do. He had no right to ask you to explain the nonexistence of self. The nonexistence of self is just the nonexistence of self. What more is there to explain? How come you didn't know this when you are so intelligent? You were actually motivated by your wish to establish connections with him because I had praised him before. Actually, I avoid mentioning anything bad about people. I even praise those who are bad, because I regard all people as Buddhas. However, I cannot guarantee that everyone is actually the way I see him or her.

People who are truly following the Path don't talk. This doesn't mean just not talking with women; it means basically not engaging in conversation, even to the point of looking dumb. When I was traveling and cultivating, all day long I kept my eyes closed and didn't look at people. I didn't chat with people. That's the way it should be done. Conversation is useless. The more you respect a cultivator, the less you want to talk with him. You have a competition to see who will talk the least. As soon as someone who understands this principle sees someone who chatters, he will look down on that person. In the past in China at both Gold Mountain Monastery and Gaomin Monastery, a person could live next to someone else for several years and still not know his name. People stayed side by side, slept next to each other, but years would go by and they wouldn't know each other's names, and would never have spoken with each other. ㅂ

NOVEMBER 2, 1973 | FRIDAY EVENING

On Turning the Tables

When Dharma Masters from China visit, you should ask them, "Dharma Master, could you please tell me why Buddhism has disappeared from China? Do you know the reasons?" Ask that that. There are a lot of principles you can question then on. When Dharma Masters come here, they have no right to throw questions at us. If we speak badly, we're just unable to talk, and that's that. If the visitor asks one of us to give an explanation—we're unable to explain. You can turn the tables on him like that. We're just incapable of speaking, and that's all there is to it. If you have pretensions and talk on and on… once you start talking, you're at fault. But if we can't talk—if we don't talk—what then? Nothing. We just can't talk. However, we can practice—tell him that and see what he says.

Basically you have no wisdom, so what's the use of talking at length? You can ask him, "How did Buddhism in Taiwan get to be such a mess? Why does Buddhism in Hong Kong only know how to hustle ceremonies for money?" Hustling ceremonies for money means going out to recite sutras for the dead, banging on the Dharma instruments "ping, ping pong." One day of "ping, ping pong" costs $80; some charge $100 or $200. If a well-known monk goes, the minimum is $200. That's Hong Kong now. None of you know how to make money. The monks in Hong Kong all have millions, amassed from their "ping, ping pong, ping, ping pong." ⌐

II. Teaching and Transforming

NOVEMBER 11, 1973 | SUNDAY NOON

On Doing Things Well

Good spiritual friends! Today here in America, Buddhism is afforded an excellent opportunity. Right now marks the beginning of Buddhism being genuinely transmitted from Asia to America. At the beginning, it is essential to make sure that the foundation is established well. The foundation must be strong so that it will withstand whatever winds and rains might rock it.

What is the foundation of Buddhism? It is everyone's understanding of rules and regulations. The rules and regulations of Buddhism are its precepts, its *vinaya*. The precepts of Buddhism are found in its propriety. Confucianism states that there are "three hundred aspects to propriety and three thousand kinds of awe-inspiring deportment." Buddhism explains three thousand kinds of awe-inspiring deportment and eighty thousand subtle aspects of comportment. The three thousand kinds of awe-inspiring deportment involve sternly guarding one's behavior in walking, standing, sitting, and lying down. To sternly guard awe-inspiring deportment is to strictly observe the precepts. The eighty thousand subtle aspects of comportment involve extremely fine details of behavior, too numerous to mention here.

Starting at the beginning as we are, we must maintain certain kinds of propriety toward our good advisors. Today we are greeting four leaders and good advisors of contemporary Buddhism from Taiwan and Hong Kong.

These four Elder Dharma Masters are leaders and wise and skillful teachers in contemporary Buddhism. The four of them have brought forth great compassion and come to the United States to create Dharma-affinities with the miserable sentient beings of Gold Mountain Monastery and the good men and faithful women of San Francisco.

This is a very good opportunity. When such a fine opportunity to draw near to wise and skillful teachers comes before us, we should definitely not miss it. On the occasion of this good opportunity, we want to practice the Proper Dharma. We should use our total and utmost sincerity to pay reverence and homage to these four wise and skillful teachers. We should consider these four good advisors as being the rarest teachers in the world. We should draw near to them, make offerings, and bow to them as much as possible, so we can plant a field of blessings. And so this time we will use the most elaborate of Buddhist rituals to welcome these four teachers. We will be as reverent, solemn, and dignified in our manners as the Catholics are when they welcome the Pope. So every single one of us should bring forth our most true, sincere, and earnest mind to welcome these four wise and skillful teachers! All of you should pay special attention to this.

We have reserved a reception room at the airport, and we'll take the four wise teachers there so they can rest for awhile. We will arrange in advance with the airline so that when the plane arrives, the four of them will be the first to come off the plane. We will send two representatives to the entrance of the airport to welcome the four wise teachers. This kind of etiquette and ceremonial ritual is no doubt unprecedented in welcoming Buddhist

II. Teaching and Transforming

monks to America. We will be writing a new page of history. All of you ought to be genuine, new Buddhists! In the future you can all become new wise and skillful teachers who can lead American Buddhists. I say "new," because there haven't been any like you before. Not only can you become new wise and skillful teachers, you can also practice the Bodhisattva Path and can one day become Buddhas. Those events lie in the future, but such is my hope for all you.

If we conduct today's event very well, it will show that you Americans are very capable and insist on perfection in the things you do.

Already, Guo Ning traveled to Los Angeles to greet them, and Guo Zhan and Guo Hu have done their part, too. We could say that today's event will cause countless sentient beings to bring forth the resolve for *bodhi*. If done well, it will make a very good impression. By going ahead and doing what we said we were going to do, we will cause the Chinese Buddhists and non-Buddhists to be moved by what they see.

At this time when Buddhism is just beginning, we need to arrange and follow through with events like this in the best way possible. Guo Zhan has been tremendously busy these last few days, and there seems to be some success to show for it. ◁

NOVEMBER 14, 1973 | WEDNESDAY EVENING

On Drawing Names in Democratic Buddhism

Master: What is everyone's opinion concerning the four lines of verse from the sutra that were explained today? Now is the time to express yourselves. Use your inherent wisdom to elicit the meaning of this stanza. If you have a unique outlook and a real point to make, you may advance it for the assembly's consideration. If there's a word or phrase that you didn't understand, you may ask that it be brought up for investigation. On the other hand, if you understood everything and don't have any opinions, we can go on to the next passage.

Our method of explaining the sutras is democratic. Everyone has the right to speak, and each person has a chance to lecture the sutra. It's not the case that one person makes baseless autocratic pronouncements that everyone else just as baselessly accepts.

> From within ignorance, further
>   ignorance is transmitted,
> So with one transmission, two don't understand.
> The teacher falls into the hells,
> The disciples burrow in after him.

Don't any of you follow a teacher who's falling into the hells, and burrow in after him. Now that I've explained it, you all understand, don't you? But you can't get out of explaining this. You definitely must explain it. And so now you disciples can explain the verse. Let's see, who should explain it?

II. Teaching and Transforming

All of you good spiritual friends should strike up your spirits. Don't fall asleep. Now we're going to investigate these four lines together to see which line was explained correctly and which line was explained wrongly. We need to find this out. Don't be tongue-tied and remain silent. We are going to look into these four lines of verse as a group. I'll be able to tell by who wants to talk or not which ones of you were asleep just now—do you believe that or not?

Disciple: I believe it!

Master: Speak up, all of you. Everybody talk at once. I'll be able to distinguish what each person says. [Editor's note: No one says anything.] Since no one is talking, I'll draw a name. [Editor's note: At the Master's Dharma seat is a container of wooden sticks labeled with each disciple's name. He pulls a name from among them and calls it out.] Come on up! You can't hide! Just say whatever you can say. What is your viewpoint on the four lines of verse? Bring up your opinions. Any parts that were not fully explained are left for you to finish. If everything was covered, you can elaborate a bit. Don't think, just speak up quickly. Once you start thinking, it's secondary truth; it's no longer truth in the primary sense. I can't believe you were happy with everything they said, or that they explained every line completely. Nor do I believe they fully brought out the meaning of every phrase.

TIMELY TEACHINGS

That's also true of what I said. All of us should examine this together so that the truth comes forth.

We don't want to follow the custom of Chinese Buddhism in the old days, the tyrannical insistence on, "What I say goes, and anything you say is wrong." As your teacher, I will definitely accept your pointing out my faults. In this democratic country, I am determined to practice democratic Buddhism.

I'm not afraid of opposition. Any disciple who opposes me is a good disciple of mine. Those who don't oppose me are my bad disciples. [Editor's note: The Venerable Master asks a visiting Dharma Master if he had ever heard anyone talk that way before, to which the Dharma Master replies he never had.] I'm not afraid of people opposing me, undermining me, scolding or slandering me. I welcome any of you having the talent to scold your teacher. Speak in Chinese first, then in English. I can't tell you to speak in English first, because the sutra text is in Chinese. [Editor's note: Several disciples explain the verses.]

NOVEMBER 24, 1973 | SATURDAY NOON

On Mutual Interchange Being the Intent of Meetings

[Historical note: What follows is a discussion of the first meeting with members of the California Dreamers at Gold Mountain Monastery, San Francisco, on November 23, 1973.]

Master: Yesterday we had a meeting, and now we will continue and investigate the meeting. All of you should bring up your opinions.

Guo Sui: I don't think one person should be allowed to monopolize a meeting.

Master: Everyone has the right to speak, but what one says should be principled. For example, when Guo Jie [Editor's note: The leader of the California Dreamers] said she wanted to raise a question, any one of you could have answered her. Any other people could answer questions any of you might raise. This is mutual exchange of wisdom. If I don't understand something, I ask someone else who does. If someone else doesn't understand something, but I do, then I can tell the other person. That's the intent of the meetings. ⊢

NOVEMBER 24, 1973 | SATURDAY NOON

On Speaking Dharma Suited to the People's Potentials

Are there any other opinions? [Editor's note: People raise a translation question, and there is a discussion.]

As to the question of whether or not to put an end to desire, the text in question was discussing the dharma door of the Sudden Teaching. In the Sudden Teaching's approach to Dharma, desire must be cut off—otherwise one is fundamentally not in accord with the Sudden Teaching. What most people are afraid of is not the words "cutting off". They fear the Sudden Teaching, because they don't want to become enlightened and realize Buddhahood that fast, but would rather take their time. It's a matter of speaking Dharma that is appropriate for a person with that kind of potential. If it's not suited to the person's potential, then no matter how well it's phrased, the person won't accept it. On the other hand, if it matches the person's potential, then even if poorly stated, the person will still become enlightened. The problem lies with matching or not matching potentials.

II. Teaching and Transforming

NOVEMBER 26, 1973 | MONDAY EVENING

On How Achieving World Peace Starts with One's Own Peace of Mind

Homage to the everlasting Buddhas
of the ten directions.
Homage to the everlasting Dharma
of the ten directions.
Homage to the everlasting Sangha of the ten directions.
Homage to the *Great Flower Adornment Sutra*
of the Buddha's Mahayana Teachings.
Homage to the Buddhas and Bodhisattvas of the
Sea-Vast Flower Adornment Assembly.

I remember that, not long after I came to America, the Soviet Union and the United States almost went to war over Cuba. At that time I thought, "I have just arrived in this country, and have not been of any help to its citizens. If war were to start in Cuba between this country and the Soviet Union, it would result in a great loss of human life and property." Since at the time I didn't understand English and was also not able to go out, all I could do was to make a vow in the Buddha Hall to fast for five weeks, praying that there would be no war. Regardless of whether or not it was a response to my sincerity, war in fact did not break out in Cuba. At the time, President Kennedy was very adamant with Khrushchev, and scared Khrushchev into backing down. Khrushchev was sufficiently frightened to withdraw the missiles, and there was no war.

TIMELY TEACHINGS

Right now [November, 1973] war has started in the Middle East. Israel is at war with the Arab nations. Two monks have committed themselves to the Bodhisattva Path and are currently bowing once every three steps, praying for world peace. The fighting in the Middle East seems to be abating now, but there is still a great war coming along in its wake. For that reason, they must continue to work hard in their quest for world peace.

Today both of them, Guo Yu and Guo Dao, are here at Gold Mountain Monastery with us. They have stopped bowing once every three steps; they have come to protect our Precept Platform, because we have several novices who wish to receive the Ten Novice Precepts. That's why we sent Guo Hu to bring them back today. After the precept transmission, they will continue to pray for peace in the world. If a great war were to break out, it would be far worse than the Second World War, and so we hope there will not be such a war.

There is an energy crisis right now in America, and fuel is lacking. The fuel shortage is a reflection of all the incidents that have happened in the Middle East. However, that's just the beginning. If the world is not at peace, humankind will have to undergo tremendous suffering.

It pleases me that these two monks are maintaining their resolve. Every day I wish their vows will be accomplished, and that the world will be peaceful. For that reason, I hope the gods, dragons, and the rest of the eightfold pantheon will guard and protect them. In that light, when they return to their bowing, it would be best if there is no rain in the area where they are bowing, perhaps for ten miles or twenty miles around them, and no snow either. After they have bowed through an area, rain and snow can fall. That would be a response to their sincerity, a response bestowed by the gods, dragons, and others of the eightfold pantheon who

II. Teaching and Transforming

are protecting them. Therefore, when they go back this time, if rain and snow fall, they should increase the sincerity of their resolve and bow sincerely, not fearing the difficulty. If they can overcome that difficulty, the gods, dragons and others are certain to protect them. This is a test of their vows. If they can keep going in the face of great trials, it indicates their vows are being accomplished.

Now I have told people to bring out two benches. Would all of you like to hear about their experiences during this period of more than a month that that they have being bowing? If you would like to listen to this, we can first welcome the two of them. How should we make that welcome? In America, you usually do it by applauding. If you want to welcome them, then you can applaud. Otherwise, you may just sit there in silence.

[Editor's note. Everybody applauds, and the two monks take their seats on the Dharma Platform, Bhikshu Heng Ju on the Master's left, and Heng Yo on the Master's right. After they report on their pilgrimage, the Master asks for opinions, which people volunteer.]

Master: Now I will give my opinion. The kind of cultivation you two are engaged in is very difficult to do. It's easy to bow for one day or two, three or four days, six or seven days; but to bow every day, day after day, not fearing rain or snow, is really hard. However, if you can do what is hard to do, then it becomes easy.

Buddhism is just beginning in this country and needs such individuals to bring forth this kind of Bodhisattva resolve as an inspiration for people. Nonetheless, this also brings out people's jealousy. Even when the Buddha realized Buddhahood, the demon king was angered and objected, "Why do you want to become a Buddha?" All the sentient beings who were part of the

Buddha's retinue were delighted, but the members of the demon king's retinue all wept.

Situations that you encounter on the road, whether good or bad, are your tests. That's why I say: "Everything's a test to see what you will do." That was spoken for you. "If you fail to recognize what's before your eyes, you'll have to start anew."

How do you start anew? Just continue to bow. That doesn't mean returning to San Francisco and starting the bowing journey all over again. Rather, when you fail to recognize a situation, continue to bow. If you didn't know how to respond to a situation before, once you've been through that experience, just keep bowing. Bow so that you become peaceful inside. If you want the world to be peaceful, you must start by having internal peace. What's meant by internal peace? It means not having any idle thoughts whatsoever. You merge with space. You bow to the point that there is no self, no others, no sentient beings. At that time, you become one with the natural order of things. When that happens, you could not prevent your enlightenment even if you wanted to. This kind of work requires concentration. As it is said, "If you are concentrated, there will be a response. If you are scattered, nothing will happen."

Therefore, to seek world peace, start by developing your own peace of mind. Have no war in your mind. What sort of mental battle could there be? There is the battle between reason and desire. Reason is the essence of True Thusness. If you quell the war inside, there will be no war outside. If you really achieve a great spirit of selflessness, you will have no demonic obstacles, and you won't fear anything. This is the second time I'm addressing the two of you. The first time was when I went there to see you on the road. As I said then, I say again now: I hope you will "try your best."

II. Teaching and Transforming

NOVEMBER 27, 1973 | TUESDAY EVENING

On One Sentence Expressing the Wonder of the Path

I'm very happy today that six people have received the novice precepts. Today I heard Guo Yu say a sentence that he would not have been able to say before he did Three Steps One Bow. You might remember what he said. That one sentence expresses the wonder of the Path. What did he say? "You have shaved your head; now you should shave your mind." [Editor's note: Shaving the head can represent shaving off one's afflictions.] I thought people might not have understood, so I made a point of mentioning this tonight. Someone is thinking, "Oh, anyone could say that." Well, how come you didn't say it? ◁

NOVEMBER 28, 1973 | WEDNESDAY EVENING

On How to Protect Cultivators

To have chatted with the bowing monks like that is really terrible. They might even have been on the verge of enlightenment, but when you went there they got all distracted. That's not the way to support them in their practice. Had you helped them to bow a few more times or bowed along with them, that would have been fine. You could bow with them for ten hours or twenty hours, and that would be fine. For example, Guo Hui went to bow with them. That is fine. Chatting with them is not. Originally they were very sincere and extremely concentrated, but as soon as you talked with them, their minds were no longer concentrated.

Do you understand the principle? You should help them to bow so they won't be wasting the time. Every day, the time is extremely precious. When you went to talk with them, you should have said what you needed to say and no more. You shouldn't have made it into such a big thing, as if you were holding a meeting. You delivered meals to them many times in the past. What was the longest time you were there? Didn't you feel you were obstructing them from practicing the Path then?

It's not just causing trouble, it's obstructing others from practicing the Path, hindering them from bringing forth the *bodhi* resolve. You thought chatting with them was a good thing. Do you know how much merit and virtue you caused them to lose in that conversation? Yes, they can still bow tomorrow, but they'll have to bow more than usual. It may take them one day, ten

II. Teaching and Transforming

days, twenty days, or a year—it's not for sure. If you hadn't obstructed them, then it would be their own business and wouldn't concern you. Do you understand now?

What happened before is over and done. Everyone should be more careful in the future. You shouldn't go there to gossip or chat. Avoid that kind of talk. When you say such things to them, they immediately start having random thoughts and who knows how many days they'll have to bow before they can regain their concentration. Basically they had forgotten about all worldly affairs, but when you go there and remind them, you were imperceptibly ruining their cultivation.

If you want to ask them for something, such as material for an article, that's fine. But don't ask them, "How's your family doing? How's your dad? And your mom?" They have no idea on these matters. I won't worry about how much anyone talked with them in the past, but in the future I will care, because they are now going through a time of great anxiety.

This rule is being made today because when Guo Hu went today, he probably drank some Coca-cola with them, and that's why he didn't return. What happened in the past doesn't count. For example, Guo Zhou, when you stayed with them for three or five hours, you weren't breaking the rule because the rule hadn't been made yet.

I want to ask Guo You about this, because I think he understands my intent. For example, if an employee stops his work and starts chatting with visitors, the boss will certainly be displeased. In this case, the Buddha had just gained two sincere disciples who were working hard, but when you went there, they stopped and took a rest. When the Dharma protectors saw that they had no work to do there, they left. With the Dharma protectors gone, they would have had a very difficult time when they started bowing again. The Dharma protectors took their time and were very lazy, as if they hadn't had enough sleep: "All right, we'll come back and watch over you again." See, even the Dhama protectors were being lazy. How can that be allowed?

Haven't people said that the monks have had the response of Dharma protectors coming to protect them? You don't have to ask whether the Dharma protectors have been moved or not. When one of the monks ripped his pants, he came across another good pair of pants. When people aimed soda bottles at their heads, the bottles missed hitting them by an inch. Those people were driving by very close to them and could easily have bashed their heads in; how can you be sure it wasn't a Dharma protector who shielded them from the blow? From all these incidents, it is clear that they have had many responses. And so you should not ruin their chance to gain responses. Do you understand now?

I like it when people deliver food to them, but you should not stay too long. It takes a long time just to get there and come back, and so it doesn't make much sense to stay there a long time. ◁

NOVEMBER 30, 1973 | FRIDAY EVENING

On Proper Procedures for Translating & Publishing Sutras

Now I have a matter to tell all of you. At Gold Mountain Monastery, the monks and nuns and laypeople work together to translate the sutras of Buddhism. We first translate those sutras that we've understood, and after the translations are done, we print them. However, it is not the case that the translator takes his or her own translation and goes to find a printer and arrange to print it. That is not the correct way to do things.

After our first translation, of the *Sixth Patriarch's Platform Sutra*, was completed, it was printed in the name of our Buddhist Text Translation Society. We printed it. But in Hong Kong, one of our monks did not like the idea of using the name of the Buddhist Text Translation Society, so he did away with it. That was a great mistake. In the future, no matter who translates the sutras, they cannot go by themselves to make arrangements for printing.

With the *Earth Store Sutra*, Guo Ning personally approached a wealthy and influential layman who came to visit Gold Mountain Monastery. Guo Ning recommended himself and his translation of that sutra, and went about quietly convincing that layman to publish his translation. This has been one of the most shameful and worthless things that someone from Gold Mountain Monastery has done.

Now some other translations are done, and some monks are following that precedent-setting mistake that Guo Ning made.

TIMELY TEACHINGS

Promoting your own translation and trying to get it printed is a terrible mistake. It shows a selfish heart, a heart that is after fame and profit. You have not liberated yourself from the wish for fame and profit. All of us at Gold Mountain Monastery should avoid being like common, worldly people. If we do not see this point clearly, how are we any different from anyone else in the world?

Now the translation of the *Lotus Sutra* has been completed, and those three monks in Hong Kong have taken charge of printing it. To do that is not in accord with Dharma. It is totally wrong. In the future, whenever someone finishes a translation, he or she has to hand it over to the Buddhist Text Translation Society, which will send it to be printed. That's the right way to do it. If you don't want to do that, then you needn't bother translating. ⊣

II. Teaching and Transforming

DECEMBER 1, 1973 | SATURDAY EVENING

On Patience

Someone is asking about the meaning of "patience with beings", "patience with dharmas", and "patience with the nonexistence of people and dharmas". The first is this: If sentient beings scold you, beat you, or kill you, you are able to patiently bear it. What is patience with the Dharma? [Editor's note: In this case, the Master is interpreting *fa* as "the Dharma" meaning the Buddha's teaching, rather than as "dharmas" meaning phenomena.] Take a look at the Buddhadharma—it's as deep as the great sea. If you were impatient, you would not be able to study the Buddhadharma. You would say, "There's so much Buddhadharma. I could never study it all." That shows a lack of patience with the Dharma. Patience with the nonexistence of beings and dharmas is a state of mind in which one does not see even the smallest dharma come into being or perish, such that people and dharmas are both empty.

Patience with beings requires that one understands the emptiness of people. When you reach the state in which you see people as empty, you can attain patience with beings. When you also see dharmas as empty, you attain patience with dharmas. When people and dharmas are both empty and gone, you have patience with the nonexistence of beings and dharmas. One sees not the smallest dharma come into being, and not the smallest dharma perish. This kind of state can only be borne in one's heart; it cannot be expressed in words. Do you understand? You do? You must have realized the emptiness of people and dharmas, right?

I fear that you are so lazy about practice that after studying, you still don't know anything. ♮

DECEMBER 8, 1973 | SATURDAY NOON

On Invisible but Viable Influences

Last night when Guo Hang and Guo Ning went to the lecture, some weird creatures—neither ghosts nor spirits—that wanted to absorb people's vital energies, got them to start laughing hysterically, so that their attention was distracted. Once they were distracted, these creatures that were neither ghosts nor spirits sucked up their vital energies as if smoking marijuana, but Guo Hang and Guo Ning didn't even realize it. They thought it was a lot of fun, but they were actually taking a loss. ⊣

DECEMBER 13, 1973 | THURSDAY EVENING

On a Warning to Be More Careful

I have some important news for everyone. The two monks who are doing Three Steps One Bow have encountered ghosts and been bullied by them. They've written a letter to Gold Mountain Monastery, and I'm going to read it to you now. Why is it that when they are so sincere in doing Three Steps One Bow, the Dharma protectors have failed to protect them and they have encountered ghosts? Everyone can speak up and explain the principle behind this. Didn't we talk about the wisdom eye earlier? This is to see whether you have the wisdom eye, and whether you are a wise and skillful teacher with clear vision. There is a definite reason for this. You can't just say that in cultivation one is bound to meet up with demons. That's not the case. There's a specific reason. Who can tell me the reason? Who knows?

I'm asking you this question in order to see how you look at each matter, to see whether you recognize the principle, whether you understand a little bit of true principle. That's why I want you to give your opinions.

First of all, in a recent phone call with the monks, I said to one of them, "The most important thing is to stay away from women. Have you been in that situation recently?"

He thought for a moment and said, "Yes."

"Well, what happened? Were you influenced by the situation?"

II. Teaching and Transforming

He said he'd been influenced a little bit mentally, but not physically.

I said, "That's good. Be more careful in the future." That very night, he caught a ghost and called me on the phone. I told him not to be afraid, that I would help him through whatever state he encountered. He knew enough to ask for help when he encountered that state.

But the two of them have to behave. They didn't have any *samādhi*. When they encountered that kind of state, they forgot about Three Steps One Bow, and when that happened, the Dharma-protecting gods, dragons, and the rest of the eightfold pantheon all took a rest, thinking it was pretty meaningless to protect people who indulged in idle thinking. Once the Dharma-protecting spirits took a rest, the *kumbhāṇḍa* ghost came. It couldn't find them directly, so it found his grandmother to lead the way so it could disturb them. This was just a warning that they should be more careful. On the phone I told them to be extra careful no matter what.

Today we are investigating this matter: Every cultivator should avoid indulging in idle thinking. Don't let your *samādhi* power get dispersed. Once your *samādhi* scatters, you incorporate with the ghosts. You form a company with them. If you have *samādhi*, you open a company with Bodhisattvas. It's an unlimited corporation, not a limited one. It's not a fixed company. It depends on how you act. These are very important issues, so I wanted to discuss them before the sutra lecture today.

MAY 8, 1974 | WEDNESDAY EVENING

On Being Familiar with the Principles in the Sutras

[Editor's note: The Master is recounting a trip to Asia.] Upon arriving back in Taiwan, I lectured on the "Chapter of Universal Worthy's Conduct and Vows." When I reached the passage that described how the Buddha "peeled off his skin for paper, split his bones to fashion brushes, drew blood for ink" in order to write out copies of the *Flower Adornment Sutra* stacked as high as Mount Sumeru, I asked them if they had any questions to bring up for discussion at that point. Do any of you have questions on this passage? I have explained this passage here before, and now I want to hear your judgment. What do you make of it?

Elder Layman Ma in Taiwan who was in his eighties but still had a resonant voice, asked about this passage. I won't explain my answer until you have told me how you would answer his question. [Editor's note: Various disciples discuss the passage in question.]

All of you have your own opinions, like the blind men who each felt different parts of an elephant and each drew their own conclusions about what elephants look like, based on whether they felt a leg or the trunk or the belly of the elephant. This is an excellent way to investigate the principles. Each person applies his wisdom and expresses his opinion for others to consider.

However, at that time, I didn't have that many people to study the question with, so I answered it by myself. I said, "First of all,

II. Teaching and Transforming

the Buddha was speaking hypothetically, supposing that there might be a person who'd make such a great resolve and use his bones to fashion brushes. He could have made brushes out of other material. Why did he use bone, which is not usually used to make brushes? It was to show his sincerity. Why did he use skin to make paper instead of using some other material? It was also to show his sincerity towards the sutra. Using his blood to write out the sutra was another way of demonstrating his sincere resolve, which made him unafraid of pain, suffering, and hardship. Although bone cannot be made into brushes, he was going to do it. Skin basically cannot be used as paper, but he used it as such. Blood is not used for ink, but he used it that way. He undertook ascetic practices that others could not do. The text says "bone," but that doesn't mean he used all the bones in his body. Just now one disciple said it would be enough to chop off a finger. He's right. A brush made from the bone of a single finger can be used to write many characters. As for skin, he did not peel all the skin off his body to use as paper. Perhaps he peeled the skin off one arm or one leg. Since he has two arms and two legs, he can peel his skin four different times, sometimes peeling in one place and sometimes in another. After the skin is peeled off, the wound will slowly heal. When the skin is peeled off, one naturally bleeds. That blood can be used to write out the sutra. Therefore, the person would not die. This is only a hypothetical situation, but if a person really did those things, he would not die, for he is not using up all the skin, blood, and bones in his body.

Elder Ma agreed with my explanation. I said that this was merely a hypothetical case; there is no such person in reality. The sutra brings up this principle to encourage people to bring forth the resolve for *bodhi* by thinking, "Someone may use his bones to make a brush, his skin as paper, and his blood as ink. If he can undergo that much pain, what about us?" This thought exhorts them to resolve their minds on *bodhi*.

I gave him another explanation: There might be three brothers who accomplish the deeds mentioned in the sutra cooperatively. Perhaps the eldest brother offers some of his bone to make a brush, the second brother peels off some of his skin for paper, and the third brother says, "Fine, I'll use my blood." Not only will the three people not die, they will be able to cooperate like this in life after life.

This is similar to how the two monks from Gold Mountain Monastery are practicing Three Steps One Bow together. One of them bows every third step, and the other pulls the cart a hundred or so yards ahead and bows in place. They work as a team. It's not that one monk carries the supplies and doesn't get to bow, but only waits as the other monk bows.

In the situation mentioned in the text, if several people cooperatively carried out the task, how could they die? They would not be in danger of dying.

If the situation is hypothetical and there is no such person in reality, who would die? If a person uses only a small part of his body, then he would not die either. Further, if there were three people carrying out the task together, they would not die either.

When Elder Ma heard my explanations, his doubts vanished and he was very happy. He told me, "When I first heard the principles in the sutra, I could not sleep at night. I wondered, 'How could it be this way?' Now I'll be able go to sleep when I go home."

II. Teaching and Transforming

You should not underestimate the principles discussed today and think the question was a minor one. We should be very familiar with the principles in each passage of the Buddha's sutras. You should not be unable to answer when people bring up questions for discussion. If you study on a regular basis, you will be able to resolve any problem that arises, like a sharp blade slicing right through something.

MAY 9, 1974 | THURSDAY EVENING

On Not Disturbing a Snake in Its Own Territory

Today I will say a little more about what happened in Taiwan. There are many wise people in the world, but the foolish people are also very numerous. This time when I lectured in Taiwan, I was accompanied by three American Dharma Masters, all of whom ate only one meal a day and slept sitting up. This aroused some jealousy. Someone called, saying he was from the National Assembly. He said, "You people are just putting on an act when you eat one meal a day and sleep sitting up. If your practice were right, then Taiwan's Buddhism would all be in the wrong. If Taiwan's Buddhism is right, then you are just trying to appear different from Chinese Buddhism."

How would you answer him? Think it over. You could hardly say that Taiwan's Buddhism is right. However, we cannot say that Taiwanese Buddhism is wrong, for 'a green dragon would not oppress a snake in its own territory.' He was the host, the local boss, and we were guests. We weren't on familiar ground, and we couldn't very well put the host out and take over. Now, how would you answer him? Later we investigated, and there was no such person in the National Assembly. Someone within the Taiwan Buddhist circles had deliberately arranged for this person to come give me trouble. Dragons are basically superior to snakes, but they will not bother snakes.

I said, "In the United States, we are right. In China, you are right." I couldn't say that they were wrong, nor could I mention

II. Teaching and Transforming

the issue of the Proper Dharma versus the Dharma's Ending, for that would have infuriated them too. ⊣

MAY 19, 1974 | SUNDAY EVENING

On the Journey to Sagehood Starting with the First Step

What America needs right now are sages in the Sangha and enlightened people, those who have become sages. America needs the Proper Dharma. It doesn't need Dharma in decline or members of the Sangha who prefer to remain mute. It has no need for ordinary Sangha members who don't know how to do anything except eat. You who have left the home-life in America must cultivate vigorously and quickly realize enlightenment. Once you have realized enlightenment, nothing presents any difficulty. Don't be afraid. Fear is useless. Hurry up and realize enlightenment.

I need disciples who have realized enlightenment. The first, second, and third people to realize enlightenment are my true disciples. We can distinguish three levels and nine grades. Whoever wants to can be in the first grade. You also have a chance to join the second or third grade. It's not the case that you reach three levels of enlightenment and that's it. There are infinitely many levels. Already there are some who have become enlightened. However, I cannot tell you who they are. Once you know, you'll do anything to make offerings to them, thinking, "Those are sages. I've got to make offerings to them." Then the merit and virtue would be all yours. Thus, I cannot tell you who they are.

Among the rankings of first, second, and third, let's see where you fall. There are the first, second, and third of the top level,

II. Teaching and Transforming

and those of the bottom level. What I need are people who realize enlightenment, not people who spend their time sleeping.

Some object, "I've bowed in repentance, and it doesn't help. All that
seems like superficial work. How can I realize enlightenment?"

Don't seek outside. You must work on the false before the true can
appear. If you don't work on the false, the true cannot manifest.
If you wish to become a sage, you must cultivate the Bodhisattva
Path to the end of time. Since we have not yet attained the true,
we can start by working on the superficial aspects. When we have
accumulated plenty of merit and virtue, we will naturally realize
enlightenment. We haven't realized enlightenment yet because
our virtue is insufficient. When we have cultivated blessings and
wisdom to perfection, we will naturally become sages. Our cultivation can be compared to constructing a building. Skyscrapers
are built from the ground up, not from the sky down.

> To travel far, one must begin nearby.
> To climb the heights, one must start from below.

Every journey begins with the first step. It's impossible to skip the
first step and start with the second or the tenth step. To reach a
high place, you must start climbing from below. You can't simply
leap up to the top of a skyscraper. You can't get up there so easily,
unless you take a rocket or an elevator, but that's another matter.
That's relying on technology, not on your own strength. ◁

MAY 26, 1974 | SUNDAY EVENING

On *Samādhi* Water

Question: What is *samādhi* water?

Master: *Samādhi* water is water that has been blessed by someone reciting a mantra over it. For example, if you recite the Great Compassion Mantra over a cup of water, that can also be considered *samādhi* water. Water over which the Śūraṅgama Mantra has been recited is also *samādhi* water. Such water has been aided by the power of *samādhi*. "*Samādhi*" means concentration, so we're talking about "concentration water." Why is the water characterized by "concentration" or "*samādhi*" after a mantra has been recited over it? It's because when one recites a mantra, one becomes single-minded and no longer has random thoughts. The absence of false thinking is *samādhi*, hence the name "*samādhi* water." ◁

II. Teaching and Transforming

JUNE 24, 1974 | MONDAY EVENING

On Good Roots

This summer, many people came from quite a distance to study here. These are all people with abundant good roots. Perhaps they came from the heavens, other planets, or other worlds. To be able to encounter the Buddhadharma in a country where Buddhism hardly exists, one must have massive good roots. They spent the "golden days" of summer engaged in a most worthwhile activity—investigating the Buddhadharma. Therefore, none of you should fear hardship or too much homework. Bring forth your patience to study the Buddhadharma. Then your trip to Gold Mountain Monastery will not be in vain. Having come here, you should not return empty-handed. ⹂

JULY 11, 1974 | THURSDAY EVENING

On Sincerity in Praying for Peace

On the 20th, we're going to Seattle to conduct a big ceremony for World Peace. How many participants will there be? I don't know. With lots of participants we will pray for the peace of the world; if there are few participants, we will pray for world peace all the same. If we are sincere, for sure there will be a response. In the past we started to be sincere; however, we need to be even more sincere now and in the future. What are we sincere about? When we are bowing the Repentance, everyone should contemplate, "On the 20th, no matter what, it shouldn't rain." I said yesterday, "Should it rain on that day, then I'll hit Heng Lu and Heng Kong 100 times each." This is because I told both of them to make sure it would not rain. All of you should apply effort to help them. If it rains, then I'll hit each one of you 100 times after we return. Each one of you would deserve a beating because your lack of sincerity caused there to be no response. Therefore, when you are bowing to the Buddhas, you should pray to all the Buddhas of the ten directions to bless the ceremony so that it is auspicious, perfect, free of any trouble and demonic obstacles. ⊣

II. Teaching and Transforming

JULY 16, 1974 | TUESDAY EVENING

On Keeping Our Objective in Mind

Today Guo Dao called and said they were doing fine staying in the park, and that the two monks making a Three-Steps-One-Bow pilgrimage from San Francisco have nearly reached Seattle. They've reserved a hall at the university there, and we will give lectures there on Friday, Saturday, and possibly Sunday.

During our trip to Seattle, we have to constantly remember that our purpose is to pray for world peace, and that we are not going just to have fun or to go camping. The world is in a dangerous situation. The world is still here today, but if there is no peace in the world, it may be destroyed tomorrow. Humanity may become extinct. If we sincerely pray to the Buddhas and Bodhisattvas to aid the world, then the human race will not perish so soon.

The drivers for the trip should be especially cautious and on the alert. When we go camping, everyone should dress warmly and avoid freezing. No matter where we are, we should be praying for world peace. We can't slack off for a moment. We can't act like a bird that flies about hysterically after being let out of its cage. When we go out, we should stay in a group. Don't wander off by yourself. Remember our objective of seeking world peace and avoid doing things that don't contribute to peace. ◁

JULY 28, 1974 | SUNDAY EVENING

On the Detriment of Manmade Powers

At the present time, demonic dharmas are strong. I'm referring to extraordinary powers that result from scientific advances. These are not true spiritual powers. Science will be even more advanced five hundred years from now, but this is only progress of a worldly sort, not world-transcending Dharma. No matter how advanced science becomes, it cannot help us end birth and death. The extraordinary powers I'm referring to are things like the television and the telephone. These are manmade psychic powers. It is not the case that the Dharma becomes stronger in the Dharma-Ending Age. Otherwise, why would the Dharma come to an end? We have to eliminate the manmade element in order to find what is genuine. I am not trying to scare you when I tell you this. ⊣

SEPTEMBER 1, 1974 | SUNDAY EVENING

On Being Sincere & Respecting the Rules

In listening to the Buddhadharma, you obtain benefit according to how sincere you are. An insincere person derives no benefit from the Buddhadharma. If you recite sutras and bow to the Buddhas with utmost sincerity, not being the least bit casual, you are sure to receive a great response. Some people recite the sutra on the one hand and daydream on the other, perhaps thinking, "Later, I'll have a cup of tea." That shows a total lack of sincerity.

After the sutra recitation when the Dharma Master is preparing to lecture, some people go running around doing other things. This shows a complete lack of sincerity. Such people cannot absorb the Buddhadharma. If they want to receive the Buddhadharma, how can they go running around? What do they hope to achieve? Why can't they stay still? They have no respect for the rules. They may think these bad habits are not a problem, but they would not be allowed to act that way in a large, public monastery. Even in our own monastery, we should not be so careless and unruly. Why don't you take care of your business earlier? Why do you run off to the kitchen as soon as the sutra recitation is over? If you had any sincerity at all, you wouldn't act like that. I hope everyone will learn to behave better as time goes on.

SEPTEMBER 14, 1974 | SATURDAY NOON

On Commemorating the Bowing Pilgrimage

Tomorrow is the fifteenth of September, and we will celebrate the return of the two monks from their pilgrimage for world peace. Last October 16, they made this *bodhi* resolve. On August 17 of this year, they completed one stage of their vow. And so we can set September 15 as a day of Complete Peace. We can hold a celebration on this day not only this year, but every year, in memory of these two cultivators who are the first in America to make a Three Steps One Bow pilgrimage. In Buddhism, whoever is virtuous and diligently practices is a true disciple of the Buddha. I have seen these two cultivators sincerely work hard for the sake of Buddhism, and as a result people have been influenced by Buddhism. This makes me especially happy. ⊣

Monks and laymen sitting in meditation in the main hall of Gold Mountain Monastery

III | Monastic Life

OCTOBER 15, 1972 | SUNDAY EVENING

On Searching for an "Excellent Site"

Last Friday at midnight, some of us took a trip. It wasn't a holiday or a trip for fun; we were out searching for an "excellent site" for Buddhism. [See *Sixth Patriarch Sutra*, BTTS, 2002, p. 47. A Tripiṭaka Master from India uses the term "excellent site" in describing the area where Nanhua Monastery was later founded.] Several years ago we found a place at Magic Mountain that was quite a bargain, but our two Bhikshunis went there and declared that it didn't qualify as an "excellent site." So we are still looking for an "excellent site"—a place that can produce sages. It's too bad that no Venerable Tripiṭaka Master has come to this country. No one has made any prophecy to the effect that after 170 years, a Bodhisattva in the flesh will proclaim the Dharma here. [Editor's note: See *Sixth Patriarch Sutra*, BTTS, 2002, p. 42. This prediction was made by the same Tripiṭaka Master from India when he arrived at Guangxiao Monastery in Canton City—the monastery where the Sixth Patriarch entered monastic life and received precepts.]

Buddhism has only just begun in this country. There are many "excellent sites" in this nation, it's just that no one has looked for them yet. That's why we were out at midnight, hunting for an "excellent site." This entire country is excellent—very efficacious; but the people haven't become outstanding yet. There's a Chinese saying, "If the people are outstanding, the place is excellent." When people are outstanding and heroic, the land

III. Monastic Life

will be efficacious. When people are sages, any place they go to will become an "excellent site."

That place near Magic Mountain which we found several years ago was basically an "excellent site", but since we ourselves are not sages, we didn't recognize it as such. Our midnight trip this time was certainly not a vacation. Let me tell you frankly: There are no vacations for us in this life! Why not? It's just because we took vacations before that we haven't reached Buddhahood yet. Realizing our mistake and knowing that "having fun" isn't all that fun, the four of us—three male disciples and myself—went out at midnight.

As we went out the door, I told one of those three, "I'm giving you an order—it must not rain today. If it rains, I won't show any mercy. When we get back, you'll have to kneel for forty-nine days straight at Gold Mountain Monastery, during which you won't be allowed to eat, use the restroom, stand up, or sleep." The worst thing would have been not being allowed to sleep, because for one of these disciples, going without sleep is equivalent to a death sentence. He just can't go on without sleep. I often see him in the sleeping *samādhi*.

That order I gave him scared him and he meekly accepted my mandate. As it turned out, it really didn't rain. Rain would have made it impossible to visit the place. That's why I had to threaten a foolish disciple, thereby indirectly scaring the rain spirits into thinking, "We had better not make it rain, or else that disciple will be in big trouble." The rain spirits felt sorry for my disciple! They weren't afraid of me; they only feared that my poor disciple would suffer, so they didn't let it rain.

At noon, I told him, "It didn't rain this morning, so your merit is complete. If it rains in the afternoon, you don't have to kneel when we get back." Then I announced to the other two disciples: "If it rains in the afternoon, it has nothing to do with this disciple."

When we got back, my disciples spread the good news, informing everyone: "That place certainly is an 'excellent site.' The *feng shui* ['wind and water'] is good, and so is the rainwater [a pun on *feng shui*]." Why did they think so? The lake there is called Long Ear Lake. When Patriarch Bodhidharma first went to China, he went to Bear's Ear Mountain and sat in meditation for nine years. Well, this place may or may not be equal to Bear's Ear Mountain. Let's take a look and then decide. I haven't seen what kind of lake it is yet—maybe it's a human ear lake or a dog's ear lake; it's not for sure. And what is the mountain called? Gold Mountain! Which seems to imply that this site was meant just for us at Gold Mountain Monastery. The location is better than "Old Gold Mountain" [Editor's note: the Chinese name for San Francisco]; its *feng shui* is superb. So tomorrow at noon, we're going out again. This time, we'll take a laywoman along. If we didn't include her, she wouldn't be able to sleep tomorrow night. She'd be worrying about us out on the road. She'd spend her time and energy speculating about what demons and ghosts her teacher might be subduing. However, let me repeat: these trips are not vacations. ⊣

III. Monastic Life

OCTOBER 23, 1972 | MONDAY EVENING

On Looking for Property

Let's listen to the disciples who went looking for property.

Bhikshu Heng Qian: In three weeks of working with local real estate agents and looking day after day, we found two places that might suit our requirements. One is in Sandpoint, Idaho, near Lake Ponderay. It's pretty nice. Another one is near Roseburg, Oregon. The Abbot [Editor's note: The Venerable Master] traveled to Roseburg and on to Sandpoint to inspect both those properties.

When we met the Abbot in Oregon, I related to him what I had been learning, "Real estate agents can talk a dead person back to life. They can really talk up a storm, but you just can't believe any of it. It's too bad the government and the lumber companies own vast amounts of land in the Northwest. The railroads own a lot of it too, which the government gave them. And nobody's selling. The only properties for sale are small private places sandwiched between the good parcels of land; none of those are suitable. Out of all the places we looked at, there were only these two, and they are far from perfect. You have an ideal place in your mind, but you just can't find it." That's my report on the trip. ⊣

OCTOBER 24, 1972 | TUESDAY EVENING

On Cooperation & Vigor

Tomorrow is the anniversary of Guanyin Bodhisattva's entering the monastic life. Buddhists will come to the monastery to celebrate this occasion. And so tomorrow, Gold Mountain Monastery will hold a Great Compassion Repentance Session during which the Repentance will be held twice in the morning and three times in the afternoon — five times in all.

Tomorrow, a group from Gold Mountain Monastery will travel to Carmel to visit Chang Dai-chien, a world-renowned painter who is a Buddhist. Those who make this visit will be working hard; those who remain at the monastery will also be working hard.

Today, Guo Xiu asked me if she could be excused from going on the visit. Others also requested to be excused. Again I say, those who go on the visit will be working hard; those who remain at the monastery will also work hard. In general, tomorrow will be a day in which everyone will toil. No matter how evasive you may be, you cannot avoid the hard work. No matter how much you try to slip out of things, you still have to toil. Why must we toil?

> Enduring suffering puts an end to suffering.
> Enjoying blessings uses up blessings.

That's why. The trip may involve suffering, but we are doing something meaningful by making the effort to go. We are not

III. Monastic Life

going to visit Chang Dai-chien just to have fun. We are doing it in the hopes of making Buddhism flourish and causing more people to believe in Buddhism in this country.

The Great Compassion Repentance ceremony at the monastery is equally important. As Buddhists, we should show our sincerity to the Bodhisattva. On the anniversary of Guanyin Bodhisattva's entering the monastic life, we certainly want to practice together and not let the time pass by in vain. So, tomorrow's two events are both worthwhile endeavors done for the sake of Buddhism. ◁

OCTOBER 25, 1972 | WEDNESDAY EVENING

On Strictly Upholding the Precepts

People who have received the precepts cannot casually violate them. If you have transgressed, you should quickly confess, repent, and reform before the assembly. A monk or nun who has committed a serious transgression should move back in line and walk with the novices or even the laypeople. It is not permissible for a monastic to continue to act in a casual manner and look lightly upon the violation of precepts. Buddhism has just begun in this country, and we cannot afford to be casual. If we are casual now, there's no knowing how far off we will end up in the future.

Therefore, anyone who has broken the precepts should be honest about it and seek forgiveness from everyone. You should let everyone decide how to deal with it. Don't think that if no one knows you have transgressed, you can get by. With that kind of attitude, you may end up falling in the hells, the animal realm, or the realm of hungry ghosts, and no one will be able to save you. ◁

OCTOBER 27, 1972 | FRIDAY EVENING

On Trying to Fly Too Soon

One of my monastic disciples, Guo Hu, wants to go and stay at a monastery in New York. What makes you think you can go there? They don't allow just anyone to live there, you know. Especially you—if you're alone outside, you'll definitely break the rules. You won't survive without someone watching over you. If you want to go off and live outside, fine—but wait till you're enlightened. When I certify your enlightenment, you can go. Before you're enlightened, if you go outside, you'll just waste your time. What use is that?

Your concern right now should not be with finding a place to stay where you'll be provided one meal a day so you can keep from starving to death. Your immediate concern should be with applying yourself diligently to your studies and never slacking off at any moment. Only then will you have some success in the future. How can you expect to fly before your wings are fully grown? If you go off to live on your own, I know for sure that you will fall. You ought to know that, too.

[Editor's note: Later, on September 9, 1981, the Master wrote a verse about this monastery.

> Turn from the small and go toward the great.
> Renounce the deviant and return to the proper.
> Establish a great monastic community.

Get rid of superstitious practices.
Bring forth the resolve for *bodhi*.

The disciple in question did go to New York and soon afterward went back to lay life.] ⊟

III. Monastic Life

DECEMBER 4, 1972 | MONDAY EVENING

On Exploiting Situations

At Gold Mountain Monastery, monastics and laypeople, men and women, should all know our three principles:

> Freezing, we do not scheme.
> Starving, we do not beg.
> Dying of poverty, we ask for nothing.

Do not spoil the good reputation of Gold Mountain Monastery. Don't try to exploit the situation as soon as some laypeople show up at the monastery. When influential or wealthy people from another country come and visit, you shouldn't ask them to do favors for you, saying things like, "I'm out of books. Could you get me a sutra?" Or, "I've run out of clothes. Please have some clothes made for me." Or, "I've run out of this and that; please get them for me." You may have thousands of ways to get laypeople to do things for you, but you are making a big mistake if you use those methods. In the West, where Buddhism has just begun, everyone should be high-minded and incorruptible. Don't cause others to look down on you. If you do, you will be of no help to Buddhism.

The bitterness that we undergo is part of our lot. We don't want anyone to pity us. Some laypeople saw that we were living in this cold icebox and offered to install a heater for us, but we refused the gift. Why? Because the colder it gets, the less we are afraid. We want to be like the hardy pine tree that remains evergreen even in winter. Every one of us should aspire to be like the lofty and noble cedar. Don't make yourself totally worthless. ⊟

III. Monastic Life

JANUARY 5, 1973 | FRIDAY EVENING

On Honoring Tradition

Every morning, our ceremony includes the Śūraṅgama Mantra, the Great Compassion Mantra, and the Ten Small Mantras. For the evening ceremony, we alternate between the *Amitābha Sutra* and the Repentance before Eighty-eight Buddhas. On odd-numbered days we recite the *Amitābha Sutra*, and on even-numbered days we recite the Repentance before Eighty-eight Buddhas. Yesterday was the first of the lunar month, and so we should have recited the *Amitābha Sutra*. The day before yesterday was the 29th, and there was no 30th of the month. Today, we should have recited the Repentance before Eighty-eight Buddhas, but instead you recited the *Amitābha Sutra*. You aren't very clear about the lunar calendar. Tomorrow, you should recite the *Amitābha Sutra*, even though you already recited it today. It looks like you're deliberately being different, and the Chinese Buddhists who come here don't know what's going on. If you want to continue this way, it's your choice. After all, in the Buddhadharma we cannot have attachments. ⊣

FEBRUARY 2, 1973 | FRIDAY EVENING

On Maintaining the Monastic Schedule in All Situations

Normally, during the Lunar New Year period, we sincerely bow every day from the lunar first to the lunar tenth. But there are special circumstances this year. On Monday, the 5th, seven of us will go to New York. From New York, two people will go to Canada on the 7th, and then return to New York on the 8th. We have been invited to attend a conference on the translation of sutras. Seven people are going to attend that conference.

Gold Mountain Monastery will still have three monastics and one layperson to look after things here. The Sutra lectures will continue each night as usual. The monastics here can work a little harder and give the lectures. The language classes will also continue as usual. One monk or nun can teach Chinese; another can teach Sanskrit or German. If you don't know those languages, you can teach English. The instructors for the French and Japanese classes will be here as usual.

Do not change the schedule. The daily afternoon lecture from 1:30 to 3:30 should continue, too. You can even have two daytime lectures. Don't take a break. The three of you monastic disciples can lecture on whatever you like. If nobody comes to listen, the three of you can listen to one another. We don't want to take a break from the lectures. Otherwise, people may come expecting to hear a lecture, only to find out that the schedule has been changed and there is no lecture. That wouldn't be right. The lectures should go on as usual.

III. Monastic Life

Don't think that we will be idle while we are in New York. We will be explaining Dharma and holding meetings—even on the plane. When we get there, we will continue to have a Dharma talk or sutra lecture each evening as usual. We, too, will stick to our schedule. Whether we are in the monastery or outside, we can't be lazy. Only through such diligence will we be able to propagate Buddhism and make it flourish. Don't think that this trip to New York will be relaxing. You should know that people who accompany me don't get to relax! I know that in the past, when five of you went to New York on your own, you didn't have to bother with much. But be forewarned, if you accompany me, you will surely have work to do! ⊟

MARCH 18, 1973 | SUNDAY EVENING

On Fulfilling Monastic Responsibilites

Today about thirty people took refuge. Guo Su is getting more and more "intelligent" to the point that he doesn't even know how to handle the refuge ceremony. If you don't even know how to handle such a ceremony, how do ever expect to be a qualified well-rounded practitioner of the Path? Your cultivation cannot be one-sided. You should be well-rounded and know how to do everything. Take, for instance, playing the Dharma instruments. In China, the monks and nuns do not look at the books or music while they play the instruments. They have the score clearly committed to memory, so they do not have to look at books. So much time has elapsed, and some of you are still looking at the books when you play the instruments. And not only that, you play them wrong on occasion. Although playing the Dharma instruments is not a very important thing, nonetheless, you should play them properly. For example, you led the new refuge disciples in bowing to the Buddhas, but you did not do it properly. I was not very pleased when I heard the chanting. Besides, I waited fifteen minutes upstairs for you to finish your bowing. Maybe it was twenty minutes. I waited up there, but I could hear their bowing and it sounded more and more awful. The sound was very short. I don't know whether you were bowing alternately, or having people bow only on one side, or having everyone all bow together at the same time. But the sound was very short and abrupt. I don't know whether you had time to actually make a full bow. The interval would have allowed people only time

III. Monastic Life

enough to lower their heads, and then people on the other side would get up and sing. Maybe you simply sang but did not even make a full bow. That will not do. ♩

MARCH 18, 1973 | SUNDAY EVENING

On Respecting the Monastic Sangha Order

Next week I will go to Brazil. In the temple, everyone should listen to Guo Ning and Guo Zhan. If evil-natured monks refuse to listen to instructions, they will have many problems in the future. It's not okay for you to have no respect for your elders. Guo Ning was the second monk to leave home, and Guo Zhan was the fourth. When I am here, if you don't obey instructions, you might still be excused. But when I am gone, if you refuse to obey the instructions of those two, that will be the same as not listening to your teacher's instructions. Be clear about this point. It cannot be the case that a younger Dharma brother refuses to listen to his elder Dharma brothers. ⊣

AUGUST 14, 1973 | TUESDAY EVENING

On Observing Monastic Traditions

The daily ceremonies at Gold Mountain Monastery include the morning and evening recitations, and a sutra lecture in the evening. The boards should be struck fifteen minutes before the evening recitation and sutra lecture, to remind people to get ready. Not only do people have to get ready for the ceremonies and sutra lectures, all the good spirits who protect the Dharma—the gods, dragons and the rest of the eightfold pantheon—are also waiting to protect the *bodhimaṇḍa*. Therefore, we cannot be sloppy. If the person assigned to hit the boards occasionally forgets his job, others should remind him so as to avoid wasting time. This evening, the boards were not hit until 7:10 P.M. That was a major mistake. From now on you should be especially mindful of this. ⊣

JANUARY 26, 1974 | SATURDAY EVENING

On Behaving with Integrity

On Wednesday I will be going to Asia. This time I will be back within two months. During that time, you should all behave with integrity. You should each think about what kind of person you really want to be. Don't let it be like last year when I went to South America and Gold Mountain Monastery was nearly deserted! If that happens, you'll all have to fend for yourselves. Bhikshus, in particular, while you're at Gold Mountain Monastery, may not bully the Bhikshunis. Bhikshus may not casually scold Bhikshunis. Can Bhikshunis scold Bhikshus? That's even less acceptable! Bhikshunis should observe the Eight Dharmas of Respect towards Bhikshus. They may not look down on Bhikshus or entertain impure thoughts. ◁

JANUARY 26, 1974 | SATURDAY EVENING

On Being Scolded by Young & Old Alike

If you are a monk and another monk scolds you, beats you, or even kills you, you should remain unmoved and feel that the experience is as sweet as if you were eating honey, not as bitter as eating *huanglian* [the bitterest herb in Chinese medicine]. The monk might be a junior or senior Dharma peer, or he might be a disciple of one of your Dharma peers. It could even be a case of a disciple scolding his teacher.

Let me tell you that after I became a monk and was resident in a monastery, old monks and young monks alike scolded me. The middle-aged monks also did their share of scolding. For no reason that I could see, they would scold me. As soon as they set eyes upon me, they would start in. They would stand at my door and jump up and down as they berated me. One of my disciples heard them and broke down crying. She said, "Teacher, you are so patient. I myself can't bear it, yet you still can take it."

"You say you can't bear it, but what could you do about it?" I asked her. "I ought to bear it. Why do they rail at me like that? It's because I'm lazy. I don't do enough work in the monastery. I'm not helping them build the monastery. That's why the disciples of the abbot and the disciples of those disciples are scolding me. They say I'm not doing my share of the work." So, my own disciples couldn't take it, but I still endured it. There was truly no anger inside of me. I felt as cool as if I were eating ice.

JUNE 20, 1974 | THURSDAY EVENING

On How Serious Vows Are

All the Bhikshus at Gold Mountain Monastery have made vows. Some have retreated from and forgotten their vows after two-and-a-half or three days, however. This indicates their lack of resolve to cultivate. It also indicates their wish to return to lay life. If they retreat from their vows, they might as well return to lay life. All of you must clearly recognize your goals. Once you make your vows, you should not change them. If you make a vow knowing that you will follow it for only three days, you are heading for the hells. ⊣

JULY 15, 1974 | MONDAY EVENING

On Not Imposing On Others

Some of us will be going to Seattle this week to attend a World Peace Conference. There may be a thousand people coming to participate. When we go there, we won't impose upon laypeople for lodging. I'm planning to stay overnight in a park; I'm not going to stay at my disciples' homes. If the park doesn't permit overnight stays, then I can stay in an inexpensive hotel. We are going in order to sincerely pray for world peace, and it doesn't matter where we stay for a couple of nights. The nuns can go camping; they'll be the first American Bhikshunis to go camping. Two novice monks have gone there to fast. It's not for sure how long their fast will last. If they can't endure more than one day, then they can start eating on the second day. If they can't take it after two days, they can eat on the third day. All of us who are going are prepared to suffer. Although we are happy to be praying for world peace, we're ready to suffer. ◁

AUGUST 2, 1974 | FRIDAY EVENING

On Criteria for Entering Monastic Life

In the future I won't casually accept people to enter monastic life. I definitely won't accept people who have no patience and are up to no good.

People who enter the monastic life have to be able to endure what others cannot endure, and yield what others cannot yield. They cannot be selfish and seek to benefit themselves, thinking only of themselves and never of others. One of my disciples is always coming to the monastery and making everyone upset so they become unable to apply effort in their cultivation. That shows a very bad character. And how can he demand that the monastery provide him with a private apartment when he has only recently become a monk? That's the worst kind of behavior. Even so, I'm willing to let him have his way. That's because I want to see if he can reform. Cultivators should not crave comfort. If they do, they won't be able to follow the Path.

Those who want to follow the Path have to first learn forbearance, and then learn *samādhi*. They have to bear what they cannot bear, and be in *samādhi* when they cannot be in *samādhi*. They cannot be stubborn. No matter how stubborn they may have been before, they now have to learn to be compliant and gentle. They cannot have a temper. Otherwise, even though they have become monks, they will not be able to realize enlightenment. If they cannot become enlightened, then not only will nothing good come of it, but there is the possibility that they will fall into the hells, which is very easy to do.

In the future, I will not casually permit people to become monks. I will examine and observe very carefully anyone who wants to enter the monastic life. ⊣

SEPTEMBER 29, 1974 | SUNDAY NOON

On Monastics Not Watching TV

Ordinary people are all hooked on TV. How do I know? Because even some monastics and laypeople here are confused by television. One of my disciples said, "TV is even worse than women." TV is in first place then. So you women had better smash the TV. If there's a TV set in the house, your husband will love the TV and forget about you. That's how seductive it is. Guo Zong, you can send your TV to the monastery, so the monks can watch it and see all the bizarre things of the world. Or you can send it to your parents. They're old and have enough experience, so it's nothing special to them. If young people watch it, they get hooked. Even little Guo Fang would rather watch TV than eat candy. This is just defiled dharma. Sometimes, the TV screen goes blank and there is nothing but light; that's pure dharma. But sometimes ghosts and demons, such as models who wear next to nothing, appear on the screen. That's why cultivators cannot watch TV. "But there's a TV in your room," someone says. Yes, but that's because I confiscated it from downstairs. It's facing the wall, so only the wall can watch it. I confiscated it because I saw a lot of people turning it on and watching it downstairs, getting caught by its lure. From now on, if you like to watch TV, I'm going to confiscate your TV. This applies to laypeople as well as monastics. The TV's will be confiscated because they are so addicting.

In the past I criticized a certain monk for watching TV all day long. Now the problem has come to Gold Mountain Monastery, so no matter what, I'm going to confiscate all the TV's.

Before you have ended birth and death, you may not watch television. If you do, it's easy to break the precepts. The novice precepts include one that says you can't play music, sing, dance, or deliberately watch or listen to such performances. There was no television in those days, so the precepts don't specifically mention it. But watching or listening to such performances also refers to watching such shows on TV. Most of the entertainment on TV is defiling, not pure. We must hold the Buddha's precepts and not be deluded by these worldly things. This is very important. ⊦

Preparing lunch in the

kitchen of Gold Mountain Monastery

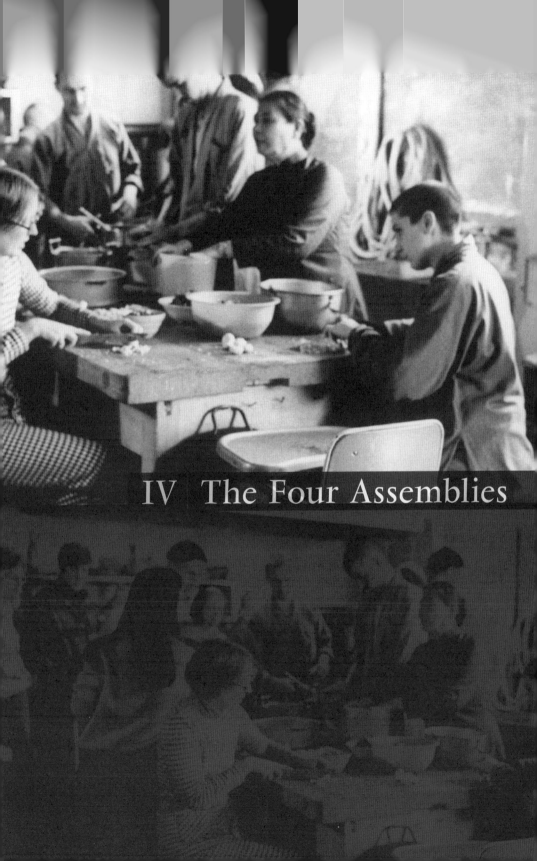

IV The Four Assemblies

OCTOBER 22, 1972 | SUNDAY NOON

On Following Rules

It's been almost two years since we moved to Gold Mountain Monastery. Since coming here, I have seldom talked about rules, so some people have become very casual. It's not that people are deliberately lax; it's because I haven't mentioned rules for so long, you have tended to forget about them. I feel remorseful that the laxity was mine in failing to remind you.

So, once again, you should all realize that:

> This day is already over,
>> And our lives are that much shorter.
> We are like fish in an evaporating pond:
>> What joy is there in this?
> Great assembly! Be diligent and vigorous
>> As if saving your own head.
> Be mindful of impermanence, and
>> Take care not to be lax.

You don't know what day the ghost of impermanence will arrive. Don't casually disregard the rules.

Gold Mountain Monastery is the first Buddhist monastery in the West [Editor's note: to have Westerners forming an orthodox monastic Sangha]; it is the fountainhead of Buddhism. You could say that everything we do is first in the world and first in Buddhism. We must resolve to make the Proper Dharma last a long time. In order for this to happen, everyone must observe the

IV. The Four Assemblies

rules. We can't act as if there were no rules. Monastics and lay-people must both conduct themselves well. "Without a compass and a T-square, one cannot make circles and squares." If there are no rules, we cannot accomplish our work in the Path. Therefore, I will now review the rules of Gold Mountain Monastery as a reminder to both monastic and laypeople.

In the Buddha Hall, we must be absolutely respectful. We should contemplate that the Buddhas are surrounding us; they are right above us, to our left and right, in front of and behind us. The Buddhas and Bodhisattvas are watching us at all times, wherever we are. Therefore, we should not chat casually or be lax. If people have proper business that needs discussed, you can go to the sitting room upstairs. But don't have a noisy conversation as if you were in the marketplace or at a theater during intermission.

It's essential for people to abide by the rules and behave with decorum here. If you yourself don't want to cultivate, fine; but don't hinder others from cultivating. If you chatter nonsense instead of cultivating, other people will be influenced. People are not sages, and even if there were sages among us, others would still be affected. Therefore, no matter what, we should protect, support, and respect this *bodhimaṇḍa*, and not do things to undermine or harm it. Everyone should pay attention to this point.

All of us here are intent upon following the Path. We don't come here to discuss business. If we truly wish to study and practice the Buddhadharma, we must do it sincerely. Don't just idle your lives away. We only have a few decades of life, and they pass by in a flash. If you lose this opportunity, next time around you may not even have a human body. If you don't apply yourself in this life, you'll be sorry in the next life. All of you should take note of this.

NOVEMBER 7, 1972 | TUESDAY EVENING

On the Four Assemblies Not Bothering Each Other

Monks should not give people trouble. At no time should monks criticize the faults of nuns or laypeople. Nuns and laypeople also must not give the monks trouble. What does giving people trouble mean? If you cause people to get upset, whether you do it intentionally or unintentionally, you are reducing your own blessings. If you get upset with people, whether intentionally or unintentionally, you are also reducing your blessings. These are both cases of giving people trouble.

People may be intent on spiritual practices, and then, for no good reason, you decide to interrupt their practice and bother them by engaging them in a conversation. Or, perhaps you bring up somebody's name and then indulge in idle gossip about that person. When you do things like that, you decrease your blessings because you yourself aren't practicing and you're disturbing others' cultivation.

Therefore, laymen should not bother laywomen; laywomen should not bother laymen. When people are quietly concentrating on their practice, you must not bother them. If you do, not only are you diminishing your own blessings, but because you have obstructed people in their cultivation, you will not be successful in your own practice. None of you should entertain too high an opinion of yourself, thinking, "I understand more than anybody else. I know all about you." That kind of attitude is a mistake.

IV. The Four Assemblies

Laypeople should not get together in pairs and talk about the faults of monastics. So, too, monastics should also not discuss the faults of laypeople. The Bodhisattva Precepts state clearly that we should not discuss the faults of those in the four assemblies.

Given that, why do you people keep bothering each other from morning till night, knowing no shame? If you have this fault, you should quickly change and repent. Otherwise, in the future when you fall into the hells, I won't pay any attention to you. ⊣

AUGUST 19, 1973 | SUNDAY NOON

On Staring or Looking Someone Straight in the Eye

Free from every arrogance and defilement, the Buddha's body is the most splendid and pure, the most wonderful and majestic. He is endowed with the Thirty-two Hallmarks and Eighty Subsidiary Characteristics. People want to keep on staring at the Buddha, never letting up their gaze.

They behave like you Westerners. Your eyes tend to fixate when you look at someone—you stare unblinkingly. [Editor's note: Westerners might consider it polite to look directly at a person when addressing him or her, but Asians generally consider it impolite to stare directly at another person's face.] 뉴

SEPTEMBER 17, 1973 | MONDAY EVENING

On Not Talking while Driving

When you pick up guests and drive them anywhere, whether they are Dharma Masters or laypeople, don't talk much in the car. A car is not the place for conversation. As soon as you start talking, it's easy to have an accident. If that happens, everyone will say, "Oh, look, cars from Gold Mountain Monastery get into accidents like anyone else. What spiritual response do they have?" So be careful. Don't create problems. The best thing is not to talk at all in the car, no matter who the guests are. If they want to talk to you, just tell them, "I can't talk while I'm driving because there are too many cars and too many people in the city. I have to pay close attention to what I'm doing in order to stay safe." To avoid accidents and ridicule are very valid reasons for not talking in the car. ᛁ

SEPTEMBER 29, 1973 | SATURDAY EVENING

On Being Punctual & Finishing What We Start

All monastics and laypeople alike must follow the rules and respect themselves. Don't look down on yourselves. People who have no self-respect will misbehave. People who respect themselves will abide by the rules.

People who wish to bow the Great Compassion Repentance should arrive at the monastery fifteen minutes before the ceremony is due to begin. Whenever there is a Dharma assembly in the *bodhimaṇḍa*, whether it is a sutra lecture or some other Dharma event, people should arrive before it begins, not in the middle of the event. Don't procrastinate. You should do a complete job of things; don't do thing halfway. If you do things completely, your merit will also be full and perfect. If you only attend half of the ceremony, you will only have half the merit. There should be a beginning and an end. In other words, finish what you start. If you attend from the beginning and stay until the end, then your merit will be complete. For example, if you want to listen to the sutra lecture, you should also attend the evening recitation preceding the lecture. That's the complete way to do it.

When the sutra lectures are moved to Washington Street, laypeople who don't have cars can take the bus wagon from Gold Mountain Monastery. People who have cars can give rides to those who don't. We should all help one another out. Everyone should understand this. We should benefit ourselves and benefit

IV. The Four Assemblies

others, enlighten ourselves and enlighten others, liberate ourselves and liberate others. ⊣

OCTOBER 14, 1973 | SUNDAY EVENING, AT WASHINGTON STREET

On Rallying When There Is Work to Be Done

[What follows is a discussion of how the Opening of the Light (a consecration ceremony for the International Institute for the Translation of Buddhist Texts) at Washington Street had gone. One disciple notes: Really, the whole back area that was to hold the reception had not been cleaned up or arranged at all, and everything had to be done just before the ceremony was going to begin.]

This morning I was rather pained, because the laypeople from our monastery all showed up very late. Many others came, whereas few of our regulars did. When there is an activity at the *bodhimaṇḍa*, each and every Dharma-protecting layperson should strive to be the first to come. When you see that there is work to be done in the *bodhimaṇḍa*, you ought to come and pitch in.

This morning I arrived around 5:45 A.M. and we got a lot done. We moved the Buddha image and did the work that did not get finished yesterday. People even washed the garage this morning.

The people in charge of the donation box were not here, and there were many visitors, but no one took care of the sign-in book. And those are not the only things that were not taken care of properly.

IV. The Four Assemblies

I'll tell you the truth. After working and walking around all day, I barely have the strength to walk now. My feet won't listen to me anymore. All of you are my disciples, and yet you act as if the monastery's affairs are not your business. You have been remiss in your responsibility of protecting the Dharma. Why do you pay no heed when there are matters to attend to in the *bodhimaṇḍa*? You act as if the affairs of the *bodhimaṇḍa* have nothing to do with you. This pains me greatly.

All of you think it over. When there is work to be done, if our own Dharma protectors do not pitch in and help, doesn't it seem that you have failed to fulfill your responsibility as Dharma protectors?

OCTOBER 26, 1973 | FRIDAY EVENING

On the Necessity of Real Practice

All of you laypeople and monastic disciples here at Gold Mountain Monastery should be courageously vigorous, because this is the beginning of Buddhism in the West. There is a need for people to become enlightened and realize levels of sagehood. If there are people who become enlightened sages, then it will be easy for Buddhism to spread far and wide.

The two monks who are bowing once every three steps are not the only ones who have the potential to become enlightened sages. The other three monks here also share that potential; the nuns as well. That's because in this country it's "ladies first," so now you nuns should be first in becoming enlightened and first in realizing levels of sagehood. Right now we need to examine and select such people of talent.

There is a layperson—I don't know whether it is an Upasaka or an Upasika—who is displeased. That person is thinking, "Are monks and nuns the only ones who can become enlightened sages? Why hasn't there been any mention of laymen and laywomen?"

Now I'll correct the omission: Laymen and laywomen also can become enlightened sages, but they have to engage in spiritual practice. Without spiritual practice, even a Buddha wouldn't be a Buddha. But if you do practice, then even though you aren't

IV. The Four Assemblies

a Buddha right now, you can become one. It all depends on whether or not you practice. ◁

OCTOBER 31, 1973 | WEDNESDAY EVENING

On Constructing Tight Fortifications so People Can't Invade

[Editor's note: The Venerable Master asks a disciple to read an article from the *Napa County Record* written by Guo Zhou (David Rounds, the *Record* editor), dated October 31, 1973. The article was about two monks, Heng Ju (Guo Yu's ordination name) and Heng Yo (Guo Dao's ordination name), who were making the first American Three Steps One Bow Pilgrimage, from Gold Mountain Monastery in San Francisco to Marblemount in Washington State. They began their journey on October 16, 1973, and completed it on August 17, 1974.]

Master: What do you think of this article? If you have any opinions, bring them up. I do have one opinion myself. The part that talks about their doing this to make Buddhism better known should not be in there. It's already enough to say that Buddhists are doing this, and that they are simply praying for world peace. You shouldn't say the purpose is to make Buddhism better known or more popular. If you talk about the benefits to Buddhism from doing this, or how it will make Buddhism better known, then you are deliberately fishing for praise and reputation. You're doing it for publicity purposes. Then you've lost all the value of the original intent. It loses all its worth. So it's best not to bring up how beneficial to Buddhism it is, or how it will influence people. Don't mention that. Other people can say it, but the article quotes Guo Yu as saying it. That's not okay. They shouldn't have that idea. Whoever is going there tomorrow should tell them right away not to have such ideas after this,

IV. The Four Assemblies

and that they shouldn't talk about this benefiting Buddhism in some way. As soon as you say such things, people will consider it a deliberate publicity campaign for Buddhism, something you Buddhists have dreamed up to do because you don't have any other way to get publicity. Do you understand what I mean?

Disciple: Yes, I understand.

Master: You give people an opening, a place to get at you, either to criticize or to scold you. However, if people scold them, the more they are scolded the better. If people hit them, it doesn't matter. The worse people treat them the better. Go tell them that. Whoever is going to see them tomorrow should inform them immediately about this. As soon as they talk like that, they lose the value of the whole thing. All of you think it over, isn't that what would happen?

Master: What do you think, Guo Zhou?

Guo Zhou: I wish it were not too late to change the article.

Master: Never mind—just be careful next time. You should think things over using your wisdom and intelligence. Don't take the Buddhist standpoint. Use the outlook, for example, of a non-Buddhist religion. That way you'll understand a lot more. Basically the article could say what it says, and it would be fine. However, when Buddhism is just beginning, you shouldn't give people an opportunity to attack it, a chance to fight. If we construct tight fortifications, then others can't invade.

There are people who would be happy for an atomic bomb to hit our building, because we speak the true Dharma. It was already that way in the time of Great Master Yongjia, who said, "They can't stand not to see it destroyed like a tile smashed to smithereens." When you speak the genuine, proper Dharma, they want to do away with you immediately. That's why you need to be careful. To them, everything we do is wrong. You try to do something right, and people try to smash you the way a tile smashes when you dash it on the ground. You should all deeply fathom this principle and truly understand it. ◁

IV. The Four Assemblies

DECEMBER 15, 1973 | SATURDAY EVENING

On Vows Being Essential

What we are discussing reminds me of the first group of disciples, three monks and two nuns, who went to Taiwan to receive the precepts; the second group of four monks who went to Taiwan for ordination; and the third group who were ordained right here in Gold Mountain Monastery. All of them have made vows. However, none of the novices who recently entered monastic life and took novice precepts have made vows.

If you wish to make vows, you should let me know first. You have made a commitment to follow the Bodhisattva Path and to become a Buddha. That is very good, but you must first make vows. Actually, all of you in the fourfold assembly at Gold Mountain Monastery should make vows. After making vows, you should practice in accord with those vows. In a few days there will be an appropriate time for making vows, so do not delay. Each of you who wants to make vows has to submit your vows in writing. If you don't know how to write, ask someone to write them for you. Making vows is a golden rule at Gold Mountain Monastery.

JANUARY 23, 1974 | WEDNESDAY EVENING

On Vows Being Up to You

Vows express your own wishes. They are something that you want to do; they don't have to do with anyone else. If you wish to ascend to the heavens, then ascend to the heavens. If you wish to go down to the hells, go down to the hells. It depends on what you yourself want. For example, the beings in the hells right now are there because they made vows to go there. If they hadn't made such vows, they wouldn't be able to go there. Those who become Buddhas are able to do so because they made vows to realize Buddhahood. There is total freedom. You can do whatever you wish, and no one's wishes will be criticized. ◁

SEPTEMBER 24, 1974 | TUESDAY EVENING

On Not Being a Parasite that Feeds on Its Host's Flesh

It's very important that we all support and protect Gold Mountain Monastery rather than try to destroy it. Don't be a "parasite on the lion's body feeding on the lion's flesh." You don't want to rely on the Buddha for food and clothing, and then relieve yourself in the Buddha's almsbowl. Anyone who does that will surely fall into the hells. Gold Mountain Monastery is the mother of Western Buddhism. If you don't want to be filial to the mother, at least don't kill her. Every Buddhist should protect Gold Mountain Monastery. Don't be like certain laypeople and monastics who are intent on destroying Gold Mountain Monastery. When we hold sutra lectures here, they take a loudspeaker out onto the streets and tell people not to come. They say the lectures are always disrupted by noisy children. It's not the case that there are children here everyday. When there are children, they tell people not to come. But even when there are no children, they themselves still don't come. Isn't it strange? ⊣

Listening to a Dharma talk at lunch in the dining hall of Gold Mountain Monastery on a special occasion

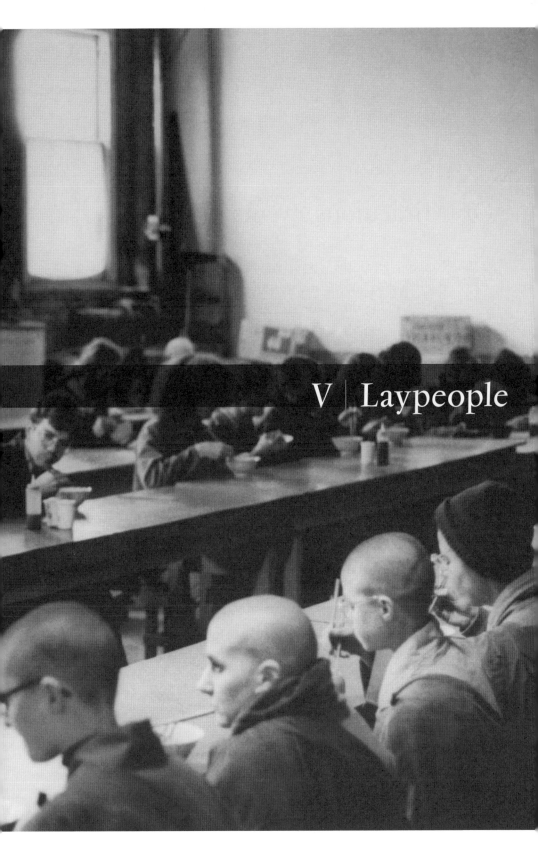

V | Laypeople

OCTOBER 25, 1972 | WEDNESDAY EVENING

On Miraculous Events

Not only was the *bodhimaṇḍa* where the Buddha realized Buddhahood inconceivable, this very *bodhimaṇḍa* where we are explaining the *Flower Adornment Sutra* is also an inconceivable place where all kinds of events occur. Several days ago, a "stone man" came to listen to the sutra lecture. Perhaps one day a "wooden man" will show up as well. The "stone man" stayed here quite a few days, but no one recognized him. Before his arrival, a ghost came—quite an inconceivable one. It was not a good ghost, but a hungry ghost that loved to eat things, especially apples. That was a miraculous event. I'm not joking. When you encounter someone you don't recognize, he or she may very well be a Bodhisattva or a Buddha or an Arhat. Or the person might also be a ghost or demon or monster—it's not for sure. In general, these are all possibilities.

Today, on the anniversary of Guanyin Bodhisattva's entering the monastic life [October 25, 1972], several of us went to visit a manifestation of Guanyin in the form of a layperson [Upasaka Chang Dai-chien]. This layman has forgotten his connection with Guanyin Bodhisattva and has gotten caught up in the five desires. However, since his inherent nature is not completely confused, he still believes in Buddhism.

You can find this transformation of Guanyin Bodhisattva as a mighty hero among the Great Compassion Mantra manifestations. [Editor's note: See *Great Compassion Mantra Verses*, BTTS,

V. Laypeople

2000, p. 38, line 30: *two la two la*.] That's who we visited today. You could say that our reasons for going to see him were not insignificant. We went intending to influence him and to remind him of his actual calling. So, some of us set out at five o'clock this morning and others left around six. Professor Hsieh accompanied us. She also has many good roots and has deep affinities with this transformation of Guanyin Bodhisattva.

This was the first time I ever visited an artist at his studio. Although there are other artists who also do excellent work, I have never had the time to visit their studios. You could say that this particular artist has been a fellow cultivator of mine for a long time, so I have special affinities with him. When we chatted with each other we found that we did have deep bonds. I found him to be honest and frank, not obsequious or crafty.

Hopefully this layman can bring forth the *bodhi* resolve—if not now, then in the future. We ought to watch over him and help him out. One needs to use different ways to cross over living beings. Today we went through some hard work to do this. As to whether this transformation body of Guanyin Bodhisattva will recognize his original face and go back to the source, only time will tell.

[Editor's note: Later, the Master wrote a verse about Chang Dai-Chien.

For the Great Chinese Painter Chang Dai-chien

> Foremost in Chinese painting is my fellow
>   cultivator from another life.
> Your name is heard throughout the cosmos.
> In the past and present, in China and abroad,
> Your work is widely known, and no
>   one wants to miss it.
> It's quick as a lightning flash in space,
>   reaching higher than the heavens.
> Guanyin manifests the appearance of a great hero.
> Amitābha himself would praise your
>   elder's countenance.
> Playing in *samādhi* is delightful,
> But don't forget your purple-golden lotus in the West.

Given by the mountain monk Hsuan Hua on October 9, in the 2999th year of the Buddha.] ⱶ

OCTOBER 30, 1972 | MONDAY EVENING

On Offering to the Sangha

Yesterday Guo Tong (Penetration) and Guo Tong (Cooperation), two of my disciples who were married at Gold Mountain Monastery, came to express their wish to make an offering to the Triple Jewel on Thanksgiving Day. Generally we decline invitations to accept offerings outside the monastery, but seeing their sincerity, I decided we could enjoy a little good food, and so I accepted. I don't know if other people want to come along or not; everyone can make his or her own decision. You may say, "My teacher may like to eat good food, but I certainly do not." That's fine. From now on, people are free to come along or not come along on such outings as they please. You don't have to find an excuse for not going. 中

NOVEMBER 5, 1972 | SUNDAY NOON

On Laypeople's Role as Dharma Protectors

Lay Buddhists are also called Dharma protectors. Their responsibility is to protect and support the Triple Jewel, to draw near and make offerings to it. As Dharma protectors, they must not destroy or slander the Triple Jewel. They cannot come to the *bodhimaṇḍa* and find fault with everything, causing trouble and spreading gossip in a place that was originally free of trouble and gossip.

A couple of my lay disciples who basically know very little about Buddhism have decided they want to boss the Sangha around by having laypeople take charge of temple affairs. They contend that all articles published in our monthly journal have to be written by laypeople, and that monastics should not be allowed to write. I don't understand who taught them this approach. They also maintain that the journal should be given free to people.

Now if you were the founders and sponsors of this publication, then you could select whatever content you wanted. But, frankly, you haven't paid a single penny toward the journal's expenses, so what right do you have to suggest that they be given away free? Why should the journal be given away free? You don't understand the least bit about the Buddhadharma, but you rely on your personal whims and opinions and want to become the managers of this monastery and to boss the monastics around. Such an attitude greatly displeases me.

V. Laypeople

These two people asked another disciple to run copies of my lectures. Initially, they invested $20 in the making of those copies. Then they turned around and charged other disciples $12 per set, and insisted that the $12 be handed in to them, that others are not allowed to take care of this business. Think it over: Is this fair or not? They say that the journal should be given away for free, yet they charge money for copies of lectures.

Now the lectures printed on those copies are delivered by me, a monastic, not by these lay disciples. To charge money for their own lectures would be reasonable. But they spend $20 making copies of someone else's lectures, and then charge people $12 per set. That's a pretty good business! I myself wouldn't have thought of a way to make such a big profit.

I didn't want to talk about this, but I notice that other laypeople are being influenced by these two, so I have no choice but to bring up this matter. All of you should reflect on the principle involved. They don't live in the area and hardly ever come to the monastery, but when they do come, they find fault with everything here. They complain to other disciples, who get confused by the 'spell' they are chanting and don't know how to answer their questions.

All of you pay attention: In monasteries established by me, I won't allow laypeople to run monastic affairs. This particular couple thinks they want to take over our monastic management. I believe that if they were actually in charge, they'd be so overwhelmed with the responsibility that within a month they'd be running 108,000 miles away. Why do I say that? Well, this monastery is just getting established; it doesn't yet have a solid foundation. Three months ago, we borrowed $1,400, and last month we scraped things together and paid back $700. If they were to take over, they'd become so nervous trying to make the monastic accounts balance that they wouldn't be able to sleep at night.

On Friday three of my monastic disciples are going to Hong Kong to propagate the Dharma. In 1969, when five of my disciples went to Taiwan to receive the precepts, many people chipped in for their travel expenses. The most that someone donated was $300, while others gave smaller amounts.

The second time, when four of my disciples went to Taiwan to take precepts, not a single layperson donated any money for the trip. However, one of those four monks told people in Taiwan that laypeople had paid their airfare. That shows his utter ignorance. Which layperson contributed to those transportation fees? What do you mean by going to Taiwan and exaggerating about laypeople that way?

This time, the three monks going to Hong Kong are a little more fortunate than those who went to Taiwan last time. Someone gave them $5 each, and I, borrowing their light, also got $10. Actually, their airfare and their expenses have all been provided by me.

You laypeople can stop speculating about whether the monastery paid for these monks. The fact is, I myself borrowed money to buy them round-trip tickets. Laypeople, pay attention to what I'm saying: if you find fault with the monastery every time you come, you are making a mistake. ⊣

NOVEMBER 16, 1972 | THURSDAY EVENING

On Recognizing One's Position

A lay disciple who visited here few days ago made the following claim. He said he was in essence a monastic, since he had not drawn near his wife for over twenty years. I told him, "Although you yourself make such a claim, nobody else will recognize you as a monastic."

"That's true," he said.

"Well, in that case, you can't claim you are a monastic," I responded. "Why do you want to set yourself up to be something you are not, and claim that you are just the same as a monastic? Basically, you enjoy pleasures and do not practice much. How can you make such a claim?"

He said, "But I've taken part in a few meditation sessions, so I think I pass."

"What kind of meditation session did you attend?"

"Well, we sat in meditation for seven days," he said.

"You probably have never heard of what our meditation sessions are like," I told him. "We get up at 3 o'clock in the morning and sit and walk straight through until midnight. Did the sessions you attend maintain a similar schedule?"

"No," he replied. "We started at eight in the morning and ended at five in the evening."

"Well, that's quite a different case."

After he heard that, he realized he could not make the grade. ⊣

FEBRUARY 27, 1973 | TUESDAY EVENING

On Protecting Supporters of the Monastery

At Gold Mountain Monastery, we lecture on the sutras and speak Dharma every day, and this is helping all of humankind. As we lecture on the sutras, the monastery is surrounded by auspicious clouds and a wholesome energy. From this day on, sick people who come to Gold Mountain Monastery will certainly recover from their illness. Of course they will recover from their illness while staying at the monastery, but even when they go home, they will not experience a relapse. That is because the gods, dragons, and the rest of the eight kinds of ghosts and spirits come to protect the Dharma and they will also guard and protect supporters of the monastery.

After we got back from New York, we stopped over at Los Angeles and San Diego. Upasika Guo Wu came up with us and has stayed at Gold Mountain Monastery for over two weeks. Tomorrow she will go home. This evening, when we bow in the Repentance before Ten Thousand Buddhas, we can dedicate the merit to her with the wish that she will recover from her sickness. I see that the time is about right for her to get over her illness. We can also dedicate merit to Guo Jin, who is still quite sick after a week. Her illness has become so serious that she's not eating or drinking. So all of you should bow to the Buddhas seeking a response for both these laywomen to quickly recover. ⊣

MARCH 3, 1973 | SATURDAY

On Sincerely Dedicating Merit

Yesterday evening since everyone was bowing in the Repentance before Ten Thousand Buddhas on behalf of Guo Jin, she has recovered somewhat from her illness. However, since not every one of you has been entirely sincere, the response is not as great as it can be. This evening, everyone should be even more sincere in requesting the ten thousand Buddhas of the ten directions to aid Guo Jin so that she will definitely recover from her illness. If she fails to get well, it's a sign that we have not bowed in repentance sincerely enough. We must bring forth a determined resolve, and our united efforts will most certainly move the Buddhas. We should ask for the Buddha's compassionate aid to help this laywoman get well. ᵈ

MARCH 7, 1973 | WEDNESDAY EVENING

On Being Attentive to Guests

I've reminded you so often to pay special attention to newcomers. But, someone new came, and you don't even know when he left. There are so many of you here, yet nobody knows when that guest left. That just goes to show that you have skill: You've perfected the *samādhi* of It's-Not-My-Business.

The problem with *samādhi* is that you quickly come out of it when it's time to eat. And when it's time to sleep, you seem to be in limbo—having neither gotten back into that *samādhi* nor gotten completely out of it either. ⊣

MARCH 7, 1973 | WEDNESDAY EVENING

On Being Attentive to Food

Well, for those who like to eat, there's good news today. On Saturday, Guo Ming [Editor's note: former Miss Chinatown] will make a vegetarian offering to the assembly. Buy vegetables on Friday and Mrs. Wang will cook them on Saturday. You can make room in your stomachs. Don't eat so much food now in order to save space to fill it up on Saturday. But do not fill your stomach to capacity, because there is still another meal offering on Sunday. Mrs. Wang herself wants to cook and treat the group to a vegetarian meal. Also, Professor Yao and Professor Hsieh will be our guests on Sunday.

And so, prepare more room in your stomachs for this weekend so you can eat more food. You may wonder why I am encouraging you to eat more food. If you eat more, you will have more strength for cultivation, and you will become even more adept at entering *samādhi*.

But the food that we cultivators eat should not be excessively delicious. I already warned Mrs. Wang to not make the food too tasty or delicious, because I fear my disciples might stuff themselves until their stomachs burst. And then, not only would there be no merit and virtue involved, the donor would have created offenses. In Hong Kong she cooked a vegetarian meal for my three monastic disciples and they told me that the following day they had no appetite at all. ◁

MARCH 9, 1973 | FRIDAY EVENING

On Remembering Details

We will begin a week-long session tomorrow during which we chant Om Mani Padme Hum. Last year was probably the first time such a session had been held in the world. [Editor's note: The disciples requested that session. The Master advocated steady daily practice and did not advocate intensive twenty-four-hour sessions, but he responded to his disciples' wishes and permitted it in this case.] We are continuing that tradition this year.

Om Mani Padme Hum is the mind-seal Dharma of Guanyin Bodhisattva. The 19th day of the second lunar month is the birthday of Guanyin Bodhisattva We will purify the boundaries at seven o'clock tomorrow evening. Since I did not attend the session last year, I will not attend this session this year either. I will take a rest. But I will lecture on the sutras as usual on Sunday. All of you should work hard on your own; don't ask others to help you out. Don't think just because I am not attending the session that you have lost something. Whether I am here or not, it is the same. You should understand this principle. Whether I am here or not, it is the same. Whether I am not here, or here, it is still the same. This is an inconceivable state, if you can understand it. ᄇ

AUGUST 12, 1973 | SUNDAY NOON

On Youth Being the Hope of the Future

Some young children whom I am very fond of have been coming often. The very young Guo Fang and Guo Zhi have been coming regularly, and some teenagers are also showing interest. These young people will have a bright future. Some of you dislike young people, but that is a great mistake. Young people will shoulder the responsibility of Buddhism. Therefore, you should put effort into training the young, the next generation. Buddhism needs new blood. All of you wily old folks are useless. I hope that the young people will quickly acquire spiritual powers. Then the older people will be in no position to look down on you young people. ◁

AUGUST 24, 1973 | FRIDAY EVENING

On Reacting to Circumstances

People are affected by circumstances. When they see others join the monastic life, they resolve to join the monastic life. When they witness a marriage, they think they should look for a marriage partner, too. Soon Gold Mountain Monastery will witness the wedding of Guo Yao; some people may have a change of heart when they see that. Then later on, Gold Mountain Monastery will be initiating people into monastic life and transmitting precepts to them. I believe that will cause many people to experience another change of heart. ⊣

SEPTEMBER 11, 1973 | TUESDAY EVENING

On Sincerely Recognizing the Importance of Dharma

Today, Guo Yang and Guo Yao were married here at Gold Mountain Monastery. Their sincerity toward the Dharma is evident, because they have come to listen to the sutra lecture this evening. They did not immediately escape for a holiday in the mountains or by the sea. Instead, tonight they came back to listen to the Buddhadharma.

I have married other disciples here at Gold Mountain Monastery, but those others did not bother to come back in the evening to hear the Dharma. And so, comparatively speaking, the two disciples I married today are unusual.

Why do I mention this? I want to make the point that the Dharma is essential; it should be people's guiding principle. The fact that these two disciples still have come to listen to the Dharma on their wedding day shows how much importance they place on the Dharma. This makes me very happy.

We are here studying the Buddhadharma together, but while some regard it highly, others do not. Some place emphasis on worldly dharmas. They obscure the Buddhadharma with worldly dharmas. They fail to illumine the five *skandhas* and see that they are empty. You should look into this. If you are one of those, take note: if you were to study Buddhadharma with the same kind of intent, effort, and earnestness with which you study worldly dharmas, you would really get somewhere.

V. Laypeople

Today is the 15th of the eighth lunar month. When you go home, recite the Great Compassion Mantra a few more times and drink a bit more sweet dew. ⊣

SEPTEMBER 14, 1973 | FRIDAY EVENING

On Seeking Liberation

Today all of you heard one of my disciples using his personal experience to reveal the Dharma for us. Before he got married, he asked me several times if he could become a monk. He made that request the first time he saw me. Later, I don't know what "passage into liberation" he entered, but he didn't become a monk.

Now, he's asking again to become a monk. I don't know if the person who wants to become a monk now is the same person who didn't become a monk before. If he is the same person, what made him seek two different things? If it's two different people we're dealing with here, then why do both of them ultimately want the same thing—to become a monk?

We'll have to do some research on this. It's interesting that the couple who just got married didn't come tonight. They would have heard about this disciple's marital problems. Actually, it would have been more timely if he had discussed this topic a few days ago before those newlyweds tied the knot. Anyway, when this disciple who wants to become a monk got married, his wedding caused some monastics to think about returning to lay life. And when those newlyweds got married recently, more monastics were having false thinking. But now, this disciple who wants to become a monk has given his personal testimony concerning so-called marital bliss, which may help quell some of the monastics' false thinking. That's why I had him talk about his experience. ⊣

OCTOBER 5, 1973 | FRIDAY EVENING, AT WASHINGTON STREET

On Gentle Guidance for Laypeople

Recently we've had many guests, including Guo Man's son, her son-in-law, and other relatives. It's been pleasant having them here; unfortunately, they are leaving tomorrow. I had hoped they could stay for the Opening of the Light Ceremony (a consecration ceremony for the International Institute for the Translation of Buddhist Texts), but they have urgent business to attend to in Argentina. They are planning to open the frontiers of Buddhism in Argentina. Those areas untouched by Buddhism are waiting for them to blaze the trail. This is important work indeed.

Professor Hsieh also left today to return to Taiwan. This time she behaved very well. Although she is given to crying, especially during partings, today she remained resolutely obedient. Her sister was crying so hard she couldn't even talk. Although tears came to Upasika Hsieh's eyes, she did not dare let them fall because she had promised me that she would definitely not cry. As it turned out, she handled herself admirably. Before she left for Taiwan, I told her to go quickly and come back quickly, and she promised to return soon. ⊣

NOVEMBER 14, 1973 | WEDNESDAY EVENING

On Parents' Responsibility
to Discipline Children

[Editor's note: A disturbance by children interrupts the lecture.] All of you parents who bring children here have to watch over them and not let them make such disturbances. When they were too young to understand, you said they wouldn't obey you. But now they have reached the age of understanding, so you should make sure they don't squabble and shout as they please in the *bodhimaṇḍa* [monastery]. ⊣

Exterior of Gold Mountain Monastery, 15th Street

Recitation before lunch in the improvised dining hall of Gold Mountain Monastery

JANUARY 10, 1973 | WEDNESDAY EVENING

On Reasons for the Flu Epidemic

> When you reflect on the suffering of sickness,
>   Having no illness becomes a blessing.
> When you reflect on the suffering of hunger and cold,
>   Eating your fill and being warm
>   becomes a blessing.
> When you reflect on the suffering of calamities,
>   Dwelling in peace becomes a blessing.

Recently many people have come down with the flu. Yesterday Guo Ning told me that many of you had gotten food poisoning and that he feared you would die. He wanted to tell Guo Su not to eat that stuff, but he knew Guo Su wouldn't listen to him, so he came to tell me so that I could tell that monk. So, today we didn't eat yesterday's food. Potatoes, after they have been mashed, should be eaten on the same day. Don't eat them the following day, because by then they will change color and a chemical change will have taken place.

Guo Jin, how do you feel today? If you're sick, you should rest more and drink a lot of water, or take a hot bath, and you will recover faster. The newspapers report that over 50 people in this country have already died from the flu epidemic—that's a low estimate, I think. Over 1,000 people have died from the flu in London. So, the situation is grave. Everyone should be more careful. Put on more clothes.

VI. Karmic Conditions

I can suggest two possible sources that have brought on this current flu epidemic. One source could be the poisons that are released into the air during nuclear experiments. Those toxins that are polluting the atmosphere are a plausible underlying reason for the flu epidemic. Another possible source may be from experiments carried out by satellites launched into space. Some eject poison into the atmosphere in order to test human tolerance levels. These experiments are part of the development of biochemical weapons that can be used in wars of the future. Both of these are possible reasons. ◁

FEBRUARY 14, 1973 | WEDNESDAY EVENING

On the Karmic Retribution of Hunger

On Monday [Editor's note: February 5] the week before last, seven of us—four monks and three nuns—went to New York. We had to go hungry on the airplane, since there wasn't enough food to fill us up. Especially Guo Hu. Since he could not get his fill, he got into an argument with his elder brother, blaming him for not arranging the meals better. Actually, you should know that a karmic retribution like having to go hungry will not necessarily be limited to just one day.

The next day, when we got to the conference, the layman hosting it was rather stingy and prepared very little food. He thought it would be enough, but many people turned up, and there weren't enough rice and vegetables to go around. And so on the second day, we had to undergo the same karmic retribution of going hungry. Then I said to Guo Hu, "Never mind, don't cry. I promise you that on the third day you will eat to your heart's content." And so, on the third day, I took him to Canada.

When we went to the Buddhist Association of Canada, a Dharma Master and several laypeople had prepared plenty of rice and vegetables in advance, and we ate our fill there. However, although we ate our fill, the other five people who stayed over at the conference site in New York still did not get enough to eat. And so, on the first, second, and third days they were there, they did not get enough to eat. On the fourth day, we just made do with it, since the conference came to an end at that point. But the fact

VI. Karmic Conditions

that we did not get enough to eat was an overriding impression and so nobody could muster much enthusiasm for the conference, which came to a rather muddled conclusion anyway. ⊢

AUGUST 15, 1973 | WEDNESDAY EVENING

On Karmic Hindrances

Some of you do nothing all day. Instead of listening to the sutras, hearing the Dharma, or learning languages, you meet with the Duke of Zhou in your dreams. That's a Chinese expression. When you say, "I've just had a meeting with the Duke of Zhou," it means you were dreaming.

You do not cultivate vigorously. When people suggest we bow the repentance, you are the first to oppose it. Actually your karmic obstacles are opposing it. It may not be the case that you yourself are opposing it, but your karmic obstacles prevent you from cultivating. They don't want you to bow the repentance, recite the Buddha's name, or cultivate in any way at all. Therefore, when people suggest a method of cultivation, you get angry. "Why do that?" you say. Since you don't want to do anything, go right ahead and do nothing. That's wonderful.

Actually, monastics must be sure to do everything in a genuine way. We cannot "hang up a sheep's head but sell dog meat." We cannot claim that we cultivate, but not actually do it. That would not be true practice. And if you lack true practice, you will not be able to realize the highest enlightenment.

Wise teachers! All of you have higher wisdom than I. I am just a fool. If you want to listen to my Dharma, go right ahead. If you don't want to listen to it, then don't listen. I won't force others to listen to my Dharma. Why? It's only to be feared that what I

VI. Karmic Conditions

speak is not the Dharma. If it is the Dharma, even if people do not listen to it, ghosts and spirits will listen. And even if ghosts and spirits do not listen to it, gods, dragons, and the rest of the eightfold pantheon and Bodhisattvas of the ten directions, will listen to it. It's no big deal if a handful of you refuse to listen.

AUGUST 27, 1973 | MONDAY EVENING

On Cause & Effect

Why do people violate the precepts? It is because they do not understand. They are confused. That's why they create karma. And, having created the karma of killing, they will undergo the retribution for killing. The karma of theft will bring about the retribution for theft. The karma of lust [sexual misconduct] will bring about the retribution for lust.

This morning a laywoman said that her sister and brother-in-law do not get along. That's because the husband misbehaves and the couple cannot see eye to eye; they have diverging opinions. I said to her, "This is what you should tell your sister: When you were a man in the past, you treated women this way. Now a man treats you the same way you treated others—this is your retribution."

You will undergo the retribution for whatever karma you create. If you kill someone's father, someone will kill your father. If you kill someone's brother, someone will kill your brother. Retribution is evident in many situations. That is the process of becoming deluded, creating karma, and undergoing retribution. Take a look at how much karma people create. The karma each individual creates is very complex; it is not only one kind of karma. Therefore, their karma is as powerful as a great sea. People are blown and tossed about by its winds. ◁

AUGUST 28, 1973 | TUESDAY EVENING

On Vows About Memorization Skills

We were just discussing why Guo Yi has such a good memory. Her good memory came about because in a past life when she cultivated, her Dharma peers and her teacher were all able to memorize sutras whereas she was unable to. She was quite stupid. Then she made a vow to praise cultivators who had good memories. She also vowed to bow to the Buddhas and ask the Buddhas and Bodhisattvas to aid cultivators so they would all be blessed with especially excellent memories. For those reasons, now she has a sharper memory than anyone else. Because she wanted everyone to have a sharp memory, she herself has a good memory. She was not jealous. This is a matter of cause and effect. ◁

SEPTEMBER 5, 1973 | WEDNESDAY EVENING

On Binding Oneself Up

Guo Ning is not well physically. About a year ago I had the hunch that he might have a relapse, and so I suggested that we do the Medicine Master Buddha Repentance, because that repentance can help people eradicate their karmic obstacles. Who would have guessed that he would object to bowing in repentance! Well, then his illness did come back, and he got angry every day. If he was not scolding other monks, he was scolding the nuns or the laypeople. Nobody was okay; everybody was at fault. He refused to cultivate, and he did not want others to cultivate. He wanted to stop our language classes, also our meditation, sutra lectures, and all other courses and work. He wanted to put a stop to everything. He didn't want to do anything at all. That was when I decided to go to South America. When I got back from South America, he was still distraught and said some crazy things to me. One thing he said was, "I scolded the nuns. I said, 'Our teacher really made a mistake this time. He should never have transmitted the Dharma to the monks—allowing the monks to wear yellow robes and don the red precept sash. He should have transmitted the Dharma to you nuns instead.'" When I heard him say that, I immediately replied, "Fine. I can transmit the Dharma to the nuns right now. Go to them and bow down! Tell your brother Guo Hu to go with you. Quickly!"

Guo Hu took a few steps forward and then came back, probably because he still put on airs himself and felt that bowing to nuns

VI. Karmic Conditions

would cause him to lose face. Then he rationalized. "If I really did bow to them, how would they react..." He added a few more things, but I won't bring them up. You've forgotten them and I don't remember either. So let's drop it.

However, be clear that I'm now letting you know that all that has transpired for the past year has been brought about by Guo Ning's karmic obstacles. Currently, I've arranged for him to take a rest and he's gone off somewhere. He wants to translate the *Flower Adornment Sutra*. We'll take a look at his translation. His has been a case of "Ensnaring and shrouding oneself with the delusion of evil karma," as mentioned in the sutra. Such people bind themselves up. ⊐

OCTOBER 7, 1973 | SUNDAY EVENING, AT WASHINGTON STREET

On Responses that Sincerity Will Bring

[Speaking of a disciple doing Three Steps One Bow] If he bows sincerely, people will deliver food to him. Not only human beings, but heavenly beings will send food to him. Even the Buddhas and Bodhisattvas may give him food. If he is not sincere, however, not even human beings will take food to him. ⊣

OCTOBER 10, 1973 | WEDNESDAY EVENING

On Greeting Monastic Guests at Airports

Tomorrow a Dharma Master from New York will be coming to San Francisco as our guest. We'll be going to the airport to welcome him. All the monks and nuns and laypeople from Gold Mountain Monastery should go. The laypeople are especially invited to go. I hope many people will be there to welcome this Dharma Master.

When I went to New York this spring, no one welcomed me at the airport. Guo Xiu asked me, "How come not a single monk was there to welcome you?" The reason no one gave me a welcome was that I had not welcomed others in the past. We are going to change that pattern by greeting guest Dharma Masters at the airport when they come here. No matter whether *that* Dharma Master greeted others in the past or not—no matter what kind of monk he might be—we will give him a welcome.

Tomorrow, everyone is invited to go and welcome that Dharma Master. When we plant a seed, we reap the corresponding fruit. When we welcome others, others will also welcome us. ⊣

OCTOBER 13, 1973 | SATURDAY EVENING

On a Response to a Sincere Request

Several days ago Guo Yao went home to see her parents. Her mother had undergone surgery for a brain ailment. After the operation, she remained in an extremely dangerous coma. Guo Yao kept calling long distance—five or six times—hoping that the monks, nun, laymen, and laywomen of Gold Mountain Monastery would sincerely pray on her mother's behalf, so that her mother could get well.

Originally I promised her I would tell everyone last night, but my memory is poor and I forgot. Nevertheless, I myself transferred merit to her mother. She called again today overjoyed, to say that her mother has regained consciousness. Although her mother is now conscious and Guo Yao herself is happy, we should continue to transfer merit to her mother when we recite the Buddha's name, bow to the Buddha, and recite sutras, because the power of the great assembly is inconceivable. ⊣

OCTOBER 13, 1973 | SATURDAY EVENING

On Not Following the Assembly

A laywoman who arrived in San Francisco on the first of this month has been staying at the Translation Institute but hasn't been coming to Gold Mountain Monastery to attend lectures and events. But that is not how we do things here. At our monasteries, the assembly does everything together. You should do whatever everyone else is doing. You shouldn't do your own thing and try to be special or different from others.

Although I'm usually quite strict, since this laywoman is so advanced in years, I let her be when she didn't come to the sutra lectures. Little did I know that by letting her do as she pleased, she would encounter a demonic obstacle. This morning she telephoned to say that she had encountered a demon. The demon caused her to be unable to stand steadily. She kept tripping and falling. That's how bad it was. She also felt as if her mouth and eyes were contorted.

She called and asked me to hurry over to the Translation Institute and subdue the demon for her. I told her, "I haven't even subdued my own demons; how can I subdue yours? What's more, I don't have time right now. I have to eat first." After lunch, I went to Washington Street and saw that she was indeed half-paralyzed. I said, "So now you really can't go to sutra lectures. Since you didn't want to go, now you've contracted this sickness that prevents you from going."

"It's not that I didn't want to go to the sutra lecture. I simply wanted to use the time to write essays," she replied.

"Whether you write your essays is not the issue. However, you should not miss the sutra lectures. Since there are lectures going on right at Gold Mountain Monastery, why are you staying at the Translation Institute and not coming to Gold Mountain?" She didn't even come for meals, because she wanted to sleep in.

Today I took her to an acupuncturist, who said, "Fortunately you came early. If you had come later, she would certainly have been half-paralyzed permanently. If you had come tomorrow, it would have been too late." When she heard that, she realized how serious the matter was. Afterwards, I sent her back to Washington Street. Originally, we planned to cut the sutra lecture short today and go over to finish some work at Washington Street. However, I've decided that we don't need to do that. We can instead go there a little earlier tomorrow morning and finish the job. Otherwise, we might get so worn out working that we wouldn't be able to wake up tomorrow. So, we'll bow the Repentance before Ten Thousand Buddhas here as usual, and then transfer some of the merit to this layperson. May she be free from disasters and sicknesses; may she cultivate the truth and enter the spiritual Path without trouble from demons. ⊣

OCTOBER 19, 1973 | FRIDAY EVENING

On an Amusing Response

Some amusing news arrived today. What is it? It's about the two [Bhikshus] who are doing Three Steps One Bow—Guo Yu and Guo Dao. Guo Dao was bowing along and suddenly noticed: "My pants are ripping!" With the next bow he said, "My pants are ripping even more!" It reached the point that he couldn't keep his trousers on anymore, and he hadn't brought a change of pants, so he said to Guo Yu, "I'm afraid it's not going to work! How can I bow with no pants on?"

Then just at that time a pair of trousers appeared right in the middle of the road. The trousers were neither too large nor too small, not too long and not too short. They were exactly his size. Wouldn't you say that was strange? ⊣

OCTOBER 27, 1973 | SATURDAY EVENING

On the Magnitude of a Celestial Calamity

This potential calamity [Editor's note: the Comet Kahoutek, which was headed for Earth] does not involve only one country; it is a calamity that would affect the whole world. But there are two monks who have resolved to carry on a bowing pilgrimage to pray for world peace. Many people may regard them as stupid and see bowing as a dumb way to act. In actual fact, with that dumb and old-fashioned method they are using, their practice could help to avert a collision with a comet that could destroy the planet. ◁

OCTOBER 29, 1973 | MONDAY EVENING

On a Reward More Precious Than the Gift

What we've been talking about reminds me of something that happened in the past. What took place is very clear. It could have happened yesterday, or last year, or two years, three years, four years, five or six years ago, or even a hundred years ago—that part is indistinct.

At the time, I owned some foreign-language dictionaries, giving the Chinese equivalents for English, Sanskrit, French, Spanish, Portuguese and German. Those dictionaries were like precious jewels to me. However, some of my fellow students didn't have those dictionaries, and when they saw me consulting my dictionaries, their faces would drop, and they would even shed tears. I don't know if it was from jealousy or admiration or what. The first day I didn't think anything of it, nor, the next. But by the third day I began wondering, "What's wrong with them?" And I realized, "Oh! It's because they don't have dictionaries."

From that point on, I no longer wanted the dictionaries—which were like precious treasures—for myself. I gave them away for everyone to use. After that, I no longer needed to look words up in the dictionary to know what they meant. I recognized them without a dictionary. I myself didn't know why, and I still don't. ⊣

NOVEMBER 15, 1973 | THURSDAY EVENING

On Reflecting on Retributions

It's not all that easy to lecture on the sutras. Don't consider it a very simple thing to do. Once you start lecturing you'll know it's not easy, especially if you haven't heard the sutra lectured before, so that you don't know which interpretation is right. Also, you may be unaware of misprints in the sutra text. That's why it's not easy to lecture on sutras.

Not only do I make mistakes when lecturing, very few Dharma Masters can avoid doing so. If the explanation is wrong, don't listen to what is wrong. When you are translating the sutras, don't translate the wrong way. Don't deliberately find fault and say, "Our teacher made a mistake when lecturing." If you know your teacher made a mistake, you ought to correct it. Who's forcing you to accept the error? Who stops you from correcting it in your translation?

Why do people say I make mistakes when lecturing? It's my retribution. Previously I didn't fear falling into the hells, and I criticized other people as lecturing wrong. If you find fault, then when you lecture on the sutras in the future, your disciples and your disciples' disciples will criticize you. That will be your retribution. You think it's a lot of fun now, but later on you will know, just as I now know I'm undergoing retribution. ◁

DECEMBER 16, 1973 | SUNDAY EVENING

On Causes & Conditions
Affecting One's Decisions

Tomorrow someone is coming to borrow the tapes for the *Heart Sutra* and the *Vajra Sutra* to make a copy. The person in charge of the tapes should be ready to give those tapes to him. This person is a Mormon, but he is interested in studying the Buddhadharma. His mother is a Buddhist and hopes that her son, who is a college student, will also believe in Buddhism. The mother thinks that if her son hears these tapes, he might convert to Buddhism. That's just an idle thought. Whether or not it can come true depends on the person's causes and conditions. ⊣

JANUARY 23, 1974 | WEDNESDAY EVENING

On Instructions Concerning Vows

Members of the fourfold assembly at Gold Mountain Monastery have made a commitment to seek unsurpassed *bodhi,* and have made great vows. In the recent past, this was rarely done in Buddhism anywhere in the world. If we are talking about the past—up to limitless eons ago—there have been many Buddhists who made vows. In this century, however, there have been very few. That's why we have entered the Dharma-ending Age, where everyone has forgotten about cultivation.

Just now, people have made their individual vows. You should constantly review your vows and become very familiar with them. Keep them securely in mind. Don't just forget your vows after you've made them. That will never do. At all times, you should remember the vows you've made.

The two monks bowing once every three steps also made vows in the past to practice what others could not practice. These two made vows to follow me wherever I go and be my great protectors, enduring what others cannot endure and practicing what others cannot practice. They wanted to engage in such ascetic practice. Regardless of whether or not they succeeded at it, they were determined to undertake ascetic practice.

In cultivation, making vows is very important. Patience is also of the utmost importance. Anyone who can be patient will surely succeed in realizing the Path. Patience is the ability to endure

VI. Karmic Conditions

adversity as if it were as pleasant as eating honey, without getting the least bit upset or angry. In the future, I hope everyone can cultivate patience. It is so important.

Today when people made their vows, I listened carefully and noticed that no one made a vow to be patient. However, before you made your vows, I couldn't very well tell you what vows to make. Your vows have to be made of your own initiative; people cannot tell you what kind of vows to make. Vows that other people tell you to make are their vows, not yours. ⊐

JANUARY 23, 1974 | WEDNESDAY EVENING

On Gender

[Editor's note: The Master replies to a question.] It's not a matter of who is better. Since women have more complications to deal with in cultivation than men do, women have 348 precepts while men have 250. In general, it is not as convenient for women to practice. However, the issue is not one of who is better.

Since this nun's vow has been brought into question [Editor's note: To which the Master's reply in the above paragraph is directed], I suggest that she may want to consider this vow she has made. If she wants to retract this vow of hers, she may still do so. However, I believe it is not because she scorns women that she made a vow not to be one. In the past, she herself was a woman too many times. Her current vow pertains to that experience. She merely felt that being a woman was not very convenient. [When asked if she wanted to retract her vow, she said no, she always wants to make that vow.] You see, that is what she wants to do. Slowly you will understand. When you have trouble and inconvenience, then you will understand. ◁

JANUARY 25, 1974 | FRIDAY EVENING

On Watching Over Others Being Unadvisable

Students of the Buddhadharma should recognize the importance of the Dharma. If we study the Dharma every day without realizing the importance of the Dharma, we will not take our cultivation seriously. If we fail to cultivate, we will attain nothing and have no wisdom. Wise people do not live in places characterized by ignorance. Ignorant people do not live in places of wisdom. "Places of ignorance" refers to dark places. Ignorant people live in darkness and don't feel that it is dark. Wise people know that darkness is wrong and so they seek a place of light. Light represents the lack of anger. Ignorance is anger. If you get angry, you are ignorant. If you have no anger, you are wise.

We ought to reflect upon ourselves daily and watch ourselves so that we do not entertain ignorant thoughts all the time. Instead we should develop wisdom in thought after thought. Once we develop wisdom, we will not get angry at others. Ignorant people like to lose their tempers.

As we study the Buddhadharma, every day we should become more and more intelligent, not more and more confused. If you can endure being scolded by others, then you have real skill in patience. Don't scold others or lose your temper at them. Not to mention your Dharma peers, you shouldn't even get mad at those who are your juniors. It's understandable that you might lose your temper once in a while out of ignorance. But you cannot let your ignorance flare every day.

All of you continually endure tremendous hardship here, rising early and retiring late. It would be a great mistake to try to watch over others instead of watching over yourselves. ⊣

JANUARY 25, 1974 | FRIDAY EVENING

On Being Scolded

What we have been discussing reminds me of when I was living on Sutter Street in San Francisco. I was alone at the time and had no one to help me. And so I decided to sponsor a Dharma Master from Taiwan to come to the U.S. Initially, I got all the paperwork in order for him to come, but then he decided not to come. The fact was that he had solicited a lot of money in Taiwan by saying that he need travel money in order to go to America. After laypeople donated a substantial sum, he canceled the trip.

A year later, after he had used up most of those donations, he again said he wanted to come. I again hired a lawyer to prepare the visa application for him. In all, I must have spent $800 U.S. This time he came. Once he arrived, he promised to work with me and help me out with monastic duties. But instead of keeping his word, he began to go to another Buddhist Association every evening. There, he secretly signed an agreement to move to that Buddhist Association, which meant he would not be staying at my monastery any more.

When I found out what he had done, I formally bid him farewell one morning after morning recitation. Five or six laypeople were witness to this. Well, the monk became furious. He had brought a knife for cutting fruit with him from Taiwan. The knife was about a foot long, including the handle, and was extremely sharp. He grabbed that knife and pointed it at my throat, saying, "I'm going to kill you!" I closed my eyes and paid no attention. I thought, "If you want to kill me, go right ahead. If I killed you in some past life, then you can kill me now. If I didn't kill you in the past, you won't kill me now."

"Why must you close your eyes?" he ranted. It was a crime to close my eyes, I guess. "Why won't you talk?" he raged. Not talking was a crime as well. He scolded me and wanted to kill me. This went on for three days. As soon as he saw me, he would scold me and want to kill me. After three days, he still had not killed me.

During that time, when he scolded me, I didn't say anything. Eventually, since he could not do anything to me, he left and went to the other Buddhist Association. After less than a month there, he couldn't take it and wanted to come back. I said, "Fine. I will give this Sutter Street building to you—no strings attached. I, however, will go somewhere else." He was afraid to accept the building, so he ended up returning to Taiwan. Since then, I have heard that he went deaf and is often ill. I learned from that experience. When people scold you, it is a test to see if you have enough *samādhi*. ⊣

JANUARY 27, 1974 | SUNDAY EVENING

On Changing Minds to Change the World

Two monks from Gold Mountain Monastery are doing a Three Steps One Bow pilgrimage towards Seattle, to one of the highest mountains there, a place where the Buddhas and Bodhisattvas congregate.

Are they simply bowing to the Buddhas and Bodhisattvas? No. They are praying for world peace. They are praying that the evil in people's minds will change to good. In that way, a world full of calamities, disasters, and miseries can change into a peaceful world filled with peace-loving people. ⊟

JANUARY 26, 1974 | SATURDAY EVENING

On Being Responsible for the Options One Chooses

> Contemplate vicious words as merit.
> Then the person becomes your wise and skillful teacher.
> Without his slander leading you to choose between
>   hostility and friendship,
> How could you demonstrate the power of compassion
>   and patience with nonproduction?

If someone can scold you, no matter who he is, he is actually helping you to cultivate. However, if you help others to cultivate in that way, you yourself will accrue offenses. Who helped Śākyamuni Buddha to become a Buddha? It was Devadatta, who tried to ruin the Buddha but failed. The Buddha became a Buddha, and Devadatta fell into the hells alive.

Suppose a nun wants to be a monk's wise and skillful teacher — to the point of hitting him or even killing him. If you want to be a wise and skillful teacher, then you can't be afraid of incurring offenses and falling into the hells. You have to want only to help people follow the Path. Do not assume that by taking on the appearance of a *rākṣasa* ghost you will actually be able to help people cultivate. Anyone who wants to be a *rākṣasa* ghost can simply lose her temper and scold people. If you want to be a Bodhisattva, simply be cheerful and happy.

> Good and evil are two different paths.
> You can cultivate the one or commit the other.

VI. Karmic Conditions

If you want to follow the Path, you can; if you want to commit offenses, you can do that. It's up to you. The teacher can only bring you in the door. You yourself must cultivate. If you don't cultivate, your teacher can do nothing. You must end your own birth and death, just as you must eat your own food to get full. ⊣

JANUARY 29, 1974 | TUESDAY EVENING

On Selecting Your Own Practice of *Samādhi*

Gold Mountain Monastery is a fountainhead of Buddhism in the West. There's a saying: "When the eight immortals cross the sea, each displays his supernatural powers." Each person can make his own resolve. If you make a resolve to eat, you can study the eating *samādhi*. Don't think that eating is such a simple matter. It is not easy at all. For instance, people who know how to eat will not eat too little or too much; they know how to stay healthy. An example of someone who didn't know how eat is a monk I knew in Manchuria. He ate only one meal a day, but had a huge bowl which he filled three times in that one meal. His bowl was bigger than any of ours. What he ate in one meal—three bowl-fuls—was more than I could have eaten in ten days and then some. In fact, I could probably have survived on one of his bowl-fuls for ten days. He truly resembled a hungry ghost.

When he was living in the town of Lalin, he would eat for one or two hours, taking his time. However, in the large monasteries, only thirty minutes are allotted for a meal—in Taiwan it is only ten minutes. He couldn't eat his fill in thirty minutes, so he would always make sure to sit next to the food server. Wherever the food server was, that's where he'd sit. He had to eat fast. In the time it took people to finish one mouthful, he would be done with his first bowl and getting seconds. By the time others had eaten a second mouthful, he would be finishing his second bowl and starting his third. Although he ate like a glutton, he

VI. Karmic Conditions

was virtually skin and bones, with no flesh at all. Would you say he knew how to eat or not? It could be said that he didn't know how to eat.

If you know how to eat, you will not overeat or under-eat. You will not go to either extreme. That's part of learning the *samādhi* of eating.

You could also study the sleep *samādhi*.

"Oh, I know what that is," someone says. "It must mean that you sleep both day and night, being totally oblivious to the waking world and always being in a deep, sleep-like *samādhi*." That's not it. If you attain the sleep *samādhi*, then it doesn't really matter whether you sleep or not. It's fine to sleep, and it's also okay not to sleep. There's no problem.

Then there's the *samādhi* of wearing clothes. It doesn't mean wearing fine garments and wearing lots of clothes. It means that you aren't even aware of whether or not you wear clothes. Again, it's not an easy state to attain.

And so, each person cultivates his or her own *samādhi*. The two monks are practicing the bowing *samādhi*. You could perhaps study sutra-recitation *samādhi*, mantra recitation *samādhi*, or the *samādhi* of bowing. The choice is yours. However, you should at all costs avoid learning the *samādhi* of fighting, the *samādhi* of being obstinate, and the *samādhi* of oppressing others. ◁

MAY 7, 1974 | TUESDAY

On Slander

Do you prefer to listen to the *Flower Adornment Sutra* or hear about the situation in Hong Kong and Taiwan? [Editor's note: Disciples were interested to hear about Asia.] Venerable Elder Guangqin, who now resides in Taiwan, is originally from Fujian Province in China. His monastery in Taiwan is called Chengtian. His practice is especially rigorous: He never lies down or eats cooked food. He eats only fruit, and so he is called the "Fruit Monk." When I was lecturing on sutras in Taiwan, I mentioned him three times, which caused quite a flurry. People said, "Don't talk about him so much. None of the monks in Taiwan like him. The Dharma Masters disapprove of him, saying that he is an illiterate, a mute sheep in the Sangha who is of no benefit to Buddhism."

Imagine that. He abstains from cooked food and cultivates diligently all day long, yet he gets accused of being useless to Buddhism. However, he is actually very useful. He had a disciple who was planning to take a vacation. He told that disciple not to travel for forty-nine days. His disciple waited for forty-eight days and then figured that it wouldn't matter if he went out on the last day. As soon as he went out, he was in a car accident that resulted in the amputation of one of his legs. Someone told the Fruit Monk, who responded, "The Buddhas and Bodhisattvas were pretty kind to him. If he didn't work for Buddhism and believe in the Buddha, he would have lost his life."

VI. Karmic Conditions

That disciple later told others, "I didn't listen to my teacher. My teacher told me not to go out for forty-nine days, but I thought it would be okay to go out after forty-eight days, and so I lost one leg." Think it over. Before anything happened, the Fruit Monk was able to warn his disciple to stay home for forty-nine days. Since the disciple didn't listen, he endangered his own life.

Despite the diligence and caliber of this monk's cultivation, all the Dharma Masters slander him and try to ruin him. However, their attempts are futile. The laypeople in Taiwan still want to take refuge with him and bow to him as their teacher. Taking refuge with him is fairly easy, and as a result he has many disciples, all of whom respect him greatly. Despite all those Dharma Masters' efforts to ruin his reputation, the laypeople can judge for themselves and still want him to be their teacher.

Here's how ridiculous it gets: having nothing better to accuse him of, the Dharma Masters allege that he eats on the sly. What do they say he eats? Rice gruel! Someone came up to me and whispered, "Don't tell anyone else, but people say that he drinks rice gruel on the sly. He says he doesn't eat cooked food, but he's lying." I say: even if he does drink rice gruel, that's not an offense, is it? What's wrong with that? I said as much publicly while I was in Taiwan: he has every right to choose whether or not to eat cooked food. He has total freedom in that respect.

There's no rule in Buddhism that says one can't eat cooked food, or that one commits an offense by doing so.

Why do those people accuse him of eating gruel on the sly? They have nothing better to do and they are afraid everyone will believe in him, so they spread rumors to slander him. People who lack wisdom might lose faith in him after hearing such rumors, but wise people will not care in the least. He eats gruel—so what? If he wants to eat gruel or rice, he can do so. Whether or not he eats gruel or rice or cooked food is his own business. No one can force him into it.

MAY 10, 1974 | FRIDAY EVENING

On Studying with the Teacher, not a Fellow-Disciple

You should understand that I cannot be over-permissive, because then everyone would get confused. You should still study with the teacher, not with a fellow-disciple. If you study with my disciple, beware that although he might be right on some points, he could very well be wrong on other points. He is not necessarily reliable. He isn't firmly grounded and often drifts here and there, being swayed by praise, ridicule, misery, joy, benefit, loss, slander, and fame. If someone praises him, he is exultant. If someone criticizes him, he gets upset. ⊣

SEPTEMBER 2, 1974 | MONDAY EVENING

On Advice to Slanderers
of the Monastery

People who cultivate the teaching of the Buddhas should fear
only that they will fail to truly cultivate. When you truly cultivate, then even people who may slander you and try to ruin
your practice will not succeed. That is why it doesn't matter what
people say about this monastery. They won't be able to destroy
it, because it's made of *vajra*. Although many people praise
this monastery, many others criticize it. Outside the monastery
and even right within it, there are lazy ghosts and lazy worms,
gluttonous ghosts and gluttonous worms. These people say the
monastery is no good because there's too much work to do here,
not enough time to sleep, and no time to talk. As a result, these
lazy people aren't able to enter the "sleeping *samādhi*." However,
that's their own problem.

If you look into this, you won't find another place in the entire
world where people cultivate as diligently as the people here do.
So, each of you should be very careful not to do anything that
would cause you to fall into the Hell Where Tongues Are Pulled
Out. No matter who you are, you won't be able to destroy the
monastery, because it is made of *vajra*. If you slander the monastery you will fall into the Hell Where Tongues Are Pulled Out.
What is meant by slandering the monastery? Suppose you engage
in gossip that is designed to confuse others, saying things like,
"The people at this place don't cultivate; the Dharma Masters
here don't know what they're doing." The reason you don't know

VI. Karmic Conditions

what they're doing is that you are just an ordinary person. If you were an enlightened sage, you would immediately come here and be bowing to the Buddhas morning till night. People with such improper viewpoints, who speak ill of people in the monastery are definitely headed for the Hell Where Tongues Are Pulled Out. No one else is making you fall into the hells; you yourself are preparing to plummet straight into them. And so, whoever you are, go ahead and try to cause dissention in the monastery if you aren't afraid of becoming a mute. However, you won't succeed in destroying the monastery or in disrupting the Sangha here. Why not? It's because the Sangha members here don't seek anything. To them, "Everything is okay." How could you possibly disrupt them? It's impossible, because it is of no concern to them whether they are treated well. It doesn't matter to them whether or not people believe in them. ⊣

Bhikshu Heng Ju on
Three Steps One Bow pilgrimage in 1973

VII | Afflictions

NOVEMBER 3, 1972 | FRIDAY EVENING

On Being Evasive

With these three people going to Hong Kong, there is a possibility that Buddhism will flourish there. When they return to the U.S. next year, they will first stop in Taiwan and speak Dharma in various places. Maybe they will help those who are evasive learn not to be so evasive. Today in the car I told you all, "I won't allow you to be so evasive. Did you hear me?" When you get to Taiwan, you can preface your talks with this sentence, "Our teacher didn't teach us anything else. He only taught us this: not to be mentally evasive. That's his first method. His second method: we cannot be too fleet-footed, because that would only facilitate our running away." If you aren't able to subdue demons, you can run. ☐

DECEMBER 3, 1972 | SUNDAY NOON

On Being Jealous & Obstructive

There's a bit of news about a disciple of mine whose real name I never really knew. No one seems to know if his surname was Liu or Yang. When he took refuge, he recorded the surname Yang, but people have also said his surname was something else. He registered with a false name even when he was taking refuge, so to this day we still don't know his true name. He said that he himself didn't know his last name.

Why was he so evasive? He hadn't come for Buddhism. He had come to study *gongfu*—martial arts. I first saw him at Guangzhou Temple. He ran after me as I came out of that temple and asked me where I was from. Later, he came here to San Francisco. He somehow had the idea that all Chinese monks know martial arts. He thought all monks were like the monks from Shaolin Monastery, where they specialize in Shaolin boxing and Arhat boxing and have impressive martial skills. And so when he saw me, he thought that I had some *gongfu*. He could tell whether or not a person has skill by the way that person walks.

He came and took refuge with me, but his purpose was not to become a Buddhist, but rather, to learn *gongfu*. Since he hung around the monastery, I found him some work and let him translate for me. But he was not a reliable translator; he often omitted important principles that I explained. He translated only the superficial things. Since he himself had not managed to learn martial arts from me, he was afraid that others might.

From morning to night he was jealous, obstructive, and selfish. He was particularly jealous of two young men who came here. I also had a jealous disciple in Hong Kong, who acted in much the same way.

Once, he accompanied me to Los Angeles and on that visit, many people wished to take refuge with me, but this jealous disciple obstructed them and discouraged them from doing so. Since he had come with me, people listened to him and no one took refuge.

He also followed me to Arizona to attend a religious conference held on a Native American reservation. I recited the Śūraṅgama Mantra for them. Some people wanted my address, but this jealous disciple wouldn't give it to them. Some others wanted to give me their addresses, and he also refused to take those addresses. As a result, those people never did manage to locate me.

Why did this disciple do things like that? He was terribly afraid that people would draw near to me and learn the Dharma and *gongfu*, and he wouldn't have a chance to study them. So he jealously kept others away from me.

Several years ago he went to Hong Kong and probably studied martial arts there. Upon his return to America, he no longer came here. A couple of months ago, he died. He was only in his thirties. Even so, he'd made some money—over $70,000 in his bank account. He left it all unconditionally to his elder brother.

When he was alive, he had money but he refused to use it to create merit and virtue. Now that he is dead, even if he wanted to create merit and virtue he would have no chance to do so. What a shame! There's a lesson to be learned here, so I decided to tell everyone this story today. ⏎

DECEMBER 5, 1972 | TUESDAY EVENING

On Wishful Thinking

In the lecture series on the *Sixth Patriarch Sutra*, I discussed the lives of many patriarchs, and went into great detail about the lives of the first six patriarchs in China. Now, in our Saturday classes, we investigate the lives of patriarchs as well. Although we have discussed so many patriarchs, no one has aspired to emulate any one of them for their cultivation, virtue, or erudition. No one wishes to do the work. There may be some who want to be patriarchs, but they want to be lazy patriarchs, gluttonous patriarchs, patriarchs who like to sleep and eat good food. They want to be patriarchs who enjoy life, because they have not broken the habits associated with a Western lifestyle. They think they can become patriarchs right in the midst of material comfort and pleasure. That will not be easy to do.

I also told you about Layman Pang and how he and his son, daughter, and wife were all enlightened. After hearing that story, many people began to aspire to be like Layman Pang. Even some who originally wanted to enter monastic life have decided that they would rather be like Layman Pang than to follow the monastic way of life. They argue their case this way: "Monastics can get enlightened; so can laypeople. I'll follow the example of Layman Pang." Nothing is wrong with that. However, you must become enlightened before you can consider yourself similar to Layman Pang. If you don't get enlightened, you won't be like Layman Pang, much less like a genuine fully-ordained monk.

You may make light of what I'm saying, but it would behoove you to look into the meaning behind my words.

JANUARY 8, 1973 | MONDAY EVENING

On Lack of Belief

Someone says, "I don't believe it." Of course you don't believe it. If you believed it, you would understand the Buddha's state of mind. But since you lack sufficient good roots, you fail to believe true principles of the genuine Buddhadharma upon encountering them. Why don't you believe? It is because your karmic obstacles are too weighty, and because the demons have profound power over you. The demons don't wish you to believe in the Buddhadharma. If you believed in the Buddhadharma, the demon king's retinue would decrease, and so they do not want people to believe in Buddhism. Therefore, there is no way for you to believe or understand the mysterious, inconceivable principles of Buddhism. ◁

JANUARY 9, 1973 | TUESDAY EVENING

On the Audacity of Ignorant Criticism

Some people don't know Buddhist terms and have no under-standing of Buddhist doctrines, and yet they have the audacity to criticize Buddhism, saying that Buddhism is wrong in this and that way. Actually, there is no way for them to recognize what is right and what is wrong. Living beings are so deluded that within their delusion, they continue to do deluded things; within confusion, they do confused things. This is really too pathetic.

JANUARY 29, 1973 | MONDAY EVENING

On the Difficulty of Renouncing Power & Wealth

Tomorrow you will meet a Chinese-American layman who supports the Triple Jewel. He has made a great *bodhi* resolve and advocates Buddhism. Tomorrow he is coming here to take a look at Gold Mountain Monastery, the icebox, checking out the cold meat in it. Therefore, if any of you lay Dharma-protectors of Gold Mountain Monastery have time tomorrow around noon, you are welcome to come and have lunch here and meet this layman who has made a great *bodhi* resolve. Those who are working outside won't have the time, but those who aren't working are welcome to come here.

There should be more of us gathered together, as a proof that these cold cuts haven't been frozen to the point that they can't be eaten, and to prove that you are still able to eat. You should meet this layman; it's a good opportunity. Besides, he might bring a Buddhist movie. We viewed it once before, but this time he is very sincere and says he will bring it along. Those who have seen the movie can watch it one more time; those who haven't will get to see it. But at any rate, meet this layperson. He has a good understanding of Buddhism.

A few days ago, he attended a Buddha recitation session in New York, during which he didn't answer the phone, do office work, or talk with people outside. He probably talked to the people in the session, since he had not made the vow not to talk to women or to men. Therefore, he probably talked to both men and women.

People get up at 3:30 A.M. for our Buddha recitation sessions. The session this layman attended in New York started at 5 A.M. and everyone rested at 9 P.M. The difference is that their schedule is a little shorter. I've been told that this layman has 600 Americans working for him in his office. But during that entire week of Buddha recitation, he didn't pay any attention to his work. Of course after the week of recitation ended, he went back to looking after his business. My hope for him is that he will not just stop looking after his business for one week, but that he will not do business for an entire year. In fact, I hope that eventually he won't have to look after those troublesome matters at all. That would be the very best. However, it's not easy for him to put down so much money.

JANUARY 30, 1973 | TUESDAY EVENING

On Different Approaches to Handling Money

Some people count every penny, dime, and quarter. That's unlike one of my nun disciples here who doesn't bother to count money at all—to the point that she made a mistake when depositing money in the bank. Well, I thought about her doing that and have come to the conclusion that she must have some skill! She has attained a little bit of *samādhi* and that's why her mind was not swayed by anything—even money. That's not a bad state. However, it's not too practical when you are handling worldly matters. From a transcendental perspective, your state is lofty. If you can manage to not pay attention to money, then other things are even less of a problem. On the other hand, people who pay strict attention to every penny, nickel, and dime, soon exhaust their energy. They tax their brains with calculations. They can't finish calculating in the daytime, so they continue at night, but still can't finish. It makes them toss and turn the whole night long, flipping back and forth like a flapjack, and not getting any sleep. Would you say that was happiness or suffering? ⯊

FEBRUARY 14, 1973 | WEDNESDAY EVENING

On Unmitigated Arrogance

On Thursday, we were supposed to fly from Montreal to New York. The airplane took off without us, however; we missed our flight. The reason was that Guo Hu was afraid he would not get enough to eat, and so he wanted to eat before we boarded our flight. I, too, thought we would not get much to eat on the plane, and knowing how concerned he was about food, I agreed that we take our midday meal while still in Canada.

But by the time the meal was over, our time was tight. Our host—the person who had invited me to Canada in the first place—was with us and asked me if he could drive us to the airport, assuring me that he was a fast driver and could get us there in time to catch our flight. I accepted his offer, but once on the freeway, he moved to the slow lane and literally crawled along on the snowy road. Other cars were speeding by in the faster lines, but he deliberately stayed in the slow lane, where the traffic was congested. I took one look and realized that he had no intention of helping us get to the airport on time. When he deliberately took a wrong turn as we neared the airport exit, my suspicions were further confirmed.

As a result of arriving late, we missed our flight and were forced to wait in the airport two hours for the next flight. Our host—the one who had kept us from departing on time—sat with us. I conversed on a superficial level, only to the extent that the situation required. Actually he had made us miss our flight

VII. Affliction

because he wanted the extra time with me there in the airport waiting room.

So when our flight was finally called, I scolded him before departing. I scolded him because he put on airs. He had said during our visit that he was "a great father," but from what I could see, he wanted to be "a great patriarch." [Editor's note: This man had a bit of charisma and took disciples in the name of Buddhism. He perceived himself as a father figure. Later, after this initial encounter with the Master, this man, along with some of his disciples, came to Gold Mountain Monastery in San Francisco, seeking to have the Master certify that he was the Panchen Lama incarnate. The Master didn't, of course, but that's another story.] So I said to him, "You are only aware of yourself. You think you are bigger than everyone else. If you keep at it, how will you ever be able to level your mountain of arrogance? I'm different from you. I only think about other living beings, not myself. And that's why I feel I must say this to you before I leave."

His response was something like, "Ah, then I have made a mistake!" He had. He hoped to have two extra hours with me—all to himself. But it turned out to be meaningless for me and meaningless for him. We both spend that time in vain. I told him so before we left. Then we boarded the flight and returned to New York.

SEPTEMBER 5, 1973 | WEDNESDAY EVENING

On Refusing to Learn & Vexing Others

We have been loaned a facility on Washington Street. A Buddhist layman has offered us its use for the purpose of translation. The place will be the named the International Institute for the Translation of Buddhist Texts. From now on not only will we translate the sutras, professors from all over the world who wish to translate sutras can come here to study and practice.

The Opening will take place on the 14th of October. On Opening Day, a ceremony for Opening the Eyes of the Thousand-Handed Guanyin Bodhisattva image will also be held. In preparation for those events, beginning October 1, we will bow the Great Compassion Repentance daily, requesting Thousand-handed Guanyin to release light and aid us.

Some of my monastic disciples have refused to bow to the Buddhas or to bow in repentance. They do not even know how to do it, and yet they refuse to learn. After you know how, you may say no. However, when it comes to monastic education, before you know how you cannot say, "I don't want to learn how to do this or that."

Basically you hardly know anything; you are an outsider. Having been ordained for a few days, you already start thinking you are a patriarch. Ridiculous! From now on, none of my disciples are allowed to casually get angry or become afflicted. Regardless of whether you are a monastic or a layperson, you are not permitted to vex others. If you obstruct other people's cultivation, I will no longer consider you my disciple. ◁

OCTOBER 8, 1973 | MONDAY EVENING, AT WASHINGTON STREET

On Wanna-Be Patriarchs

Tomorrow, sutra lectures (both noon and evening) will be at Gold Mountain Monastery, and will continue to be at Gold Mountain Monastery until after the Opening of the Light (a consecration ceremony for the International Institute for the Translation of Buddhist Texts). Otherwise people won't have anywhere to sit. Some people want to sit on the Buddha's feet. The disciples of the Buddha are supposed to bow to the ground and hold the Buddha's feet in their hands. But it's to be feared some may want to start bowing by sitting on the Buddha's feet. Others may want to sit on the Buddha's head. Since this place is too small, we are going to Gold Mountain Monastery where there will be more space. Some people are contemplating moving the Buddha aside and sitting in his place. What a bright idea! Once they have done that, they can start having ideas of wanting to be a patriarch. They think being a patriarch is better than being an ordinary monk. For these reasons, the (noon and evening) lectures will be held at Gold Mountain Monastery starting tomorrow. ⊣

OCTOBER 8, 1973 | MONDAY EVENING

On Being Coarse & Two-Faced

Many people are coming to attend our Ceremony for Opening of the Light. All of us should try to be more alert and aware, and not indulge in constant frivolous chatter. Bhikshus in particular should pay attention to this point and not cause others to look down upon us, thinking, "What a bunch of rowdy youths! They are so unruly!" Gold Mountain Monastery will lose its reputation right then and there.

You should not cause a big ruckus or hold conferences in the restroom. I hear people meeting in the restroom all the time. This is especially the case with the tall monk. As soon as he comes, you can hear his voice yelling and hollering in the restroom. How shameless! How pathetic!

The two people who meet in the restroom ought to know who you are—I don't need to call you by name. Not only are they unruly in the restroom, they are even worse in the dining hall and the Buddha Hall.

They should talk more softly and not be so coarse and loud, like a loudspeaker that can be heard five or six blocks away. That's completely against the rules. I've been trying to tolerate this situation and not bring it up for a long time, but today I couldn't hold back any longer. If I held back any longer, the whole Gold Mountain Monastery would collapse, as if a cannonball had struck it.

Does anyone want to say anything? Anyone who wants to speak can do so for five minutes. You can pass judgment on whether what I've said is right or not. If you disagree, openly express your disagreement. Don't keep it inside or only let it out when no one is around. I'm not afraid of opposition. In fact, I welcome it. However, you ought to clearly express your disagreement to everyone. Don't be like a certain Bhikshu disciple, who tells me he doesn't disagree with anything I say, but then stirs things up when I'm not around. As soon as I'm gone, he tries to turn everyone against me, telling them not to listen to me. Now he's living on his own, and I wonder whether he considers himself to have merit or offenses. I hope no one will repeat his mistake. He shows one face in front of his teacher, and another face when his teacher's back is turned.

A few years ago, I had planned to turn the abbotship over to this disciple. However, when I was in South America, he tried to drive all the people away. He wanted neither laypeople, nor nuns, nor monks around. He wanted to be left just by himself, alone, and then he himself would not want to stay either. But he could not run away. When I returned, I tried to chase him away, but he refused to leave. Because of his behavior, he lost the opportunity to be the abbot. I had wanted to give the position to him, but it wouldn't have worked.

After I founded the International Institute for the Translation of Buddhist Texts, many times I considered making him the director. Then I thought of how even he recognizes his problems. He's told us how from the time he was little he tried to oppress and control everyone. Well, unfortunately, he can't control himself. That's why, in the end, he lost the position of director. This matter grieves me deeply. ◁

NOVEMBER 16, 1973 | FRIDAY EVENING

On the Fire of Ignorance

At present the Bhikshus, Bhikshunis, Upasakas, and Upasikas of Gold Mountain Monastery are exceptionally fine. You could say there is no one like them in the world, and that in the future they will be the world's leaders. But for the moment they are lacking in one respect and cannot yet be leaders. In what respect? Their tempers are too big. If it were not for those afflictions and those tempers, they would already be the world's most lofty teachers, great guiding masters for the world. It's just due to that small deficiency, namely our tempers, that right now it won't work for us to go outside. If we could control our tempers; be very cordial when speaking with others; never display any anger, but treat everyone the same; never respond with anger when others are angry with us; remained unaffected when others are afflicted with us—if we could be that way, we could be said to have the power of *samādhi*. So long as we are unable to be that way, and instead, when speaking to anyone, our fire of ignorance flares up 30,000 feet, not only are we unable to teach and transform the people in the world, we can't even subdue our own ignorance. This is extremely important. Now we need to look for people with such skills, and see who can manage not to have a blazing temper, ignorance, anger or hatred. We need to find such people. The time has now come for all of us to train ourselves to be free from anger. Instead of anger we should have great compassion and be at one with all creatures. This was illustrated when the pigeons ate from people's hands. When you have no thoughts of killing or anger, then even birds who are not your pets will come to eat from your hand. Birds and beasts won't fear you. Tigers who see you, will not bite you. As the saying goes:

> One who is lofty in the spiritual Path
>> subdues dragons and tigers.
> One with formidable virtue gains respect
>> from ghosts and spirits. ╡

NOVEMBER 24, 1973 | SATURDAY EVENING

On Admonishing Those Who Think They Are Extraordinary

[Editor's note: Master responds to a question about translation.] Earlier, I discussed an ocean-ruling spirit's name as meaning either "Ever Dwelling in Waves" or "Ever Making Waves Dwell." All of you should decide which interpretation is correct. Since we already discussed this spirit, we don't need to repeat the explanation. If you remember it, you remember; if you don't, you don't. There's no need to re-lecture it. Just use one of the names. You don't have to repeat the two meanings I gave before. If there is time left, the translators can use it to translate. If they don't understand or they forgot because they weren't paying attention, that's their problem. I explained to you all very clearly, and yet you still don't know which meaning is correct.

If you don't even have the judgment or wisdom to know that, how can you think of opposing your teacher? What abilities do you have to oppose your teacher with? You talk about it, but you don't actually oppose your teacher. Most of the time, all of you think you're quite extraordinary. You think that in the heavens and below, you alone are honored. When a test comes, however, you hardly dare to call yourself honored.

Which of the meanings is more accurate, more forceful, and more complete? It is decisions like this that determine whether you have Dharma-selecting Vision or not. You should use whichever interpretation expresses the principle more fully. There might not only be two interpretations, but millions upon millions of them.

If you kept on explaining, there would be many, many meanings. And if you were to go into detailed and subtle analysis, then the meanings would be infinite and unending. However, just interpreting in a general way, which of the two meanings should be used? Do you know?

Disciple: Yes.

Master: Explain to the rest of them. ⌐

SEPTEMBER 14, 1974 | SATURDAY NOON

On Obstructing Others' Study & Practice

In spiritual practice, do you truly work hard? Or do you just go through the motions? Do you just follow the crowd? Do you recite the Buddha's name just because others are reciting it? Do you recite sutras just because others are reciting them? Or even worse, when you see others reciting sutras or the Buddha's name, do you refuse to join the recitation? Or worse than that, when you see others who are reciting, do you tell them not to recite? Do you obstruct their cultivation?

I know that some people are obstructing the language classes we're holding now. They say the language classes are terrible. They say that if they didn't have to take those classes, they would have become enlightened and become Buddhas a long time ago. They contend that the language classes are impeding people from becoming Buddhas. They find any way they can to ruin these classes. They themselves don't want to study, and they influence others to quit studying as well. That is a most despicable attitude. They themselves don't want to practice the Dharma, and they influence others not to practice, because they don't want anyone else to get ahead of them. ◁

SEPTEMBER 14, 1974 | SATURDAY NOON

On Denying Virtue & the Classics

In our practice, we have to value virtue and cultivation. One of my disciples, who considers himself an expert on Chinese literature, claims that virtue is illusory. He uses Han Yu to back up his argument. Han Yu said, "Compassion which does not discriminate is humaneness. Appropriate action is justice. Interactions with others based upon humaneness and justice are the Path. That which is inherent within oneself and does not come from external sources is virtue. Humaneness and justice are concrete concepts. The Path and virtue are illusory positions." Based on that premise, this American monk has decided that there is no such thing as virtue and the Path. He also now contends that Laozi's *Classic of the Path and Virtue,* as well as the *Analects* of Confucius and the works of Mencius—and a lot more besides—are illusory.

VIII | Cultivation

Ceremony in the main hall of Gold Mountain Monastery during renovations

OCTOBER 29, 1972 | SUNDAY NOON

On Good Roots & Virtue

Everyone who is studying the Buddhadharma here is a person with good roots in the Dharma. You must nurture and cherish your own good roots, and not casually abuse or squander them. People who study the Buddhadharma must be endowed with the greatest virtue. Not only do you yourself have to have virtue, but your parents and ancestors must also have developed virtue. It is this combined virtue that enables you to study the Buddhadharma. If you were not endowed with good roots and virtue, you would not be able to remain in this monastic setting. This monastery maintains the highest standards of any in America, in China—in the entire world. You shouldn't look lightly on yourself and think that you have no virtue. You all have virtue, but because you haven't become enlightened, you aren't aware of it.

Today I'm going to tell you a bit of news. In just two months, Gold Mountain Monastery will have been established for two years. Counting our stay in Chinatown, we've been established for four years altogether. In all these years, I have been observing the causes and circumstances, and it seems to me that there are one, two, or maybe three individuals who may be able to realize the first stage of Arhatship in three years. If you work very hard, you may be one of them. If you are lazy, you will miss the opportunity. I am telling you this to exhort you to try your hardest and not to fall back into the cesspool. Of course, if you really

VIII. Cultivation

want to fall back into it, it's your own choice. But once you fall in, you'll be sorry.

NOVEMBER 5, 1972 | SUNDAY EVENING

On the Importance of a Single Thought

My monastic disciple Heng Ding called me from Hong Kong. A while ago, he told me that he thought he was only one month away from enlightenment. The problem was, as soon as he had that thought, a demonic state came on him. After that, three demons kept pestering him and made him utterly confused. He called here and also wrote a letter asking for help.

Later, those demons behaved themselves and Heng Ding recovered from his demonic illness. I told the three monks who went to Hong Kong to visit Heng Ding, and they reported that he has recovered. His eyes no longer emit a demonic light. [Editor's note: This disciple, who passed away in 2003, accompanied the Master in the late 1940's when he left China and went to Hong Kong.]

NOVEMBER 16, 1972 | THURSDAY EVENING

On Practice being the Icing on the Cake

At Gold Mountain Monastery, lectures are given twice a day, except on Saturday, when there is only one lecture. When sutras are being lectured, not only do people attend, but all those of the eightfold pantheon of gods, dragons, ghosts, and spirits come and listen. Therefore, we must stay on schedule.

If people call and ask about our schedule, tell them that lectures are given from 1:30 to 3:30 in the afternoon, and from 7:00 to 9:00 in the evening. There's no need to tell them that we recite Śākyamuni Buddha's name or that we recite the sutras. Although the lecture itself begins at 7:30, the time for the evening ceremony, which starts at 7:00, is included within the sutra lecture. In fact, reciting the sutras and the Buddha's name is the most essential, indispensable part of the entire program—it's the actual practice. It is even more important than listening to the sutra lecture.

It's a lot like eating. When we eat bread, we put a spread on it. When we eat rice, we put some vegetables with it. You don't eat plain rice without vegetables or plain bread without butter. You put some butter on it, and if there's cheese, that's even better. In the same way, reciting the sutras and the Buddha's name is the icing on the cake—it's actually the most important part of the schedule. That is why we include it within the time for the sutra lecture.

When people call on the phone or come to inquire, don't tell them that we first recite the sutras for part of the hour prior to the sutra lecture. When you draw the picture of a person, you don't have to draw in the intestines. If you insist on drawing the intestines, then they will appear to be outside the belly. Originally they are inside the belly and invisible, so there's no need to depict them. Everyone should pay attention to this point. ⊟

NOVEMBER 27, 1972 | MONDAY EVENING

On Bowing in Repentance before the Ten Thousand Buddhas

Copies of the *Sutra of the Names of Ten Thousand Buddhas* have arrived, and it would be best for everyone to bow in repentance before the Buddhas through a section of this sutra each evening [Editor's note: following the evening lecture]. The merit and virtue derived from bowing in repentance before the Ten Thousand Buddhas can never be fully expressed. Bowing in repentance can eradicate people's karma; bowing in repentance can nurture people's roots in the Dharma. Bowing in repentance can help people who have never done any spiritual practice learn how to practice, and it can help people without good roots to develop them. When our good roots are fully developed, we will become enlightened. Therefore, the merit and virtue of bowing in the Repentance Ceremony before the Ten Thousand Buddhas is inconceivable. We will experiment with bowing in repentance for one hour every evening. Next year we can start to hold the full Repentance. Everyone should recognize the importance of bowing in repentance; only then can you derive its benefits. ⊣

NOVEMBER 29, 1972 | WEDNESDAY EVENING

On the Importance of This Repentance Ceremony

Bowing in Repentance before the Ten Thousand Buddhas is very important. If you don't participate in this Repentance, you can't really be called a practitioner of the Path. In the past, I also did this repentance practice. Therefore, in spiritual practice, you must undergo a process of hardship and exertion, and then maybe you'll have some achievement. If you aren't sincere, you won't achieve anything at all. ⊣

DECEMBER 7, 1972 | THURSDAY EVENING

On Being Mindful of the Buddha

Today we sprinkle water along the sides of the hall to purify and safeguard the boundaries, before beginning our seven-day recitation session, during which we will recite "Namo Amitābha Buddha". During these seven days, you can recite "with one heart unconfused" and attain the *samādhi* of mindfulness of the Buddha, thus enabling your great wisdom to unfold. To do that is to "dispel dark delusions." ⌐

On Seven-day Revitalization

Why do we recite for seven days? The blood and other fluids in our bodies go through a complete cycle in seven days. On the first day, our blood and energy begin a process of change and renewal. That process continues through the second and third days, all the way up to the seventh day. At that point our blood and energy are completely revitalized, and that is conducive to enabling our great wisdom to unfold. Revitalizing involves casting out the darkness. We no longer engage in deluded thinking, and so we can recite the Buddha's name single-mindedly.

We may request, "Namo Amitābha, please come rub the crown of my head." Or maybe we will see light, or flowers, or the Buddha's fine hallmarks and characteristics. We may have any number of these greater or lesser responses. Although these can't be counted as completely good states, nonetheless they indicate a certain degree of response in our recitation. Therefore, having become revitalized and full of new blood and energy, we no longer have false thinking, our great wisdom can unfold, and we can plant deep good roots, which are the seeds of *bodhi*.

It is extremely hard to get an opportunity to join a session for reciting the Buddha's name. We have only one such session each year. The seventeenth day of the eleventh lunar month is Amitābha Buddha's birthday. It is very fitting that we are holding the session right before Amitābha Buddha's birthday. All the monasteries that I've been to in the past held sessions

VIII. Cultivation

for reciting the Buddha's name around the time of Amitābha Buddha's birthday.

All of you, whether you are monastics or laypeople, should participate in this recitation session now that you have such an opportunity. Do not miss your chance. This is a *bodhimaṇḍa* for realizing Buddhahood. This is a chance for you to become a Buddha. ⊣

DECEMBER 7, 1972 | THURSDAY EVENING

On Planting Vajra Seeds

Now that you have planted *vajra* seeds, you will certainly reap the fruit of *bodhi* in the future. Once you have ingested *vajra* into your stomach, that *vajra* will never be dissolved. To recite the Buddha's name is to plant *vajra* seeds. Those seeds will never be destroyed. Don't have doubts, thinking, "What benefits could chanting 'Namo Amitābha, Namo Amitābha' possibly have?" There's no way to discuss those benefits fully.

Throughout his whole life, Śākyamuni Buddha enthusiastically praised the dharma door of reciting the Buddha's name. The *Amitābha Sutra* was spoken without being requested. From that we can see the importantce of the method of reciting the Buddha's name. By reciting the Buddha's name we can be reborn in the Western Land of Ultimate Bliss. In the past, in China, many, many people have attained rebirth in the West by reciting the Buddha's name. ⊣

DECEMBER 7, 1972 | THURSDAY EVENING

On Diligence

During the recitation session, everyone should resolve to recite the Buddha's name. Even those who work during the day should recite the Buddha's name after they come back from work. All the language classes will stop during the session. We will simply recite the Buddha's name. The sutra lectures will be replaced with instructional talks during the session. We will discuss the practice of reciting the Buddha's name. Basically, I do not wish to stop the sutra lectures [Editor's note: on the *Flower Adornment Sutra*], since this sutra is very long and each time we stop we miss the opportunity to cover a large section. However, now we must emphasize the recitation session. Even those who have jobs should join the session when they get back from work and not miss the opportunity. Don't simply take a rest after you come back from work. Don't be lazy. Because we have been lazy for countless eons until now, we are still ordinary people and have not accomplished anything. Therefore, we cannot be lazy anymore. When you aren't working, you should all come to recite.

The weather is cold, so you should put on more clothes. And if you are still cold, you should recite the Buddha's name loudly. Recite till you perspire, and then you won't be cold anymore. It's like lecturing sutras: when you exert yourself, then you perspire. If you drink a cup of warm water on top of that, you will also perspire. We should put effort into reciting the Buddha's name, so that we can end birth and death and then save living beings the way the Buddha does. Don't casually chat or gossip with others. The monastics and the laypeople staying in the monastery should recite the Buddha's name whenever they have time. Laypeople who are not resident in the monastery should also not forget to come here and recite the Buddha's name. We should have a contest in reciting the Buddha's name and see who first attains the *samādhi* of mindfulness of the Buddha That's the game we'll play. Everyone can show off his spiritual powers. Let's see who has the greatest spiritual powers and is the first one to attain the *samādhi* of mindfulness of the Buddha. Don't waste time. People who work should come on the weekends to recite the Buddha's name instead of goofing off. I like nothing better than seeing people recite the Buddha's name. Whoever recites the Buddha's name is a good disciple of mine, and whoever doesn't, isn't.

In the past, when we had recitation sessions, I did not insist that everyone come and recite and as a result, many people have slacked off. Many people took a holiday and went on vacation, going off on their yachts or in their cars, running off everywhere and wasting the time. This year, I decided that it would no longer do for me not to demand that you come. Therefore, if you want to come you can come, and if you don't want to, you still have to come. If you don't come, I won't pay attention if you get into trouble in the future. I'm telling you clearly now. If you come now, I'll be able to help you if you get into trouble. I don't have much strength to help others, since I can't even help myself. However, there are times when I can be of a little help. In what ways can I help? I don't know. When the time comes, we can talk about it. ☐

FRIDAY EVENING | AUGUST 17, 1973

On Cultivation's Effect on Family Members & One's Own Destiny

Recently, one of my monastic disciple's brother and sister came to visit Gold Mountain Monastery. I was pleased to see them and I noticed how their sincerity has increased since last time they visited. This nuns' parents will also come for another visit soon. This monastic disciple of mine has a bit of sincerity, and for this reason she has influenced her younger brother and sister to believe in Buddhism. Her mother has also taken refuge; her parents visit often. If she did not truly practice, this kind of thing would not happen. Her sister and brother both felt they had affinities with me as well, so they wanted to come back again. If this nun were not doing a good job herself, her brother, sister, and mother, would not believe in Buddhism. It is from things like that we know about a person's cultivation.

For instance, another disciple's younger brother went away, and his parents don't come to visit. Why do you suppose that happened? It's because he doesn't truly cultivate, and so no one in his family believes. Be aware that I am not just talking about those two individuals; the same applies to all of you.

A long-time disciple, Guo Jun, will visit Gold Mountain Monastery soon. He took refuge with me in Hong Kong when he was only eleven years old. He liked to visit the Monastery there. Every Saturday and Sunday he insisted that his mother take him to see me. If his mother did not take him to see me, he would cry all day in the house. He was not someone who especially liked to cry, but he would cry the whole day in the house. And so his mother had to bring him to my place. Later, when he was going to school, he used to have lunch at my place. Every day he wanted to see his teacher. If he didn't get to see his teacher, he would cry. It's fortunate that this disciple took refuge with the Triple Jewel. If he hadn't, his karma retribution this time might have pushed him into another kind of lifestyle. Because he became a disciple of the Buddha, he was able to change his destiny.

VIII. Cultivation

SEPTEMBER 4, 1973 | TUESDAY EVENING

On Being True in What We Do

Just after I returned from South America a few days ago, my monastic disciple Guo Yu asked for permission to visit his parents. I granted him permission, but said he had to make the journey by bowing once every three steps.

Well, he took me up on it! He left Gold Mountain Monastery that very next morning—at 2 A.M.—to begin his journey of bowing once every three steps, heading north to Seattle, his home. He took a backpack with him. He bowed from the door of Gold Mountain Monastery until he almost reached at the Golden Gate Bridge. He bowed for eleven hours. Many people watched him on the streets, because nobody had ever seen this kind of show before. The police also kept him under close surveillance. They did not know what he was doing, but they did not dare meddle with him either. But then he got hungry when it came time to eat and his hunger drove him to return to the monastery. Actually this disciple is very sincere; he is willing to do what I tell him to do. He has a promising future.

In this country, you have to do things that are true. If you can do true things, you can help propagate the Buddhadharma and make it flourish. If you don't do true things, then you will remain a mediocre Buddhist.

It seems this monk does have the tenacity to continue his journey from San Francisco all the way to his home. However, arriving there, he will still not have arrived at his final destination. Nonetheless, even if he will not have completely arrived, the process of his journey itself will have a positive impact for Buddhism.

On his first day out, this disciple bowed without saying anything. Even the police were perplexed. In the future, whoever is sincere in making a special resolve—perhaps to bow to the Buddhas, bow repentances, or recite the Sutras—will certainly obtain a response. During the advent of Buddhism in the West, everyone should do true things and not be sloppy in the least bit. In that way, you will have some achievement. ◁

SEPTEMBER 24, 1973 | MONDAY EVENING

On the Ease that Comes with No False Thinking

See how Guo Man [Editor's note: a long-time disciple and Dharma protector from Hong Kong], old as she is, has nonetheless left the home life and become a nun? And as a nun, she is as sincere as ever. See how she is? The Buddhas always aid her. They even help her sleep! She's so content that she can eat her fill and then fall asleep. That's because she doesn't have any false thoughts. If she were false-thinking all the time, she wouldn't be able to sleep. She said when she was on her way here from Hong Kong she didn't sleep for two days. She kept wondering, "When will we get to America? How will the flight go? When will I see my Teacher?" She had those false thoughts from morning to night, and they kept her awake. Arriving here after two sleepless nights, she fell sound asleep as soon as she had bowed to the Buddhas and greeted her teacher. Her false thinking stopped and she slept at ease. ◁

SEPTEMBER 28, 1973 | FRIDAY EVENING

On Cherishing Blessings

Everyday I find a teacup lid, but no teacup. Why? Where is the teacup? Did it grow legs and walk off? If you can't even take care of teacups, what good are you? What if I gave you a building? You'd probably let it fall into the ocean. There is also the matter of the bookmark. It has a definite place where it should be in the sutra, but sometimes it ends up in a different place. I don't know if someone wants to read the sutra, or if they want to steal the bookmark but don't quite dare to.

You should realize it's not that your teacher is attached to teacups. It's just that you can't go around losing things. [Editor's note: Also, the teapot was found burnt in the kitchen.] How could you treat the teapot like that and expect not to ruin it? We're not smelting steel here. We're not setting up a foundry as in China's Great Leap Forward. That kind of steel-forging won't work. Do you all know that today one of my disciples boiled the teapot dry? Was anyone told? Did you all know about the teapot when I asked and yet none of you told me about it? Why did none of you tell me?

There's also the matter of leaving lights on. I have told you over and over again that people must turn out the lights when they are not in a room. But every time this particular disciple is not in her room, she leaves the light on. I've noticed this many times.

VIII. Cultivation

We cultivators must be careful in all respects not to squander our blessings. We need to nurture blessings in every possible way. For example, when you let the pot boil dry while you are boiling water, you are squandering blessings. Not turning off lights is the same. Blessings are successfully cultivated through progressive, bit-by-bit accumulation. If you fail to pay attention, you won't have many blessings.

Furthermore, none of you bothers to amass blessings in the best place possible. Who would have expected that Professor Hsieh would grab the blessings of our second floor by cleaning the lavatory there. I doubt if anyone has ever cleaned that lavatory before, but today, our professor helped us clean the toilets.

I, too, like doing that kind of work. After I became a novice, I specialized in cleaning toilets. Even while I was still a layman, whenever I went to a monastery, I would clean the toilets for them. I did whatever work others were unwilling to do. It doesn't take long to perform such a task. One can finish the job quickly. Now Professor Hsieh has cleaned up our lavatory on the second floor. No doubt you're waiting for me to clean the third floor. I can probably make time for that tomorrow. If Upasika Hsieh had not cleaned the second-floor lavatory, I would have forgotten about this job. But when she volunteered, it reminded me of my work in the past. I should continue to do what I did as a new novice and a layperson, and clean the toilets. Don't you agree? ⊣

SEPTEMBER 30, 1973 | SUNDAY EVENING, WASHINGTON ST.

On Being Cautious About Praise

When Guo Yi lectured the previous stanza this afternoon, she was especially praised by Professor Hsieh—who said, "She's an American woman who has mastered Chinese to the point that she can lecture just like a Chinese person. A Chinese person couldn't lecture it better than she did." So, Guo Yi, someone is giving you a high hat to wear, but wear it cautiously. ⊣

OCTOBER 5, 1973 | FRIDAY EVENING, AT WASHINGTON STREET

On Guanyin Bodhisattva Not Permitting the Earth to Quake

It's almost time for the Opening of the Light Ceremony (a consecration ceremony for the International Institute for the Translation of Buddhist Texts). Everyone should sincerely bow the Great Compassion Repentance and cultivate Great Compassion Dharmas, so Thousand-handed, Thousand-eyed Guanyin Bodhisattva will manifest great spiritual powers and keep San Francisco from falling into the ocean in an earthquake. As you have seen, there have been several earthquakes, but they have all been far away from San Francisco—some fifty or sixty miles, or a hundred miles—and we have been safe here. That has been a response from Guanyin Bodhisattva.

Someone thinks, "Master, it was you who vowed that as long as you are in San Francisco an earthquake will not hit. Why are you now saying that the absence of earthquakes here is due to Guanyin Bodhisattva?"

It's just because I knew Guanyin Bodhisattva would come that I said that there would not be an earthquake. I said that in 1968, and I repeated my statement in 1969, 1970, 1971, 1972, and 1973. I have said it every year, not just one year. Haven't you heard me say that? ⊣

SEPTEMBER 30, 1973 | SUNDAY EVENING, WASHINGTON ST.

On Being Careful
About Cleanliness

The professor says everything here is good, except for one thing: the toilets are dirty. We should remember that. I'm also going to be checking each toilet every day, and if I find any dirty ones, I will clean them myself. What do you think of that? If the toilets aren't kept clean, people can get sick due to the poor sanitation. And I, too, know what sentient beings like in their minds. What is that? They like things to be clean. Whether you are a monk, a nun, a novice, or a layperson, you can do this work. ⊣

OCTOBER 27, 1973 | SATURDAY EVENING

On Practice Helping
Avert a Calamity

Even though this celestial calamity [Editor's note: the Comet Kahoutek, which was headed for Earth] will not be easy to avert, we have two monks who have resolved to become Bodhisattvas. They wish to act as models and express the Dharma for sentient beings through their method of practice. Therefore they have made the vow to make a pilgrimage bowing once every three steps. This is no ordinary undertaking. I'm not joking with you. What they have set out to do is real and factual. The two of them have made the resolve to pray for world peace, and they may be able to help avert a calamity, subduing the comet so it won't have a devastating effect on this world. ⊣

NOVEMBER 2, 1973 | FRIDAY EVENING

On Being Like Water, Not Like Ice

It's best not to get angry at what people say. Not one of you has reached that level yet, but you can gradually learn. Each of you should practice being very pleasant and harmonious—which means not having a temper. In your dealings with anyone, no matter who, be like water, not like ice. Water doesn't harm people. Of course, sometimes there's a lot of it, and people may drown. But that's rare. However, from people's point of view, ice is very hard, and you feel it's very cold when you come in contact with it. But you feel quite comfortable when you see water, and water can quench your thirst. You should be happy all the time, like the Bodhisattvas. Don't be like the hungry ghosts who are always pouting. As soon as you pout, you turn into a hungry ghost. If you are cheerful and happy, then you are a Bodhisattva. ◁

NOVEMBER 15, 1973 | THURSDAY EVENING

On How to Keep Our Mind on the Path

Master: Does anyone have any opinion to bring up today?

Visitor: When sitting, what should one keep one's mind on?

Master: Not on any fixed place. Your thoughts should be free of all attachment. Your mind should not dwell upon anything, thinking neither of good nor of evil. You should work on that point. Focus your attention there. Thinking in terms of good and bad are both attachments, and in cultivation you should not have attachments. You must rid yourself of all attachments whatsoever, even forgetting about your own body. If you don't have a body, then what attachment is left?

Don't think of anything except for the question "who?" "Who is it who recites the Buddha's name?" "Which one is it?" Look for the "who." When you find out "who" it is, you become enlightened. Before you've found it, you have to keep looking for it—for one day, two days, ten days, a hundred days, a thousand days, ten thousand days, one year, two years, ten years, a hundred years, a thousand years, ten thousand years. It only counts when you find it. You can't speed up the process, like taking opium and getting a fix. To attempt to rush things results in a fraudulent outcome.

When you practice genuine Dharma, you have to do the work yourself; you must make your own effort. You can't be like the farmer who tried to make his sprouts grow faster by pulling them upward. That's a mistake.

By focusing on the question, "Who is it who recites the Buddha's name?" you can cut off all random thoughts. All thoughts of desire will be ended. You could say that is to cut down the ten great demonic hordes which I talked about a few days ago. In that "who" alone, everything is gone. If you aren't mindful of the Buddha, of course you won't investigate the *chan* question "who?" and idle thoughts will arise. But as soon as you have that "who?" it's like the Vajra King's precious sword which cuts everything off clean so there is nothing at all. We're definitely not talking about attachment to some particular place. "Everything is empty and unreal. If you see all phenomena as nonexistent, then you see the Thus Come One." If you have attachments, you still have the mind of an ordinary person. If you have no attachments, your mind is on the Path. ◁

NOVEMBER 16, 1973 | FRIDAY EVENING

On Increasing Vigor

I'm adding an extra day of Chinese class. All of you are so vigorous I feel remorseful I've been so lazy, particularly since Guo Yu has written a letter saying that every day while bowing he thinks about our study of the Buddhadharma here at Gold Mountain, and how important it is. Right now, since he can't hear the Buddhadharma, he feels very pained at heart. But he is happy that all of you can study the Buddhadharma. Isn't that the gist of his letter?

Think about it: Gold Mountain Monastery has produced those two aspiring Bodhisattva sages who bow every third step praying for world peace. Yet we are lazy and don't do anything at all. How can we face the two of them? They are walking the Bodhisattva Path in the wind and the rain, practicing for the sake of the world. What should we be practicing in order to help them? Shouldn't we be doing our utmost to help the Buddhadharma spread far and wide?

They are doing Three Steps One Bow on the road, and reporters interview them. Their influence on Buddhism is very great right now. Their success will be a success for us all. Let us vow that they succeed in their practice. That will be important to this country.

We should think, "They are cultivating that kind of practice, so should we be cultivating the practices of sleeping, being lazy, or being selfish? Should we only be cultivating the practices of jealousy, greed, anger, and delusion?" We ought to reflect upon ourselves. That's why I've decided to add another sutra lecture for you and an extra Chinese class on Saturdays. I'll dedicate that merit and virtue to the two of them, and there are other things I'm doing which I dedicate to them as well. I don't need to tell you what those other things are.

You all know Guo Yu. He used to be a muddled person. When he was here, he did not realize how important our study of the Buddhadharma was. Now he has been gone for a month, bowing once every three steps day after day. Bowing once every three steps seems to have brought him an awakening. He is more clear than he used to be. He knows he is missing this opportunity. Not only is he losing this opportunity, he is also causing Guo Dao to miss this chance. That is his awakening. Thus, he hopes all of you will attentively study the Buddhadharma and wishes that you would help him study some Buddhadharma as well. His physiognomy has already changed. He resembled Hitler before, but he is really different now. Although I have not gone to see them, haven't you found him to be different? Did you notice? I feel that he is not the same as he used to be.

Guo Dao is different from the way he used to be too. Did you notice this when you went to see them last time? I see that he is different from before. You can tell at a glance. You can know when you listen to his voice, even without looking at him; the sound of his voice is different from before. They are not bowing in vain. Guo Dao would absolutely never write letters before. Now, when you read this letter he has written, you can know

VIII. Cultivation

that he has had some awakenings. I am not talking about a major enlightenment, but small awakenings.

There's another piece of news. From now on, every Friday from 12:30 to 2:30 P.M. we'll be conducting a Seminar on Proper Dharma. Anyone is welcome to attend, including followers of non-Buddhist teachings and cults. You should all pay attention to this. We are not afraid of cults or non-Buddhists—or even of demon kings. If kings of demons or members of externalist religious groups arrive, we will do our best to welcome them. Provided they really want to participate in the discussion, we are willing to discuss true principles with them. We should not get angry with them. Rather, in a pleasant fashion, we will look into the principles together and clarify them bit by bit to see who is right. Do you claim your principle is reasonable? All of us will consider it. Is mine reasonable? We will investigate it as a group and determine which is true and which is false. It will be "open talking." ⯂

NOVEMBER 17, 1973 | SATURDAY NOON

On Losing Ground
by Standing Still

Your study of the Buddhadharma should be lively, not stiff and dead. When we are investigating topics together, anyone who has an opinion may express it immediately. It shouldn't be that you would like to speak but don't dare, being afraid to talk even though you want to. For instance, one layman didn't know which of two questions to ask, and ended up not asking either one.

Those of you who have studied the Buddhadharma for many years should not hold back or retreat, so that when someone asks a question, no one answers. If you are that way, then the more you study, the more you retreat. If you retreat, then you will be overtaken by the newcomers. Therefore, all of you should ask yourselves if you have the intention to retreat. If not, then you should go forward with heroic vigor, not just wait.

An old adage goes, "By standing still, you lose two and a half miles." If, for example, the two monks doing Three Steps One Bow were averaging five miles a day, and they stopped for awhile, they would lose two and a half miles. Since you won't be going forward, you will actually be losing ground. All of you should be courageously vigorous and not retreat. ⊣

NOVEMBER 17, 1973 | SATURDAY EVENING

On Remembering Upon One Reading

I have become somewhat familiar with the *Flower Adornment Sutra* as I explain it and so I can remember each passage of sutra text upon seeing it once. I don't need to look at it many times. After one reading, I certainly won't forget it. Therefore, when a visiting Dharma Master came here a few days ago and saw that I could still lecture when the electricity went out, and I didn't need a lamp, he exclaimed, "You can lecture without having to look at the sutra text!" and then he knew. I simply glance once at the text during the sutra lecture, and then I remember it. This is through the aid of the Buddhas and Bodhisattvas of the Flower Adornment Assembly. ◁

NOVEMBER 24, 1973 | SATURDAY NOON

On Cultivation Bringing About Changes

The meeting we held yesterday went very well. I hope that we will hold these kinds of meetings regularly, and that all of you will express your opinions. This gives you all the opportunity to investigate and debate topics together. Debates don't have to be angry disputes over who is right or wrong. They should be the investigation of true principle. You examine your principle, and then I examine mine. We exchange opinions with each other. Debates don't have to be heated arguments where people get red in the face and the redness spreads to their eyes, ears, and neck, so they turn into red-faced monsters. That's not the idea. Instead we need to use our wisdom to present our point to the other person. We should be agreeable and persuasive, and avoid making people angry. That is how we should investigate.

Yesterday's discussion was very good. I hope more people will take part in the investigation. These are meetings for investigation and debate, not for arguing. Why do I tell you that each of you has the right to speak? It's because you shouldn't just rely on me. In the future I might go to South America, or to North America, East America, or West America. When I'm gone, you would be like a snake without a head, unable to budge. There's a saying that goes: "A snake without a head cannot go anywhere." I hope all of you "snakes" can go places and not be headless. After you go around for awhile, you can turn into dragons. Right now Gold Mountain Monastery is a place where snakes and dragons

VIII. Cultivation

mingle: If you cultivate well, the snakes will become dragons. If you don't cultivate well, the dragons will turn into snakes. ◁

DECEMBER 3, 1973 | MONDAY EVENING

On Welcoming Practitioners

On the ninth of this month, we will have a Buddha Recitation Session. Each day from the beginning to the end, we will recite "Namo Amitābha Buddha" without stopping. After we finish reciting and the session is over, we will ask, "Who is reciting the Buddha's name?" during two weeks of *chan* meditation. All day long, we will meditate continuously. Anyone who would like to participate is welcome.

Today practitioners from the Zen Center have joined our sutra lecture. They are both Dharma protectors and our good spiritual friends. We are delighted to have them and extend a warm welcome to them.

Are there any questions? How can one understand without participating? To understand, one must participate. ⊣

JANUARY 29, 1974 | TUESDAY EVENING

On Cultivation Being
a Serious Matter

The two monks from Gold Mountain Monastery who are bowing once every three steps informed us two weeks ago that they could not continue their bowing pilgrimage. The reason was that the roads were flooded—covered in some places by more than five feet of water—from the heavy rains. They rested for two days and then telephoned. Over the phone, I told them to resume bowing. During the two weeks between then and their next phone call, there was no rain and they managed to bow over a hundred miles.

We should all reflect deeply on this. The two of them have made such a sincere resolve and have continued to bow every three steps, undeterred by wind, rain, or snow, carrying out a practice that most people cannot do. In the West, they are the first two to practice this kind of dharma. We should all think about what dharma we want to cultivate. Our goal should not be to be number one. Rather, we want to think about what dharma we can use to propagate Buddhism and make it prosper, so that everyone will understand the teachings of the Buddha.

Right now, the two of them are making a full prostration every three steps. Their bowing has evoked a special response, such that the rain stopped. This is an inconceivable state. Every time Guo Yu bows down, he recites, "Homage to the *Great Flower Adornment Sutra of the Buddha's Mahayana Teachings* and the Ocean-wide Flower Adornment Assembly of Buddhas and Bodhisattvas." As a result, he now has some foundation for his wisdom. When he talks, he doesn't laugh or joke around. He doesn't behave too casually. Every word he says and every move he makes accords with the Buddha's precepts—the precept dharma and the precept substance. He is quite in accord with the rules.

All of us at Gold Mountain Monastery should reflect upon ourselves. How can we fail to cultivate when he cultivates so vigorously? Being so scattered and having so many false thoughts, how can we face these two who have made the Bodhisattva resolve? We are their Dharma brothers and fellow cultivators. They were ordained and received precepts at Gold Mountain Monastery in the United States and subsequently made such a resolve. We should really ponder this well. The practice of the Path is not a game or a joke. ⊣

JANUARY 29, 1974 | TUESDAY EVENING

On Virtue in the Path

Cultivators should value virtue in the spiritual Path. Such virtue takes the form of benefiting others. Put aside the concern for helping yourself and devote yourself to helping others. Be willing to take harm upon yourself in order to protect others from harm. In other words, if you want to benefit others and not harm them, it is essential to cultivate virtue in the Path. The Path is external, whereas virtue is internal. Externally, you nurture the Path by cultivating various paths. Once you are in accord with the Path on the outside, a sense of great happiness wells up within. You have attained virtue in your mind.

> When you have virtue, everyone admires you.
> When you are in accord with the Path,
>   everyone respects you.

Once your conduct is virtuous, everyone thinks well of you. If you are virtuous, then people will be delighted even if you were to scold or beat them. If you lack virtue, then even if you make obeisance to people, they will want to kick you. Virtue wins everyone's respect. Therefore, it is of the foremost importance. All of you should keep the words "virtue in the Path" firmly in mind, so that you see them as soon as you open your eyes.

Some people have no concern for virtue or the Path. It could be said that they have forgotten what is most fundamental. The most fundamental thing is virtue in the Path. Without virtue, one cannot follow the Path to its end and realize Buddhahood. Buddhas are adorned with the myriad virtues. Having perfected and realized the myriad virtues, they were able to become Buddhas.

Virtue in the Path represents righteous energy. It can be compared to the sun and moon. It is equivalent to heaven and earth. Therefore, no one can afford to overlook virtue in the Path. Virtue in the Path also serves as our place of practice. Virtue in the Path requires cultivation. If you cultivate, you can be virtuous. Without cultivation, there is no virtue.

Therefore, if cultivators fail to consider virtue, they will not be able to cultivate. Virtue in the Path consists of renouncing oneself for the sake of others. Forgetting about ourselves, we should help others; we should do that without harboring even a single thought of selfishness and without ever thinking of our own benefit. A mind devoid of selfish and self-benefiting thoughts is a virtuous mind.

Thus, in everything they do, cultivators should pay attention to virtue. Do everything within your capacity to help others. Supporting the monastery is a way of helping others. You are practicing the Path when you protect the *bodhimaṇḍa* from troubles. Therefore, each of you should use your utmost ability to perfect your virtue. Then, you will have some accomplishment.

Don't be so preoccupied with yourself that you cannot forget about yourself. To practice the Bodhisattva Path, you must forget yourself. While it is important to enlighten yourself, it is even more important to enlighten others. As students of the Buddhadharma, we ought to realize this and never forget about helping others. ◁

MAY 9, 1974 | THURSDAY EVENING

On When & How to Use Expedients

In Taiwan there are some Americans who are studying a more sophisticated Buddhism; in Australia there are some Australians doing the same. What is the extent of their sophistication? They claimed that my biography was completely false, saying it should never have been printed. They didn't like our Buddhist journal *Vajra Bodhi Sea* either. "You cannot say that what you teach is the Proper Dharma. If you represent the Proper Dharma, then it implies that what we study are heterodox teachings. You simply cannot say that!" Guo Qian tried to argue with them. You see? They didn't want us to use the term Proper Dharma, for then their teaching would be seen as wrong.

Bandits will allow themselves to be called soldiers, but they don't want to be referred to as bandits. Likewise, adherents of mistaken teachings will not accept criticism. If you tell them that their viewpoints are unorthodox, they will say, "You are the ones who have unorthodox viewpoints! What makes your viewpoints orthodox?" Therefore, in speaking the Dharma, sometimes we have to be expedient.

If we insist on speaking only straight, undiluted Proper Dharma when we lecture outside of our own monasteries, no one will want to listen. We have to intersperse our lectures with a few jokes and anecdotes to make people happy. ⊣

SEPTEMBER 14, 1974 | SATURDAY NOON

On Delusions about the Putrid Bag of Skin

Some people have a strong aversion for the hard work of cultivation. To them I say, our stinking skin-bags have a terrible odor and contain a lot of filth, but you love yours so much that you want to give it good food, good clothes, and a good place to live. You want to fulfill its defiling desires and help it commit offenses. Nothing could be more stupid. Your behavior reveals your delusions, and yet you think you are smarter than everyone else. Frankly, you just stink more than anyone else! You are filthier than anyone else, yet you have no shame! To still suffer and get afflicted for the sake of your stinking skin-bag is really pathetic. Those who cultivate the Path shouldn't be attached to anything. If you have no attachments, you can let go of anything. The *bodhimaṇḍa* is a place to create Buddhas, and whoever has a true resolve and practices with constant diligence will quickly realize enlightenment. People who are muddled and insincere will never achieve anything. ⊣

SEPTEMBER 14, 1974 | SATURDAY NOON

On Advice Upon Entering Seclusion

One of my disciples is going into seclusion. Last night he asked me about the practice of seclusion. Here's my comment:

Everything's a test
To see what you will do.
If you mistake what's before your face,
Don't start all over again.

[Editor's note: The Master changed the last line a little. Usually it goes, "You'll have to start anew"] Don't go back to the beginning; just pick up where you left off. ⊣

SEPTEMBER 22, 1974 | SUNDAY EVENING

On a Lesson about Energy

Today I went to look in on the disciple who is fasting. He was so hungry that he was lying down. He didn't move when I went in, but when I started to leave he turned his head. I asked him how he was, and he said he had no energy. I told him, "That's the very best. If you don't have any energy, then you won't get angry. There's nothing better than starving your anger away. This is where you have to practice patience. Our anger is supported by our energy. If you're so hungry that you can't even move, then when someone scolds you, you won't realize it. You won't have the strength to fight." ⊣

SEPTEMBER 22, 1974 | SUNDAY EVENING

On Rules to Uphold During a Fast

Four people are fasting here. Maybe it is because they know Gold Mountain Monastery doesn't have much rice or vegetables and they want to save on food. Whatever the reason, when people who are fasting leave the building, they have to go out in pairs, or in a group of three, four, five, or more. At least one person who is not fasting must accompany them, because that person will have enough strength to help the others.

There are reasons why someone who is fasting cannot go out alone. First of all, people here might become suspicious and surmise that you're going to buy apple pie to eat on the sly! In cultivation we should be as true as possible and avoid rousing suspicions. Moreover, if you're light-headed and giddy from fasting, and you don't see too clearly, you might get hit by a car. Even though cultivators are not afraid of death, we shouldn't deliberately try to get run over. We have to be careful at all times. It is not permissible to be lax. This is my suggestion to you. Whether or not you listen to and believe me is up to you. I don't know which of the four of you is the decision-maker. ⊣

Studying Buddhist sutras at Gold Mountain Monastery, 15th Street, (left) and at the International Institute for the Translation of Buddhist Texts, Washington Street (right)

IX | Study Habits

OCTOBER 23, 1972 | MONDAY EVENING

On Study Habits

Will someone explain the words "**upon initially realizing Proper Enlightenment**"?

[Editor's note: The Master asked his disciples to explain a passage of the *Flower Adornment Sutra*. Their explanations can be found on pages 62-65 of Chapter One, Part One]

Many people had something to say. Who gave the best explanation? Whose explanation is the most correct? Whose explanation is most helpful in our quest to realize Proper Enlightenment? Whose explanation is in accord with enlightened truth?

In any case, everyone lectured better than I could have done.

People who are reading the text should place it on a table rather than on their lap. First of all, it's not respectful to put the sutra on your lap; it's disrespectful to the Triple Jewel. We have tables here, so you can put your sutra text on a table when you are reading it. It looks bad if you put the sutra on your lap and hunch over to read it. It's also easy for you to fall asleep, and it's disrespectful to the Dharma. Before we had enough tables, you had no choice, but now that we have tables, we should place the sutras on them. Today I called on the people who were hunched over to lecture first. ⊣

OCTOBER 29, 1972 │ SUNDAY NOON

On Language Classes

My monastic disciples who are going to Hong Kong are pre-occupied all day long with the thought that they are going to Hong Kong. "We're leaving for Hong Kong on Friday. I can't wait." They daydream about their forthcoming trip morning and night. Guo Meng has even given up his study of Sanskrit and does nothing but think about the impending trip. That's really useless. He says it's too much for him to handle studying Chinese as well. Why is it that when you eat, you like to eat a variety of foods and you never think there are too many kinds, but when it comes to studying, you complain that it's too much? At lunch, you have bread, rice, butter, cheese, apples, bananas... After you finish one thing, you want to eat something else. After you finish that, you want to try the next course. You want to taste whatever food there is. But when it comes to studying, how come you can only study one subject and not another?

There's a saying, "If you don't study hard when you are young and strong, you'll regret it bitterly in your prime and old age." I know this from experience, because when I was young, I didn't have an opportunity to study. I wanted to learn, but didn't have anyone to teach me. That is true misery. Now that all of you have someone who is willing to teach you, you're really missing a good opportunity if you don't study. Once you learn something, you can use it. Of course, you can understand something and choose not to apply it, but you cannot apply something without first understanding it.

For example, you say you study Chinese at Gold Mountain Monastery every day. Do you understand Chinese? You say you don't. What about Japanese? People boast about how they study Chinese and Japanese, but you say you don't understand Chinese. Do you know Japanese then? "No, I don't know that either," you say. What about Sanskrit? "Sanskrit? Oh, we've had so many lessons on that." What about French? "I wouldn't want to learn French—it's the worst language." How can you say things like that? Why do you have that attitude? ⊣

DECEMBER 6, 1972 | WEDNESDAY EVENING

On Being Multilingual

Now, some of you have decided you don't want to study German, Sanskrit, Japanese, or English, but are content with studying only Chinese. [Editor's note: Many talented young people were resident at the monastery or actively supporting the monastery during this period. The Master recruited them to teach these language classes. It was a rare event to be able to study so many languages simultaneously from such good teachers.] That's a worthless decision and you are making a big mistake.

In the future, when you find yourself in situations where those languages are needed, you'll be sorry. Suppose I go to Germany and need a German translator; if you don't know German, you won't be able to translate for me. You will be brought to you knees then; you'll have to just join the audience. Suppose I go to Japan or France where my talks must be translated into Japanese or French. If you don't master those languages now, you'll have to yield to others then. Those who know how to translate into foreign languages will be the outstanding ones. Those with wisdom and knowledge will have senior status in the group. Those lacking wisdom and knowledge will be relegated to the rear. ⊣

DECEMBER 31, 1972 | SUNDAY EVENING

On the Value of Study

Right now we are in the process of learning many languages. Today we study German; tomorrow we study Sanskrit; the day after that we study French. We also have classes in Chinese, Japanese, and maybe Vietnamese. If someone can teach it, we will offer a class in it. If you know other languages, we can also study them and learn more. At the very least, you should know "yes" and "no" in those languages, because those terms will come in handy. You shouldn't refuse to learn, thinking this is not part of spiritual practice. Actually, studying languages is also part of practice. It drives away your other false thoughts. If you didn't pursue a course of study, you would engage in confused thinking, suddenly running off to the heavens and suddenly boring in to the earth. Your fantasies might take you off to have a chat with the Jade Emperor; at other times you might go and visit King Yama. These are all confused thoughts. If you can study something, you will acquire certain abilities that will help you to propagate the Buddhadharma in the future.

JANUARY 7, 1973 | SUNDAY EVENING

On Studying the Buddhadharma

In the past when I listened to lectures on the sutras, I especially listened to those who didn't know how to explain them. The less they knew about explaining the sutras, the more I wanted to listen to them. I didn't listen to those who spoke well. I particularly wanted to listen to those who couldn't speak well. Why was that? I believed that right within what was not so good, if I could find good points, then that would be the Path. Some of you Americans went out to attend a lecture last night, and when you came back you said once was enough; in fact, once was already too much. I certainly did not have that kind of attitude in studying the Buddhadharma. ⊣

JANUARY 10, 1973 | WEDNESDAY EVENING

On Improving Language Skills

Guo Zhou has offered to edit the English articles that the rest of you write. After he has polished the articles, they can be sent to periodicals every week. This week you have a topic to write on. Next week, if you want to, you can hand in your articles to Guo Zhou and he will bring them back, all edited, the week following that. Some of you have been saying that certain people write good English, while others don't. Since Guo Zhou is a writer, he knows how to edit articles; this is a good opportunity. You are welcome to write if you want to. If you don't want to, don't force it. If you feel you could use some improvement in your English, you can write articles. If you feel your English is already good enough, you don't have to write articles. ⊣

JANUARY 15, 1973 | MONDAY EVENING

On Preparation for Sutra Lectures

[Said after disciples explained a sutra passage.] You explained it pretty well. Guo Hu worked despite his illness and knew the names of the three wheels, which is not bad. Guo Ning was able to discuss them in greater depth. Every one of you should do this. Before I lecture, you can do some preparation and know the terms that will appear in the lecture. If I lecture correctly you can remember it, and if I lecture incorrectly you can simply forget it. That's a good method. ⊣

JANUARY 26, 1973 | FRIDAY EVENING

On Learning Buddhist
Terms & Principles

Did anyone look up the meaning of the Bodhisattva Grounds? I was hoping that some of you would, but nobody did. People who lecture on the sutras and speak Dharma should make a point of remembering Buddhist terms very well. Then you'll be able to explain them at any time, and your explanations will have a sound basis. You can't just give a random explanation that's not based on anything.

Guo Su, you've been studying the *Sutra of Perfect Enlightenment*. Have you gained an understanding of it? You can lecture on one passage from it now. [Editor's note: The disciple lectures.] Your explanation has some principle in it. Your daily study of the sutra hasn't been in vain. ⊣

AUGUST 14, 1973 | TUESDAY EVENING

On Attention & Comportment during Sutra Lectures

Avoid daydreaming as you listen to the sutras. Stay alert. Do not doze off. Sit up straight and be very respectful. Do not be lazy or sleepy. For every degree of respect you muster, you will derive a corresponding degree of benefit. If you are ten percent respectful, you will obtain ten percent benefit. If you are a hundred percent, a thousand percent, or ten thousand percent respectful, you will obtain a hundred, a thousand, or ten thousand percent benefit. When you listen to the sutras, you should act as if the Buddhas and Bodhisattvas are right before you. The Buddhas and Bodhisattvas are observing you as you listen to the sutras. If you are lazy, you are missing an opportunity right in front of you. When the Buddhas and Bodhisattvas see how lazy and insincere you are, they will pay no attention to you and let you do as you wish.

Therefore, you must be extremely reverent as you listen to the sutras. If you are reverent to the Buddha, the Dharma, and the Sangha, to all of the Three Jewels, you will benefit from listening to the sutras. The same applies to when you read or recite the sutras and when you investigate the Buddhadharma. You should also be very respectful and sit upright. Don't lean to the left or right. Don't hunch over or lean back. If you are inattentive and look lightly upon the Buddhadharma, you will derive no benefit from it. Now that I have told you this, you must be especially mindful. ◁

AUGUST 23, 1973 | THURSDAY EVENING

On Research Aiding Lecture Skills

[Editor's note: The Master asked Guo Hu to explain a passage of sutra text.] Guo Hu did a decent job of explaining the text. It's good that he did some research and knew how to explain the sutra before hearing it lectured. That's the way to learn to lecture on the sutras. Although his explanation was a little evasive, there was still some meaning in it. ◁

AUGUST 24, 1973 | FRIDAY EVENING

On Learning the Sutras Well

The person who just discussed the dragon-kings did a good job. All of you should remember what you have heard in the lectures. For example, suppose a Dharma Master were to come and ask you, "What sutras have you heard explained?"

And you said, "I've heard the *Dharma Flower Sutra, the Śūraṅgama Sutra*, and the *Flower Adornment Sutra*."

The Dharma Master might then say, "Oh, you've heard the *Flower Adornment Sutra*. Well, how do you explain the line, 'Thus, Sagara contemplates the Buddha'?"

Now suppose all you could answer was, "Huh? I don't know."

What do you think he would say? Perhaps he'd say, "Ah, you have a muddled teacher who tries to teach a muddled student. Neither one of you understands. How pathetic!" In that case, not only would you lose face, you would also disgrace your teacher. Both teacher and disciple would have their reputations ruined. ⊣

AUGUST 27, 1973 | MONDAY EVENING

On Doing the Necessary Research

We have discussed the twenty-five levels of existence many times before. If anyone remembers them, you may review them for everyone. When we were going through the prose earlier on, I did not explain the twenty-five levels of existence in detail, assuming that you would look up the list and make note of it. However, I see that you have been lazy. None of you know the list today, and I, too, have forgotten it. And so no one will try to explain that list today. Tomorrow, after you have researched the list, I will also recall it.

Right now we can explain "the realms of existence" to mean the Three Realms—the Desire Realm, the Form Realm, and the Formless Realm, which include the twenty-five levels of existence. Guo Pu mentioned some levels of existence in her discussion of the text, but not the entire list. We all need to know them. ᕷ

AUGUST 28, 1973 | TUESDAY EVENING

On the Value of Memorization

People who could not explain the twenty-five levels of existence before must pay back their debts and explain them today. [Editor's note: Disciples gave explanations.] Those of you who know them have already spoken. Those who do not know cannot speak anyway. For the time being, we'll consider those debts repaid.

Now I will ask you another question: What are the Eighteen Uncommon Dharmas? Does anyone remember? In the past we had several exams on this while riding in the car, but I fear you've already let this list slip your minds. However, this examiner is not going to let you pass so easily. You have to truly remember it for it to count. That way, you will be able to explain this list whenever you are called upon to do so. Most people cannot speak extemporaneously. They must prepare a draft beforehand and then read from their draft. But if you remember lists and terms clearly, you can explain them at any time. Then your audience will have no choice but to respect you. Having studied the Buddhadharma for so many years, how can you always answer with an "I don't know" when people ask you about a certain topic? What have you been studying?

Having studied all this time, you still haven't weaned yourself from the traditional method that is pervasive in the American education system. You pull a slip of paper from your sleeve and read while peeking at the paper. There's not much point in that. That's not your own stuff. What belongs to you is what you have committed to memory. Most of you have forgotten what you have studied over the years. Some of you still remember. Those who remember are those who work hard. They are serious. No doubt they reflect on the Buddhadharma that they have studied—even reviewing it just before they fall asleep at night. They do not engage in excessive false thinking. Those who do not pay attention have listened to the sutras for many years, and still, they have no understanding whatsoever. How pathetic!

Guo Yi has an excellent memory. Why do you suppose that is? We should look into this question. During the first summer session, there was an exam to see who could memorize the Śūraṅgama Mantra first. She was the first one to commit it to memory. However, during the actual exam, Guo Qian placed first. That disciple is also very intelligent, but his memorization was in fact just a little bit behind Guo Yi's. She took about one month to memorize the 554-line Śūraṅgama Mantra, doing her memorization for about forty-five minutes each day.

Elder Master Miao of Gaomin Monastery managed to commit the Śūraṅgama Mantra to memory after studying for only four hours. I studied it for two hours a day, for a period of three days. I studied one hour in the morning and one hour in the evening. By the third day I could recite it from memory. That's the way I remember it. It took me thirty minutes to commit the Great Compassion Mantra to memory. I was sitting on a train from Lalin to Beiyinhe [Editor's note: villages in northeast China]. I knew the Great Compassion Mantra was a rare treasure as soon as I obtained a copy of it. Therefore I studied it while on the train. By the time I got off the train thirty minutes later, I had memorized it. ⊣

AUGUST 29, 1973 | WEDNESDAY EVENING

On Advance Preparation

In a few days, I will be lecturing on the Buddha's Ten Powers. Pay attention. I am telling you ahead of time so you may do a little research. That way, when asked about the list, you won't say, "I don't know." Of course, maybe I won't ask you about it after all. If you have researched the list, I might not ask you about it. But if you don't know the list, I will quiz you on it. Someone asked a layperson about the twelve kinds of canonical text in the Buddhist canon. He said, "I know, the *Amitābha Sutra* is the first kind; the *Vajra Sutra* is the second kind; the *Dharma Flower Sutra* is the third kind; the *Śūraṅgama Sutra* is the fourth kind; the *Flower Adornment Sutra* is the fifth kind; the *Earth Store Sutra* is the sixth kind; the *Sixth Patriarch's Platform Sutra* is the seventh kind; and on and on. There are twelve kinds in all." What do you think of that explanation? [Editor's note: It was not accurate. The Twelve Kinds of Canonical Text are:

1. Prose
2. Verse
3. The transmitting of predictions
4. Interpolations
5. Dharma spoken without being requested
6. Causes and conditions
7. Analogies
8. Expanded (*Vaipulya*) writings
9. Stories of the past lives of the Buddha

10. Stories of the past lives of the Disciples
11. Rare and unprecedented teachings
12. Commentarial literature.] ♯

NOVEMBER 18, 1973 | SUNDAY EVENING

On the Value of Taking Notes

Disciple: In view of all you said about books, do you think it's a good idea to take notes?

Master:

> Before you understand, take notes.
> After you have understood, destroy them.
> When one is confused, a thousand volumes are too few.
> After one is enlightened, a single word is too much.

What does it mean to understand and not to understand? Someone who doesn't understand the Buddhadharma hasn't plumbed the depths of the Treasury of Sutras, and so does not have wisdom as vast as the sea. That's when you need to take notes. But once you have entered deeply into the Treasury of Sutras and have wisdom as vast as the sea, the sutra is you, and you are the sutra. The notes are you, and you are the notes. All notes have been recorded in your own nature, and you will never forget them. At that point, what need is there to keep the written notes? "When one is confused, a thousand volumes are too few." When you are confused, you can read a thousand volumes of commentary, and you still haven't read very much. But after you are enlightened, a single word is too much. Even one word would be a hindrance to your own nature. So, what do you think you should do?

TIMELY TEACHINGS

Disciple: I sometimes wonder if I can hear the lecture well, since I'm so busy taking notes.

Master: The notes you are taking are of the lecture, and you can look at them afterwards. I know you write notes very fast. That's why I really dislike the tape recorder. When there's a tape recorder, no one takes notes. The tape recorder makes everyone go to sleep. When there's no tape recorder, people all take notes and don't fall asleep. For that reason I think the tape recorder is an abominable thing.

It would be best if there was a tape recorder and everyone also took notes. Then people could correct any mistakes in their notes by referring to the tape. But the way it is now, no one takes notes. Everyone relies on the tape recorder. If the tape recorder were to die, everything would be finished. There would be nothing whatsoever, right? People have become too dependent.

When we started using a tape recorder, I felt the tape recorder was encouraging people to be lazy, telling everyone to fall asleep. It's there turning around and around, and probably is jealous when people take notes, and so it wants to monopolize the work. It wants to have all the work to itself, including all people's notes. It says to people, "You can fall asleep; you can take a rest. I'll do the work." Probably it wishes to be doubly vigorous so others will be lazy. That's why I think it's very unfair! ⯅

On Writing Out the Sutras by Hand

Before I discuss the situation in Hong Kong and Taiwan, I have some news to tell you, which I hope you will take into consideration. What is this news? Guo Qian, in Hong Kong, has come to the realization that typing sutras on the typewriter is not a good idea. Why not? Because it makes him go through the sutra too quickly, like a galloping horse, before he has time to ponder it over and investigate it. As a result, he is a bit muddled about the principles in the sutra. What is he going to do about this? Instead of transcribing the sutra lecture directly on the typewriter, he is going to write it out by hand. On the one hand, he can practice his handwriting and learn to write faster; on the other hand, he can reflect on the principles as he writes the text down. And so, instead of typing it out quickly on the typewriter, he is going to write it out manually.

I told you a long time ago that the tape recorder is a terrible thing. Since we have a tape recorder, no one takes notes anymore. Everyone depends on the tape recorder. People don't even think it matters whether or not they listen to the lecture anymore. They think they can doze off during the sutra lecture, because the tape recorder is turning the great Dharma wheel, recording all the Buddhadharma. They figure they can listen to the tapes later. First, people don't take notes. Second, they become dependent on the recorder and start dozing off at lectures. Those are two disadvantages. Then, they let the tapes sit there for a long time without listening to them, and as a result they forget all the principles that were lectured on. When they finally have time to listen to the tapes, their memory is already quite foggy and they can't figure out what their teacher was talking about.

Therefore, the tape recorder is not that helpful to students who truly want to investigate the Buddhadharma. It is helpful in a small way, since it can help people fill in what they missed in their notes from not being able to write fast enough. When you miss something in your notes, you can leave a space in your notebook and then listen to the tape to find out what was said. The tape recorder is helpful in this small way, making your notes more complete.

If you really want to understand the Buddhadharma, you should regularly write it out by hand. That is a very good method. ◁

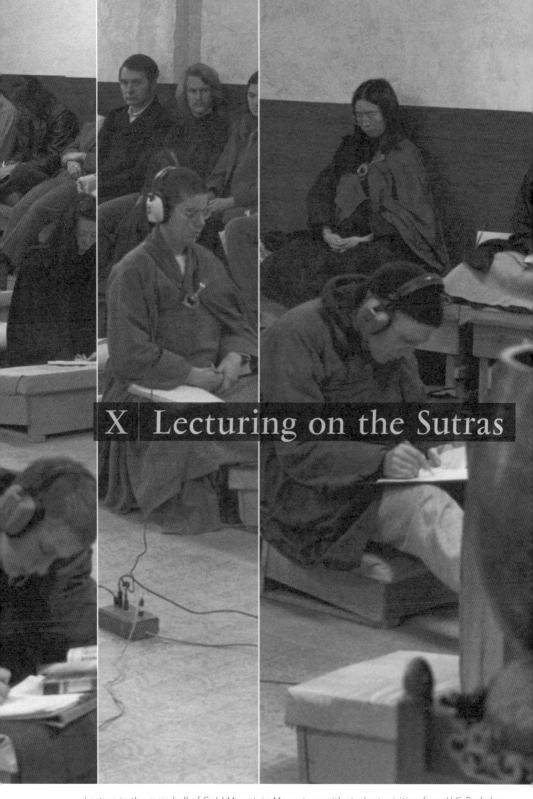

X | Lecturing on the Sutras

Lecture in the main hall of Gold Mountain Monastery, with students visiting from U.C. Berkeley

OCTOBER 12, 1972 | THURSDAY EVENING

On Learning to Lecture on the Sutras

As we are now studying the Buddhadharma and learning what's in the sutras, we should all take part in explaining the *Flower Adornment Sutra*, which is exceptionally long. Such a long text as this should not be lectured by a single individual. We should all take part. That way, when one of you is explaining a passage, I can take a rest. When none of you talk, I have to do all the talking. But I'm not as foolish as I used to be! I'm a bit more intelligent now and so every day at lecture time, I will call on one or two people to explain a little bit. On the one hand, it will prevent you from being lazy, because you'll have to study the sutra beforehand. Otherwise, it will be embarrassing if you don't know what to say when it is your turn to explain. Of course, you will look very good if you give a fine explanation.

This method will keep everyone attentive. At any time, I could call on you to explain something. Today I asked you to talk about the translator of the *Earth Store Sutra*. Tomorrow I might ask you to talk about the translator of the 'Heaven Store Sutra', and the day after that, the translator of the 'Human Store Sutra'.

"I've never heard of the 'Heaven Store Sutra'," you say. Well, you've heard of it now. You have not heard of everything there is. It's possible for there to be such a sutra without your knowing about it. Discovering something we didn't know before is really the definition of learning. Don't you agree? ⊣

OCTOBER 15, 1972 | SUNDAY NOON

On Democratic Process

If I explain something incorrectly, any one of you can address the matter. I don't have the attitude that as I'm the teacher, only I can say what's wrong, and you can't. You can always ask me a question if you think I've explained something wrong. It's only to be feared that you won't be attentive enough to bring anything up. I'm willing to discuss and look into any point that you do bring up.

A saying [in the *Analects*] goes, "If I bring up one angle and the student cannot surmise the other three, he is not fit to be taught." Confucius also said, "Hui is not my helper. No matter what I say, he never opposes me or inquires about anything. He seems to be a fool. Yet when I examine his behavior after he goes home, I find that Hui is no fool." Confucius was extremely democratic in discussing the principles with his disciples. His style was not dictatorial.

We are also investigating the doctrines in a democratic fashion. In this democratic country, we must follow democratic ways also in our study of Buddhism. We cannot employ Hitler's dictatorial regime or Mussolini's fascist rule. Our method is completely democratic: Everyone investigates together. If I correct a mistake in your explanation, then you should not only not be upset, you should be grateful and think, "If you hadn't told me, I would never have known I was wrong and would go on being wrong forever." Don't get red in the face as soon as someone criticizes

TIMELY TEACHINGS

you and sputter, "Hey, how dare you say I'm wrong!" That's not the proper attitude.

I encourage all of you to investigate together. If I lecture wrongly, feel free to correct me. Don't be like Prime Minister Zhao Gao. Zhao Gao and Emperor Qin Er Shi had a contest to see which of them was more powerful. Minister Zhao Gao summoned a crowd of people, pointed at a deer, and said, "I say this is a horse. What do you say?"

Emperor Qin Ershi said, "I say it's a deer. What do you say?" Basically, it was a deer, but because the people feared Minister Zhao Gao, they all said it was a horse. Qin Ershi was an emperor, but he lost to his minister Zhao Gao. That's how the saying, "Pointing at a deer and calling it a horse" came about. The people followed Minister Zhao Gao in calling a deer a horse, because they feared that if they said it was a deer they would be executed.

Our situation is entirely different. Here, people can correct each other's mistakes. Issues are open to public discussion. You, the citizens of this democratic country, choose to come to this monastery precisely because we are not dictatorial here. ⊣

AUGUST 26, 1973 | SUNDAY EVENING

On Dharma Filling
People with Joy

The word for "all" is *xian* in Chinese; *todo* in Spanish, and *tudo* in Portuguese. [Editor's note: The Master had traveled to South America in the spring of 1973.] Hearing me speaking some Spanish and Portuguese, you are delighted and think, "This teacher is not bad." My multi-lingual translation doesn't bring tears to anyone's eyes; it makes everyone is happy. Even the toddlers are waiting expectantly for some candy. ⊣

SEPTEMBER 17, 1973 | MONDAY EVENING

On Guidelines for Lecturing

Recently I have been lecturing six evenings a week, but for the next few weeks I have something I need to do, so I will be lecturing five evenings a week. Guo Zhan can lecture on the remaining evening. He can lecture whatever he wishes, as long as he doesn't scold people. He can't act like one of my disciples, who, as soon as he took the Dharma seat, would begin scolding everyone — the monks, the nuns, the laymen, and the laywomen. That disciple has been removed from the lecture circuit, due to his propensity to scold. He found fault with everyone else but was unaware of his own shortcomings. Now he's trying out seclusion. ⊣

SEPTEMBER 28, 1973 | FRIDAY EVENING

On an Omission with a Positive Outcome

[Editor's note: In explaining a sutra passage on spirits, the Master skips two spirits and then comes back to them after explaining the third one. A disciple advises the Master of the omission.]

Oh, it seemed to me that I had already explained these two; since I couldn't figure out how I was able to recite their names by heart otherwise. It turns out you have not been listening to the lectures in vain. Otherwise, you would not have known that I skipped explaining these spirits' names. If you were sleeping or if you had entered *samādhi*, then you wouldn't have known where I stopped lecturing last.

Now, as I fill in the sections I skipped, I will speak even more energetically. That's because I'm encouraged that you are all promising listeners. Now that I've discovered that, I'll be even less afraid of forgetting a section, for if I do, some of you are sure to remind me. Isn't that right? This is a good method, wouldn't you say? ⊣

OCTOBER 22, 1973 | MONDAY EVENING

On Being Able to Forget Anything

[Note: There was a heavy rain storm that evening in San Francisco, and the lights went out just as the Venerable Master was being requested to come to the hall. When the Venerable Master came in, he said that if there were enough candles to go around, he would lecture the sutra anyway.] If I recite the sutra text wrong, correct me right away. My memory is not very good, and I don't have the sutra text to look at. I can't see clearly and I don't have a candle. [Editor's note: The Master had instructed that his candle be given to someone else.] It's not certain that what I recite will be correct. Although my memory is not very good, my ability to forget is excellent. No one can match it. If you don't believe me, we can have a contest. I can forget anything, but all of you are unable to forget. I can even forget to eat and sleep. Try and see if you can do that. ⊣

X. Lecturing on the Sutras

OCTOBER 28, 1973 | SUNDAY NOON

On the Translation of Terms

Master: Would any of you like to comment on the meaning of any of the four passages of sutra text that were lectured today about the four space-ruling spirits? If so, bring up your opinions quickly for us to investigate together.

Bhikshuni Heng Yin [Editor's note: Guo Yi's ordination name]: As to the translation of 離障安住 (*li zhang an zhu*), 安住 (*an zhu*) consists of two characters, the first of which is the same character as in 平安 (*ping an*) which means "peaceful." The second character is 住 (*zhu*) which means dwelling, as in "without dwelling anywhere." Is the combined meaning then "peacefully dwelling," or do the two characters form a compound with the single meaning of being somewhere. My question is, when we translate the two characters into English, do we have to use the two words "peacefully" and "dwelling," or does 安住 (*an zhu*) just have a single meaning?

Master: What single meaning? How would it be translated?

Bhikshuni Heng Yin: We could say "established," which has the meaning of residing in a location without moving. What I don't quite understand is whether the two characters form a single meaning unit, or whether the meaning of each individual character is intended.

Master: Ask our American sage. How about this? Who is the sage? Sage, speak up. You're not talking? Then the left-over person [Editor's note: "leftover" sounds the same as "Sage" in Chinese] should talk. Who's the left-over person?

Bhikshuni Heng Hsien [Editor's note: Guo Pu's ordination name]: Master, sometimes a peaceful dwelling could be translated as *araṇya*.

Master: *Araṇya*? An *araṇya* is a still and quiet place.

Bhikshuni Heng Yin: It's because sometimes 安住 *an zhu* occurs in 安住道場 (*an zhu dao chang*), and to say "peacefully dwelling" for that didn't sound very smooth in English.

Master: Oh. Then what should it be?

Bhikshuni Heng Yin: Maybe we could say "established."

Master: What does "established" mean?

Bhikshuni Heng Yin: It means being stationed in one place without moving.

Bhikshu Heng Jing: Master, I think I also asked this question before. If the character 安 (*an*) in a certain passage of text is conveying the meaning of 平安 (*ping an*), then 安 (*an*) should be translated "peacefully." However, when, as in this passage, the meaning of peace is not prominent, her idea is that it's possible to use a translation like "established" or "dwelling." But she's right. If those two characters are translated as those two words in English, it doesn't sound very good. Also, the meaning of "peaceful" may not be present in all cases.

Master: Here it means not moving.

Bhikshu Heng Jing: Yes.

Master: It's related to the words "apart from obstacles." If one has obstacles, one cannot be unmoving, and one won't be

X. Lecturing on the Sutras

able to 安住 *an zhu* "dwell securely." Without obstacles one can 安住 *an zhu* "securely dwell." 安住 *an zhu* in this context means not moving. Not moving means stillness, and so it could refer to being still and quiet. Just now Guo Pu brought up *araṇya*, a still and quiet place. One could also say it is *samādhi*, to be in concentration. All those meanings are possibilities. However, when translating into English if you insist on the words "peacefully dwelling," it's true that the meaning is not completely conveyed, and that isn't the best way to say it. What was the translation you suggested for this context?

Bhikshu Heng Jing: Established.

Master: "Established" is one word, right?

Bhikshu Heng Jing: Yes, it's one word.

Master: And it isn't the meaning 安 *an*, but just the meaning of 住 *zhu*?

Bhikshu Heng Jing: The main meaning of "established" is that of being set up.

Master: Does it have the meaning of 安 *an*?

Bhikshu Heng Jing: Not really. But I remember that there is a word which has that meaning. In Sanskrit there is such a word. I don't remember the Sanskrit, but the translation is "settled in," the way a bird settles into its nest and doesn't move. That term occurs in the *Great Prajñā Sutra*. The word has the meaning of being settled somewhere in a secured manner.

Master: I don't think you have to translate "peaceful" in this context. You need to investigate what the context here requires, and then you can reach a decision. ⊣

OCTOBER 28, 1973 | SUNDAY NOON

On Various Interpretations of the Text

Master: Who else has an opinion?

Bhikshu Heng Jing: I do. I see a bit of a contradiction in Bhikshu Heng Shoou's [Editor's note: Guo Hu's ordination name.] explanation just now. If I understand correctly, what he said was, "She enters into nonattachment to everything." But if nonattachment were something you could enter into, then there would still be a place which is entered. However, if there is a place, then an attachment still remains, and the nonattachment becomes an attachment. So I think it should not be explained that way, but another way.

Master: Tell us how you would explain it. Both of you are *sheng ren*, one a Sage, and the other a leftover.

Bhikshu Heng Jing: Universal entry into everything is one meaning, indicating there is no place she is unable to enter. Being without attachment refers to how even though she can enter into every mode of dwelling, each and every location, every single spot—even though she universally enters every single one, she is not attached to that ability. Another possible interpretation is that she doesn't become attached to any place even after she has entered it. The words "strength of blessings and virtue" come before that in translating into English. She has that kind of ability, and it is because she has such blessings and virtue that she possesses the ability to enter into everything universally. Not

X. Lecturing on the Sutras

only does she enter into everything, she does so without any attachment. It's not entry into nonattachment. If there were entry into some "nonattachment," that "nonattachment" would be an attachment still remaining. It's a minor problem, but nonetheless a problem, although he says it isn't a problem.

Master: [to Bhikshu Heng Jing] Explain it in English, [Editor's note: The previous exchange had been in Chinese] and let them evaluate. [To the assembly] I'm notifying all of you in advance—get ready to judge the two of them. Best would be to bring one of them to his knees with your critiques. Now I'm giving you a chance to stand up and present a rebuttal, to bring up objections and evaluate the way the two of them spoke. It's impossible for both of them to be right. One must be right and the other wrong.

Bhikshu Heng Jing: He says he was wrong. [Editor's note: Bhikshu Heng Shoou indicates that he wants to speak.]

Master: You may speak, but do so quickly.

Bhikshu Heng Shoou: Okay, I didn't express my point very well.

Master: Don't be evasive!

Bhikshu Heng Shoou: As to "Strength of blessings and virtue for universal entry to everything without attachment," just now I was explaining "universal entry to everything without attachment." Now here it is talking about the kind of power from blessings and virtue to enter universally into nonattachment to anything. Since she has no attachments, she has a state of nonattachment—such blessings. And such blessings and virtue are uniquely supreme. Furthermore, the kind of power she has is unobstructed, and so she has the power of blessings and virtue to universally enter into nonattachment to anything.

Bhikshu Heng Jing: That explanation is somewhat problematic.

Master: On what grounds are you objecting?

Bhikshu Heng Jing: On grammatical grounds.

Master: Did you ever hear a principle similar to this before?

Bhikshu Heng Jing: Which principle?

Master: The passages into liberation that I'm talking about are passages into liberation without passages—none. There can't be liberation. That's how I explained it before. Did you hear that doctrine previously?

Bhikshu Heng Jing: If I heard it, I didn't think of it.

Master: You didn't think of it? What you said today is not bad. All three interpretations are acceptable, but there are still limitless and boundless interpretations. If we tried to present them all, we would never finish. However, the literal interpretation which Guo Hu [Bhikshu Heng Jing] just gave was in your Westerners' English. To English speakers it might sound as if there were problems in the way it was expressed. But the Chinese sounded fine. Also, since he hasn't heard this explained before, his ability to explain it as he did was quite good. If you have never heard it explained and are still able to explain it on the first try, for others to critique you is a victory for you. The victory is yours. And you, the sage, from start to finish are a leftover.

Bhikshu Heng Jing: As to this question, I have a...

X. Lecturing on the Sutras

Master: A judgment?

Bhikshu Heng Jing: No. In Chinese, we see that every phrase can be interpreted in many ways. But when translating, it's not easy to express that many meanings in a single English phrase. Therefore if, in translating, some meanings are lost, what can one do? That's because sometimes when the text is changed during translation, the meaning is also changed.

Master: When you don't understand, and there are places you can't make sense of, I'll give you a secret method. But you're not allowed to tell them. The secret is, don't think.

Bhikshu Heng Jing: What was that?

Master: Don't think. The myriad things, when contemplated in stillness, are all revealed of themselves. Do you understand? It all depends on whether you can be still or not. Do you understand?

Bhikshu Heng Jing: I understand.

Master: Do the rest of you understand? Guo Hu, do you understand?

Bhikshu Heng Shoou: Is *xiang* the word for thinking? [Editor's note: The Master stated his secret in Chinese; no English translation has been made at this point.]

Master: Don't ask what it is! Do you understand or not?

Bhikshu Heng Shoou: I understand.

Master: Really? What is it?

Bhikshu Heng Shoou: Not to translate according to that meaning.

Master: You didn't get it. I can tell by what you answered. [to Bhikshu Heng Jing] So I transmitted the method directly to you, and you received it directly. Not one of you understood the method.

Bhikshu Heng Jing: Okay!

Master: You're all lazy. Your eyes are lazy, so are your hands, and your minds are even lazier. They think, "It doesn't matter if we sleep." This tape recorder [Editor's note: being used to record the sutra lecture] is the worst thing there is. The tape makes all of you lazy. If the lecture weren't being tape-recorded, then all of you would be taking your own notes. Now you're not writing notes, so you don't keep your attention on what's being lectured, but just go to sleep. So wouldn't you agree that the tape recorder is the worst thing? Because of it, your eyes are lazy, so are your hands, and your minds are even lazier.

Disciple: What if we take notes and listen to the tape?

Master: That's good. But the way it is now, your minds get lazy and think, "It doesn't matter if we sleep." ⊣

OCTOBER 28, 1973 | SUNDAY EVENING

On Examining the Five Coverings

Master: What are the coverings? Doesn't anyone know? Are you all without coverings?

Bhikshuni Heng Yin: Greed, anger, delusion, and sleep.

Bhikshu Heng Shoou: There is also agitation.

Bhikshuni Heng Yin: This was discussed in the *Dharma Flower Sutra*.

Master: Oh, then it was the *Dharma Flower Sutra*. What were they?

Bhikshuni Heng Yin: I remember the English translation.

Master: What was the first one? We'll discuss them one by one.

Bhikshuni Heng Yin:

> Single-mindedly casting out confusion
>   removes the covering of greed.
> Staying away from foolish followers
>   removes the covering of anger.
> Drawing near to the wise removes
>   the covering of delusion.
> Collecting one's thoughts in mountain forests
>   removes the covering of sleep.
> Keeping clear of all frivolity removes the covering
>   of agitation. [verse by Great Master Ou Yi]

Master: People are speaking English and I don't understand. Translate into Chinese for me. I don't know if what you are saying is correct or not. We can decide this tomorrow. Tell me tomorrow. Look this up and get it straight. Ask your teacher, the dictionary. Okay?

Disciples: Okay.

Master: Do you know what they are, Guo Pu?

Bhikshuni Heng Hsien: I think I remember four of the five coverings which the Master discussed during the *Śūraṅgama Sutra* lectures.

Master: It doesn't matter what sutra it was. Wherever you heard it was where you heard it. I said the *Śūraṅgama Sutra*, but it could have been the *Dharma Flower Sutra* or the *Vajra Sutra*. Wherever it was, I've discussed this before. And I may not remember clearly myself where I explained it. Don't believe what I say. You should believe yourselves and have faith in your dictionary.

Bhikshuni Heng Hsien: Master, the first is lack of faith (=doubt). I don't remember the second. The third is a form of sleepiness. The fourth is something like manic depression. The fifth is confusion. But I don't know the exact Chinese terms for these. The fourth refers to constantly switching from extremes of depression and irritation to excitement and elation.

Master: What is the meaning of the term "covering" just by itself? We don't need to talk about how many there are. What is meant by "covering"?

X. Lecturing on the Sutras

Bhikshuni Heng Hsien: The Sanskrit for it is *avarana*. [Editor's note: Actually *avarana* is the term for "obstruction," and *nivarana* is the Sanskrit term used for the Five Coverings.]

Master: *Avarana?*

Bhikshuni Heng Hsien: The covering covers over purity. It's the way the Master explains it.

Master: She talked about the Sanskrit. What do those of you who were speaking English have to say? What is the meaning of "covering"? We don't have to discuss all that much—just investigate the meaning of the one term "covering." Once we understand that single concept of covering, then no matter how many coverings there are, we'll be able to understand them all. First we'll understand one covering. One covering is all coverings, and all coverings are one covering. Then we'll see which one covers you, and which one covers me. Your covering may be different from mine.

Guo You: Master, I think "covering" is something like obstruction. However, a covering prevents you from seeing your own nature—like an umbrella. If your own nature has something over it, you are unable to see. That's the meaning of "covering."

Master: So you can't see ghosts?

Guo You: No, not that. Maybe a ghost would be a covering. And ignorance is a covering.

Master: The English for this is "cover," right? Then it's just this, isn't it? [Editor's note: The Master picks up the lid of the teacup on the table.]

Disciples: Yes.

Master: Then there's nothing to say. It's just this! [Editor's note: The Master drops the lid loudly on the cup.] If you understand this, then you'll understand that. And if you understand that, then you'll understand this. Isn't that correct?

Disciples: Yes.

Master: And yet it isn't this. This is just an analogy. The light of our wisdom originally fills heaven and earth to overflowing, and shines throughout the Dharma Realm. But the problem is there is a black barrel which has no light at all inside, because it is covered by a lid, like this teacup now. There are a lot of errors in what I say to you while lecturing, so whoever knows what the right way is should tell me afterwards, because I don't know whether I've spoken correctly or not. You are all good spiritual friends. You can tell me tomorrow night. Tell me to my face, don't talk behind my back. Okay? ◁

OCTOBER 29, 1973 | MONDAY EVENING

On Working Together to Uncover the Truth

Master: Last night's five coverings are still covering us. Today we need to remove the coverings. Whoever can take off the coverings will achieve freedom and ease, but anyone unwilling to remove them will not be free and at ease. If you want to remove the coverings, then speak up quickly.

Bhikshu Heng Shoou: The first is desire, the second is anger, the third is drowsiness, the fourth is restlessness, and the fifth is doubt. Yesterday's explanation was a little incorrect.

Master: What do you think about what he said? Was it is right or not? [Editor's note: A discussion ensues.] That's from the dictionary?

Bhikshu Heng Shoou: It's from the *Discussion of Great Vehicle Doctrines*, not a dictionary.

Master: Great Master Yongjia said, "It's not that I, the mountain monk, presume there is self and others, but in cultivation one must be careful not to fall into the pit of annihilationism and eternalism." Since we are currently lecturing on the sutra, we have to make it understood and investigate it thoroughly. If everyone really understands it, then we will not have wasted our time. However, if you remain silent when you don't understand, and also remain silent when you do understand, then only you yourself know ultimately whether you understand or not, and no one else knows. In that case, it's very easy for fish eyes to pass for pearls. Hence there is a certain amount of difference between the way we are lecturing on sutras and the way it was done in China. Here, everyone has the right to speak. There is freedom of speech, and no matter who lectures incorrectly, any of you can raise the issue for investigation. Don't hesitate or say you don't dare talk. Even if I'm the one who says something wrong or explains a principle incorrectly, any one of you can bring it up for discussion. Therefore we are equal, and you should not view things in terms of rank. Don't have the outlook that there are a Master and disciples.

When it's a matter of theory or of principle, no one should be allowed to bluff his or her way through. You have to investigate honestly. Consequently, Great Master Yongjia also said, "If you have unresolved doubts," you should ask about them. If you wonder about something or don't understand something, you can ask about it. "If you have unresolved doubts, you must directly attack." We need to attack. It's not okay not to attack. What must be attacked? We should attack the truth. We absolutely have to work together to make the truth emerge. It's not for certain that the way I see things is complete, but the group as a whole is equivalent to a sage in wisdom.

We should pool our collective wisdoms. You think of things I didn't think of, and someone else thinks of something you didn't think of. Then we put it all together. The collective mind is the Buddha's mind, and the theories of the group are the theories of the Buddha. We should all speak up without formalities of politeness and bring the truth to light together. ⊣

OCTOBER 31, 1973 | WEDNESDAY EVENING

On Disciples' Explanations of "At that time"

Master: We have had the phrase "at that time" over and over already, and I've forgotten how I explained it the first time. In the recent occurrences of the phrase, we've given perfunctory explanations. Today we'll do our best to bring out what each of you understands concerning "at that time," and see if it's the same. There's not much time left today—just ten minutes more. During those ten minutes, everyone has to talk. Anyone who comes regularly to the sutra lectures, or who lives at Gold Mountain Monastery, must speak. What method shall we follow? I think we can start with Guo Hu. After you talk, you can have each one who comes after you speak in order.

Bhikshu Heng Shoou [Guo Hu]: The phrase "at that time" refers to the time when Śākyamuni Buddha was sitting under the *bodhi* tree and had first realized Buddhahood. The phrase occurs many times in the text.

Master:

> When I learn of someone else's death,
> My heart burns as if with fire.
> It does not burn for the other person,
> But because death is heading my way.

Bhikshu Heng Jing: When it says "at that time," it means "at this time." How? It's this time we're coming to, at that point in the text; or at no time.

Master: It has died.

Bhikshu Heng Jing: Yes.

Master: What has died?

Bhikshu Heng Jing: All aspects of the self have perished. It is when the Buddha first realizes enlightenment, which doesn't happen in a single time; for the time of enlightenment pervades all times, and the Buddha sees all beings become enlightened at the same time. ⊣

NOVEMBER 2, 1973 | FRIDAY EVENING

On the Reasons for Asking Disciples to Explain "At that time"

Why have we been investigating the phrase "at that time"? It's because when I explained an earlier occurrence of "at that time" in a very simple way, the visiting Dharma Master said my explanation was wrong. Thus, I am now having everyone explain it now so he can listen and see which explanation is correct. He made that criticism because he is quite young and doesn't understand much. He said, "I have an opinion about 'at that time.'" His opinion was basically a disagreement with my explanation. If he had more experience, he would not say such things. He would not say, "Your explanation is wrong." Is there any right or wrong? There is none. It's only because of attachments that we talk about right and wrong. If we had no attachments, what would we call right or wrong? If we could see that 'everything's okay,' how can there be any right or wrong? Do you understand?

Whenever you go somewhere, even if you clearly know someone is in error, unless they ask you to tell them whether they are right or wrong, you can't "nominate yourself like Mao Sui." You can't say, "I'll tell you how you are wrong." That will not work anywhere. After this, wherever you go, be careful not to find fault with people. Even if you clearly know they are wrong, unless they ask you to instruct them, you cannot criticize them. This is very important.

[Editor's note: the translator asks the meaning of "nominating oneself like Mao Sui."] There was something that weighed a ton, which no one could lift. Mao Sui said, "I can lift it—I'll carry it." Then he went over and lifted it. That's called "nominating oneself like Mao Sui." Mao Sui is the name of a man who lived in ancient China. At the time there was a high official with lots of money named Lord Ping Yuan, who regularly supported three thousand people. When something needed to be done, Mao Sui said, "I can do it; I'll take care of it," hence the saying, "Among three thousand there is Mao Sui." Mao Sui said it was something he could do, and so there is the phrase, "nominating oneself like Mao Sui." What is this like? It's similar to Guo Qian voting for himself in the election for Chairperson of the Sino-American Buddhist Association. That's an example of "nominating oneself like Mao Sui." Do you understand? ⊣

NOVEMBER 2, 1973 | FRIDAY EVENING

On Concluding Comments about "At that time"

Master: Who else would like to speak about "at that time"? Would any of the people who spoke before like to say something more? Guo Yi, you should explain "at that time." I think you were attentive whenever you spoke previously.

Guo Yi: I was thinking of the time when all the Buddha's disciples were sitting around the Buddha, and he was speaking sutras for them; he was speaking the Dharma for them. That's what "at that time" is.

Master: Guo Gui, do you have an opinion?

Guo Gui: I have nothing to add to what I heard last night.

Master: Guo Hang?

Guo Hang: I don't know.

Master: [laughs] Who taught you not to know?

Guo Hang: I don't know.

Master: Guo You, you speak.

Guo You: What I wanted to say has already been said several times.

Master: Your food has already been eaten?

Guo You: Sort of.

Master: Guo Rong? What is your opinion?

Guo Rong: It may be that I don't really understand what the Venerable Master means.

Master: Can you give a summary?

Guo Rong: It could be said that "at that time" is the time when the space-ruling spirit, Pure Light Shining Everywhere, received the Buddha's awesome power. Because the sutra text says he received the Buddha's awesome power, therefore he absolutely would not have fallen into the position of giving rise to a second thought, and so he was able to receive the Buddha's awesome power. Hence if he had fallen into the position of giving rise to second thought, probably it would not be "at that time."

Master: Guo Sui, you speak.

Guo Sui: I missed the previous discussion, and I really don't think I can say anything.

Master: [to the translator] What about the new person? Last night didn't you say he wanted to talk? Ask him if he has something to say.

Bert (the new person): Considering my very slight knowledge of *bodhi*, I could consider that it might be referring to the moment of illumination for any *bodhi*.

Master: Now I'll give you your evaluations: all of you spoke correctly. No one spoke wrongly. What I said was also right. Each person who spoke had his or her principles. Therefore, if you don't understand, you'll divide things into right and wrong. But once you understand, fundamentally there's no such thing as "correct" or "incorrect." All of it is bestowing teachings according to each individual's needs, the way medicine is prescribed depending on the illness. Dharma is spoken to suit individual people, just the way particular medications are employed to cure each type of illness. That's the principle of this sutra, and there's nothing right or wrong about it.

As for "at that time," what time is meant? Guo Ning said it: there is no time. If you try to pinpoint it as this time, this time has already gone by. If you say it is that time, that time is also already gone. The mind in the past cannot be grasped, the mind in the present cannot be grasped, and the mind in the future cannot be grasped. Since they all cannot be grasped, how can you be attached to any particular time?

Then why does the sutra mention a time? It's because at that time there were billions upon billions of Bodhisattvas and spirits, who had arrived and were surrounding the Buddha, praising the Buddha. As the visiting Dharma Master told us last night, there was no sequential time. But even though their praises were simultaneous, there has to be a linear sequence when you write them down. A single stroke of the pen won't serve to describe the whole array of Bodhisattvas, celestial kings, *yakshas*, dragons and others of the eightfold pantheon. It's the same as eating—it has to be done bite by bite. You can't eat your fill in a single gulp. Hence there is a sequence. But basically the time, as just discussed, has already gone by—what's the use of becoming attached to it?

And so, at the very beginning when I explained "at that time," I had already discussed the principles at great length. But since the visitor had not heard the explanation at the beginning and had come in the middle of the discussion, he thought I couldn't lecture and didn't understand, and so he "had an issue" with it. For that reason I didn't lecture either, and asked him to speak instead. However, he didn't speak. If he had been straightforward in his attitude, he would have talked. For him to have spoken would have been correct. He could have told us the way he saw things. But he didn't. His not speaking indicated he was not straightforward in his attitude but was evasive. Do you understand? Then I had all of you speak, and had him listen. You all gave various interpretations, but all he heard was so many things he felt were incorrect. He heard so many things wrong, but I heard so many things right. All of you think it over: That's where the difference lies.

Dharma Masters in China for the most part had the following attachment: wherever they went, they wanted to put others down so as to raise themselves up. Their aim in going places was to squash others underneath their feet and position themselves on top of people's heads. That is a serious and total error, and accounts for the current disappearance of the Buddhadharma from China. But they still can't shed that fault, and continue to cling to that bad habit, unable to let it go. Here in the West we should not adopt that unwholesome custom. We should learn to consider everyone as being right. ◁

NOVEMBER 21, 1973 | WEDNESDAY EVENING

On the Frequency & Pace of the Lecture Series

Tomorrow is a holiday [Thanksgiving Day]. From now on, whenever there is a holiday, we will add an extra sutra lecture after lunch, because on holidays everyone can attend. Tomorrow (Thursday) the lecture will be at the usual [weekend] time: 12:30-2:30 P.M. We will have this supplementary lecture on each holiday, because the *Flower Adornment Sutra* is so long: if we don't add some lectures, it's hard to say how many years it will take to complete the lecture series. [Editor's note: In all, the Venerable Master delivered more than 2,000 lectures, spanning more than nine years, on the *Flower Adornment Sutra*.] That's why a visiting Dharma Master was worried about us and said, "Each lecture you just explain one verse of four lines. At that rate, how many years will it take you to finish?" For that reason, and since we are in the scientific age, I'm going to speed up a bit. Tonight we've already discussed three water-ruling spirits, and tomorrow we can discuss three more, and bit by bit we can finish. If I make mistakes while lecturing, you can investigate the commentaries. The commentaries will tell you very clearly; certainly they have greater wisdom than my commentary. Hence you "Commentary Dharma Masters" must be careful not to stray from your commentaries! ⊣

SEPTEMBER 29, 1974 | SUNDAY EVENING

On the Definition of
Useful Answers

Today the translator asked: "Why are there so many kinds of nondifferentiation? Exactly how many kinds are there?" I don't know. But the translator obviously thought there were too many. When she asked me, I told her to ask Śākyamuni Buddha. But Śākyamuni Buddha has entered nirvana and isn't speaking anymore. Even though the Buddha entered nirvana, the Dharma is still around. So you can look into the sutras. But the sutras can't speak either. Since the Dharma is incapable of speech, you should ask the Sangha. Right now there are a lot of Sangha members here at Gold Mountain Monastery. Why doesn't each of you explain why there are so many kinds of nondifferentiation? Let's see who has great wisdom and can give an answer that everyone finds useful. I myself cannot answer this question.

You could measure the usefulness of an answer in terms of whether it reveals pure or defiling dharmas. If the answer reveals pure dharmas, then the listeners will benefit from the Dharma. If the answer reveals defiling dharmas, then the listeners may react by delighting in and enjoying those defiling dharmas. Although revealing pure and revealing defiling dharmas are both useful in their own way, your answers should be useful in the sense of helping people benefit from the Buddhadharma.

Anyone can bring up an opinion about nondifferentiation—not only Sangha members, but laypeople, too. [Editor's note: Nobody speaks.] It appears that all of you have obtained the benefit of

X. Lecturing on the Sutras

nondifferentiation. "He is me, and I am him. You are me and him. Mahasattvas pay no attention to others." So you all close your mouths and curl your tongues against the roof of the mouth and enter *samādhi*. ▯

Ceremony in the main hall of Gold Mountain Monastery during renovations

XI | Rituals & Ceremonies

NOVEMBER 29, 1972 | WEDNESDAY EVENING

On Requesting Dharma

From now on, one person at a time can request the Dharma. You can take turns. Since we don't have a lot of people right now, one person will suffice. If there is a larger crowd, then two people can request the Dharma. Nothing is certain—simply follow the Middle Way. ⊣

SEPTEMBER 16, 1973 | SUNDAY EVENING

On the Bell Song

Before the sutra lecture we have been chanting the Bell Song. When you chant it, the notes should be protracted as long as possible, and it's best to chant it so that it resonates with a full sound. Don't pronounce the Request for Dharma too fast either. Actually, it should be chanted, rather than simply stated, and slowly, not like the firing of a machine gun, as if you wanted to get it over with. The rhythm and phrasing should calm people's minds, like music that chases people's false thoughts away in preparation for listening to the sutra lecture. That's how it should be. ♩

On Learning Ceremonies

Starting tomorrow, Dharma Master Huiseng will come to teach the ceremony for sutra lectures. Whoever wants to study this should do so seriously and not be casual about it. It's permissible to master the ceremony but not use it; but don't let it happen that when the time comes to use it, you don't know how to do it.

Also, when you are learning it, don't act like it's something utterly new and startling that you've never seen or heard of before. For example, when a certain Dharma Master came here to lecture, he talked about a "stinking pickled vegetable." One of my disciples told him she'd never heard of it before. When you say something like that, you lose face for us. What he talked about was not beyond the principles that we investigate here all the time. All he did was change the name and refer to it as a "stinking pickled vegetable." What's so great about that? But she said, "We've never heard of that before." Her saying that made it obvious that she'd totally missed the point. Studying ceremonies is the same. You can study them, but don't act really surprised by them, or people will think you don't understand anything.

XI. Rituals and Ceremonies

SEPTEMBER 19, 1973 | WEDNESDAY EVENING

On Reciting & Chanting

When Dharma Master Huiseng is teaching you, allow him to speak and listen to what he says. Pay attention to how he explains the lesson. Yesterday you all studied the Flower Adornment (Avataṃsaka) Syllabary and practiced chanting parts of it. What do you think of it? Bring up your opinions and we will investigate them together.

Every day I hear you reciting the Buddha's name quite stiffly, in a most constrained way. It's not very lively. The sound from your recitation of the Buddha's name should be unconstrained and unimpeded, not as if tied up with a rope and unable to get free. Set it free. The sound should resemble flowing water that nothing can stop, and wind that rustles the grass and flowers, trees and shrubs as it blows.

That's true for reciting the Buddha's name; it's also true when chanting the Avataṃsaka Syllabary. As people chant, they should feel blissful and elevated, as if they had become spiritual immortals. They should recite the Buddha's name in such a way that the Buddha appears before them. That's how it should be, not stiff and dead with no resonance to the sound. It's fine for the recitation to be somewhat slow, but it shouldn't sound dull and lifeless. I've wanted to mention this for a long time, but up to now I haven't said anything. Also, you are not reciting with one sound; each person has his or her own sound. Although we have different mouths, we should recite with one voice.

TIMELY TEACHINGS

You should not sound as if you cannot set your sound free. That way it becomes very constrained. During the recitation of the Buddha's name, whether you are a monastic or a layperson, you should recite out loud and join in the recitation. You shouldn't just be silent and listen to others recite. All of you should recite the Buddha's name with a single mind and chant in unison. Then it will be easy to attain the Samādhi of Reciting the Buddha's Name.

SEPTEMBER 29, 1973 | SATURDAY EVENING

On the Opening of the Translation Institute

The new International Institute for the Translation of Buddhist Texts, located on Washington Street, will be dedicated to the Thousand-Handed, Thousand-Eyed Bodhisattva Guanyin. The nuns and laywomen will reside there and reverently make offerings to Guanyin Bodhisattva. At the Opening of the Institute, an "Opening of the Eyes" of the image of Guanyin Bodhisattva will also be performed. After that, Guanyin Bodhisattva will protect all Buddhist centers in San Francisco, so that all Buddhists will be able to cultivate the truth, enter the Path without being troubled by demons, bring forth the *bodhi* resolve, and realize the *bodhi* fruit.

Beginning tomorrow, prior to the Opening of the Light Ceremony (a consecration ceremony), we will hold the noon sutra lecture at Gold Mountain Monastery and the evening sutra lecture at Washington Street. That way, the gods, dragons, and the rest of the eightfold pantheon will become acquainted with the new *bodhimaṇḍa* and will constantly protect it.

Our invitation to the Opening of the Institute says that we will bow the Great Compassion Repentance at 9 A.M. every day starting on the first of the month. The Repentance will be held at Gold Mountain Monastery, in preparation for the Opening of the Light Ceremony. We are seeking a special response from Guanyin Bodhisattva, hoping that she will radiate bright light to illumine San Francisco, here in this corner of our world system.

As we sincerely bow in repentance, we should pray for world peace and blessings for the people of San Francisco. The nuns who reside at the Institute should come to Gold Mountain Monastery by 9 o'clock each day to attend the Great Compassion Repentance. In the afternoon, we monks and novices will go to Washington Street and bow the Great Compassion Repentance at 1:00 P.M. there. After that, people are free to work on translating sutras or typing manuscripts as they wish. In the evening we will have a sutra lecture there.

People who wish to bow in repentance in the morning at Gold Mountain Monastery should plan to arrive ten or fifteen minutes before the Repentance is due to begin. The same goes for Washington Street. Everyone should arrive ten or fifteen minutes early. We should all take care to follow the rules and not be sloppy.

Whenever the monastery has an activity—whether it is sutra lecture or some other event—people should plan to arrive before the event is scheduled to begin, not in the middle of the event. Don't procrastinate. You should do a complete job of things. Don't do things halfway. If you do things completely, your merit will also be complete and perfect. If you only attend half, you will only have half the merit. You should start at the beginning and finish what you start. If you attend from the beginning and stay until the end, then your merit will be complete. For example, if you want to listen to the sutra lecture, you should also attend the evening recitation preceding the lecture. That's the complete way to do it.

When the sutra lectures are moved to Washington Street, laypeople who don't have cars can ride in Gold Mountain

Monastery's van. People who have cars can give rides to those who don't. We should all help one another out. Everyone should understand this. We should benefit ourselves and benefit others, enlighten ourselves and enlighten others, liberate ourselves and liberate others.

Basically, we started out not knowing how to translate sutras. We are doing something we don't know how to do. I've explained the sutras—however imperfectly—so that the translation can get started. Once you develop more translation skills, you will be able to teach others how to translate. As more and more people learn to translate, we should translate the entire Tripiṭaka, with its twelve divisions, into English, so that the light of *prajñā* will shine upon all Westerners. That is our objective in translating the sutras.

For the past six years that we have been translating, we have made a fair amount of progress. We have acquired skills and abilities we didn't have before. Unexpectedly, the most unlikely people have praised our translations as excellent. The most unruly people have decided on their own to follow the rules. All those are good signs. Hearing this good news, all of you should work hard and advance in the work of translation. Translation will be done at the Washington Street Institute; Gold Mountain Monastery will continue to be the headquarters of our Association. ⊣

OCTOBER 5, 1973 | FRIDAY EVENING, AT WASHINGTON STREET

On the Efficacy of the Śūraṅgama Mantra

Now that an image of Guanyin Bodhisattva has come to our place, it will be even more safe and peaceful. We have set the date for the Opening Eyes Ceremony for our Guanyin Bodhisattva for the 14th. Everyone can bring family and friends here to celebrate the occasion and to be bathed in the Buddhas' light. Our ceremony for Opening of Light and Opening Eyes will be different from what others do; it will include reciting a section of the Śūraṅgama Mantra. After the ceremony, I will explain the power of that section for you. When we recite the Śūraṅgama Mantra, a canopy of jewels and a cloud canopy form overhead; it's an inconceivable state. ◁

OCTOBER 7, 1973 | SUNDAY EVENING

On Reciting Amitābha Buddha's Name

Before the lecture begins, you should recite the Buddha's name more. You should stop reciting only when I come into the hall. The more you recite the Buddha's name, the better. There's not a fixed amount of time that you should recite. ⊣

OCTOBER 10, 1973 | WEDNESDAY EVENING

On Lessons About Sutra-Lecture Rituals

After we have welcomed this Dharma Master at the airport and have returned to Gold Mountain Monastery, we will then proceed to formally ask the Dharma Master to lecture on the *Heart Sutra*.

There are a lot of things that need correcting about the way we do our lecture rituals. I've refrained from mentioning these things before, but now that a Dharma Master from outside is coming, we ought to improve ourselves.

Prior to the lecture, after the cantor chants, "We invite the Dharma Master," he should hit the big bell. Then two hand bells should be struck alternately as those making the request proceed to where the Dharma Master is waiting.

At the end of the lecture, when the Dharma Master has finished speaking and has left his seat, the cantor should chant, "Let us bow to the Dharma Master."

The Dharma Master will reply, "No need to bow."

Then the cantor should chant, "Let us accompany the Dharma Master back to his quarters."

The Dharma Master will reply, "No need to accompany me."

Those are the traditional rituals used when conducting a sutra lecture in China. Since I prefer to be a little more modern, I have

XI. Rituals and Ceremonies

not followed the old-fashioned routine. All the other Dharma Masters follow this routine, but I often change it.

As for asking the Dharma Master to speak Dharma, I have composed a verse that you can recite tomorrow when you make the request. Whoever makes the request should first recite this verse:

> We give back our lives to the Honored Triple Jewel.
> May we resolve to awaken to the Great Spiritual Path.
> Please compassionately instruct and
>   rescue everyone everywhere;
> Proclaim the teaching to transform the multitudes.

The recitation of this verse should be rather drawn out and protracted. [Editor's note: The Master sings it to demonstrate.] When the recitation is protracted like that, people can hear the words clearly. In all the things we do, we should strive to improve. We are revolutionizing Buddhism as well, so when people from other monasteries come here, we keep them guessing. ⊣

On the Ritual for Making Vows

[Editor's note: On certain special occasions (this day happened to be the Chinese New Year), the Master would encourage his disciples, whether they were monastics or laity, to make vows publicly. This was after the sutra lecture that evening.]

Everyone should join in making vows. If you want to make vows, come forward and bow three times to the Buddhas, then make your vows. Be sure to say your name first. ⊣

SEPTEMBER 9, 1974 | MONDAY EVENING

On the Ritual for Requesting Dharma

The method we use here for requesting Dharma is unique. You won't find it being done this way in any other *bodhimaṇḍa* in the world. Gold Mountain Monastery is somewhat different from Buddhism in the rest of the world. When the sutras are lectured in China, Japan, Thailand, or Burma, no one requests the Dharma as we do here. Even the Elder Master who visited us recently had never seen anything like our ritual for requesting the Dharma, and he went home thinking we were quite peculiar.

This is not peculiar; this is the method that was used when the Buddha was in the world. Before the Buddha would speak Dharma, someone would always request it of him. If no one requested it, the Buddha usually did not speak. He remained silent and entered *samādhi*. If someone requested Dharma, he spoke.

To request Dharma, you must first circumambulate the Buddha to the right at least three times. To circumambulate four or more times is also correct, because the more merit and virtue you create, and the fewer faults you have, the better. And so now we are returning to the ancient ritual of requesting Dharma, as it was done when Śākyamuni Buddha was in the world.

Whoever requests Dharma should take your responsibility very seriously and see it as an extremely important act. If you do it well, then as a reward, you will certainly be able to speak Dharma with unobstructed eloquence in the future. You will be like Purnamaitreyaniputra, the Buddha's disciple who was foremost in speaking Dharma and who had unimpeded eloquence. No doubt in the past he had always asked others to speak the Dharma, and so as a reward, he himself became endowed with eloquence in speaking the Dharma.

The opportunity to perform the ritual for requesting Dharma is very rare. The person who requests Dharma should raise a stick of incense with both hands to the spot between the eyebrows, and circumambulate with eyes cast down, respectfully and single-mindedly thinking of how the Buddhas everywhere in the cosmos are receiving his request to speak Dharma.

I am lecturing sutras for you now. Whether I speak well or not is one thing, but it's important to realize that I am representing the Buddhas and Bodhisattvas in teaching and transmitting some of the sutras; I'm not just speaking on my own. You, in turn, are just representing me in translating these explanations into Western languages. If you know how to listen whether I lecture well or not, then, "General statements and detailed explanations all express the ultimate truth." In other words, if you don't know how to listen, then no matter how profound the lecture is, you won't understand it. If you know how to listen, then even if the lecture isn't very good, you will still be able to gain a thorough understanding of the principles. ⊣

XII | Propagating the Dharma

Translation of taped lecture using typewriter and reel-to-reel recorder at the International Institute for the Translation of Buddhist Texts, Washington Street

NOVEMBER 2, 1972 | THURSDAY EVENING

On Propagating the Dharma

Tomorrow is November 3rd, and three people—Heng Qian, Heng Jing, and Heng Shou—from Gold Mountain Monastery are going to Hong Kong. Because it is so crowded, Hong Kong is now pervaded by a stench, so it's not easy to go there to teach living beings. However, after you go through the difficulties, it will no longer be difficult. If you don't go through some hardship, you won't understand what the world is really like and you'll think it's a pretty happy place. After you've been through some hardship, you'll know that the world is filled with suffering. Since it is filled with suffering, our aim is to transform it into the Land of Ultimate Bliss. Therefore, we must go to many different places to propagate the Buddhadharma. The Buddhadharma needs people to propagate it. It cannot propagate itself to people. That's why, in the spirit of propagating the Dharma, we go outside and practice the Six Perfections and the Ten Thousand Practices. ⊣

NOVEMBER 5, 1972 | SUNDAY EVENING

On Composing Buddhist Music & Articles

Today I learned that Guo Jin has composed some Buddhist songs with wonderful lyrics. In the future, I hope all of you will compose more Buddhist songs and praises. This year on the Buddha's Birthday, Guo Yi also wrote a song. I listened to it more carefully today and found it is also well-written. Those who can compose music can write more songs and we can publish the scores and lyrics in our monthly journal. There are many Buddhist songs in Chinese but few Buddhist songs in English. You are now innovators in this field, and so you should write a few more songs and show them to me. If they are acceptable, we will print them in our journal.

Also, from now on people should practice writing articles in both Chinese and English. With practice, you will be able to write good articles in both languages. Write about the principles you have heard, so more people in the world will come to understand the Buddhadharma. There is boundless merit and virtue involved in this. You should understand my intent. Don't retreat. Buddhists should always courageously advance and not retreat. Everyone should pay attention to this.

Write an article every week. Decide on the topic yourself. You can either write an essay, or compose a song or a poem to help propagate Buddhism, so that a *bodhi* tree will quickly grow in the West. [Editor's note: Editor Zhou's periodical was called *Bodhi Tree*.] The *bodhi* tree we planted here at the monastery is now about three feet high. This tree should grow tall very quickly; it's not permitted to grow slowly. Once the *bodhi* tree has matured, someone will realize Buddhahood beneath it. ⊟

NOVEMBER 15, 1972 | WEDNESDAY EVENING

On Sparking Interest in Buddhism

Today we went to an art exhibition. Those of you who have talent in painting can learn to paint, and in the future you may become great artists. For example, Bhikshuni Xiao Yun from Taiwan is a painter and shows her paintings in various exhibitions. Her exhibitions have inspired many people to believe in Buddhism. Layman Chang Dai-chien does the same. Since he is a Buddhist, he paints Buddha images. The paintings of Buddhas in his exhibitions have sparked an interest in Buddhism. This is part of propagating the Buddhadharma, so you should not look lightly on it. For example, if we put on a sutra display or a sutra-lecturing exhibition, there wouldn't be such a large turnout. But now, whether people believe in Buddhism or not, even if they are Catholics or Protestants, they still attend the exhibition and see the Buddha images, and this plants *bodhi* seeds in their minds. If you wish to become a celebrity you can begin now—there's still enough time, and you can become a great artist. That wouldn't be bad. ⊣

JANUARY 15, 1973 | MONDAY EVENING

On the Buddhist Text Translation Society

The Buddhist Text Translation Society, operating under the auspices of the Dharma Realm Buddhist Association, has been engaged in translation of sutras for five years. During this period, people who didn't know how to translate have matured into qualified translators. They are not merely capable; they do an excellent job of it. It can be said that "they are in correspondence with the Buddha's mind and they understand that potential beings have to be rescued." Now we are planning to hold a board meeting of the Buddhist Text Translation Society. You Bhikshus, Bhikshunis, Upasakas, and Upasikas can bring up your suggestions for improving and perfecting our methods of translating sutras. Starting today, you can keep a journal of your ideas and opinions. This will be handy in the future. Write down your thoughts on how we can produce the best possible translations of the sutras, so that we can inspire Westerners to make a commitment to *bodhi*—to resolve to become enlightened. Everyone should come up with a list of suggestions. Write as many items as you want. In the future, this will be very useful and important. I'm not joking. If you wish to make some contribution to Buddhism, you should bring up your suggestions for improvement. In this scientific age, what scientific techniques can we adopt in our translation of sutras so as to widely propagate Buddhism?

FEBRUARY 14, 1973 | WEDNESDAY EVENING,

On Travel Adventures

[Editor's note: The Master is recounting a trip to New York that he and six other monastics from Gold Mountain Monastery had just made. See "On the Karmic Retribution of Hunger" on page 194 for earlier comments on this trip.]

Our flight to Canada was delayed one hour, and then we had to wait two hours on our return flight. The people who had come to pick up us at the New York airport ended up waiting over two hours. It's said, "Those who have to travel are people with scanty blessings." Some people like to travel; I, however, don't find it so enjoyable.

On Friday, the resident Dharma Master at Great Enlightenment Monastery invited us for a vegetarian meal. He got fourteen monastics together—including three nuns—and some laypeople. That was a pleasant gathering, and we also got enough to eat, which pleased Guo Hu.

Another day, we went to Mahayana Temple, where we also had lunch. But this time some problems occurred at lunch. Maybe we ate too much, or maybe it was just a matter of not being used to the kind of food, but Guo Pu got a bad stomach from it and couldn't even manage to walk.

Prior to that visit to Mahayana Temple, one Dharma Master there challenged us, "I heard that one of you oversees the weather, so see to it that it does not rain or snow."

We were invited to Mahayana Temple for Saturday. So on Friday I gave the order to Guo Hu, "Make sure that it doesn't snow on Saturday. If it snows, you will have to kneel for forty-nine days as a penalty."

Basically Guo Hu did not want to display his spiritual powers, but he had no choice when he received that order. It turned out that it did not snow or rain on Saturday. A few miles away from the road on which we were traveling, there was a heavy snowfall. But no snow fell on the road we used. So you see? Guo Hu really does have some spiritual powers!

After lunch at Mahayana Temple, we went back to Great Enlightenment Monastery. The next day, Sunday, we paid a visit to the Eberles—the family of Guo Zhao [Editor's note: a lay-woman and one of the three people who completed the 98-day meditation session at the Buddhist Lecture Hall in the winter of 1970-71]. She and her family welcomed us very warmly. They were very sincere. They have very kind faces. They treated us to some Spanish cuisine, and we ate our fill. We stayed overnight there.

On Monday, we took a plane to San Diego. On Tuesday, we gave a lecture in San Diego, and today we are back in San Francisco. In other places, we are always in a furnace and feel very uncomfortable. And so it's nice to come back to the icebox where it is clear and cool.

[Editor's note: The questions and answers at Eberles were so interesting, they are summarized on the following pages.

Mr. Eberle: When someone is reborn, would he necessarily be reborn on this earth? Might he be reborn in another world-system?

Master: That is not at all certain. It depends on causes and circumstances. It's said: One goes where one has affinities, depending on which way the winds of karma blow.

Young man: Is it necessary to do good deeds and thereby acquire a greater propensity so as to better continue the quest for Buddhahood? Or should one try to transcend the creation of karma?

Master: Before one becomes a Buddha, one must act in terms of worldly karma and one must do good. It is only after one becomes a Buddha that one transcends involvement with karma. Therefore, one should always do what is wholesome.

Mr. Eberle: How does one know one has become a Buddha? Who decides?

Master: When you become a Buddha, you will certainly know it. Furthermore, all the Buddhas of the ten directions will come and verify your accomplishment. We can use the example of graduation from a University. A number of professors have to have passed you for that to happen.

Young man: Is awareness of Buddhahood like *samādhi*? What is the relationship between nirvana and realization of Buddhahood?

Master: *Samādhi* is skill that comes with cultivation. Nirvana is entered after realizing Buddhahood. At that time all effort becomes tranquil; all virtue is complete.

When one becomes a Buddha, three types of enlightenment are perfected once one has succeeded in doing all the many practices...

Another person: How many Buddhas are there?

Master: There are as many Buddhas as there are living beings. In some religions it is believed that there is only one God who is eternal and perfect, and that no other living being can be that God. Only God can be God and living beings have to be living beings. It is a dictatorial divinity.

According to the Buddha's teaching, on the other hand, all living beings can become Buddhas. They only need to cultivate, work hard, and follow the teachings in their practice and they can all realize Buddhahood. Everyone has a share.

In many religions, there is only one God and people have no share in being God. No other being can become God, no matter who he is. God is the 'only one.' Which leads one to wonder why he requires people's belief, since he's eternal—'perfect unto himself.' Wouldn't it be sufficient that he was the one and only God?

Buddha, however, is not the only Buddha. Everyone has the potential to be a Buddha. If you cultivate, you can become a Buddha; if you don't cultivate, you won't.

So the Buddha said, "All living beings have the Buddha-nature; all can become Buddhas." It is only necessary to break through ignorance and to put an end to afflictions so not a trace remains. Then you can all become Buddhas. The Buddha is neither solitary nor dictatorial. That is why the number of Buddhas is the same as the number of living beings.

If there were no living beings, it would not necessarily mean that there were no Buddhas, however. That is because the Buddhas could create many more living beings in the world. Living beings are created by Buddhas and Buddhahood can be realized by living beings. Is that not democratic, egalitarian, magnanimous, and unselfish? It is only to be feared that you won't cultivate. If

XII. Propagating the Dharma

you want to cultivate, you can become a Buddha. Therefore, in Buddhism no one says, 'You can't become me. I am a solitary Buddha. I am a dictatorial Buddha.' There is no such principle.

The Buddhadharma takes the entire Dharma Realm as its scope; consequently it includes all other teachings. It is not that the Buddhadharma is superior to all other religions, its scope is just bigger. Other religions are not inferior, their scope is just smaller. The Buddhadharma is the totality. For example, this table: other religions are like a square foot or just a corner of this table, whereas Buddhism encompasses the entire expanse of the table. That is why Buddhists should not criticize other religions—for all of them teach people to do good. But some principles are ultimate and some are not.

The difference is that Buddhism teaches principles that are ultimate, thorough, and complete. Other religions' principles are less clear, sometimes even confusing, so that they seem to be right and yet aren't. Sometimes their explanations are incomprehensible. Some say, "You must just believe, you must not question; you must just believe, you must not doubt; you must just believe, you must not disbelieve."

Some say, "If you believe in me you can go to heaven, even if you don't cultivate. I, the almighty God, will escort you to heaven to enjoy bliss. But when you get there, you can't be me, for I am the only God. You can just be my people. I am going to be the only God forever and ever and you have no way to become God. If you believe in me, the only God, then you can commit offenses and still go to heaven. But if you don't believe in me, then even if you do good, you will go to hell." In fact there is no such principle as that in the entire world, and I believe heaven is certainly not that way either.

Young man: Jesus said that only through him could one enter the kingdom of heaven. What did he mean by that? Was it an egotistical statement?

Master: Not just that statement was egotistical, but inherent in the entire doctrine of that religion is a condescending attitude toward other religions, which are viewed as the work of the devil and so forth. What he said, anybody could say. I could say, 'Jesus, unless you go my way, you can never get to heaven.' Also you must remember that the masses he spoke to were largely uneducated, uninformed, easily led. The events that took place in the past might not be so readily accepted today.

Another person: Is that really the way it was?

Master: It might have been that way and it might not have been. We are investigating a question; it is not our intention to slander Jesus.

Question: Was Jesus himself any form of enlightened being?

Master: One could say he was a Bodhisattva. Bodhisattvas dare to say anything and will do anything—even kill—and there is no offense, because they can bring beings back to life again. They are like magicians who make things appear and disappear, disappear and reappear. People who lack deep understanding are like children who see everything the magician does as magical, for they do not understand the tricks he employs.

Elder Master Zhi exemplifies this principle. Buddhists are vegetarian, but Master Zhi ate fish and pigeons. Every day he had two pigeons for lunch. One day his cook could bear it no longer and decided to taste the birds, thinking they must be indeed delicacies. He lopped off a wing and ate it. Since he served the birds minced, he figured Master Zhi would never miss the wing.

XII. Propagating the Dharma

But when the Master had finished his meal that day, he called the cook out and asked who had stolen his pigeon meat. The cook denied everything, whereupon Master Zhi opened his mouth and a whole pigeon flew out, followed by another which hopped and flopped about on the ground—because it was missing one wing. "If you didn't eat it," challenged the Master, "where did it go?"

Young man: Is it really fair for Jesus to have performed tricks? Was he just out to cheat people?

Master: Not only did he cheat people at that time, he cheated them before he was born and he cheated them after he died. What I mean is, the principles he taught were unclear. The beliefs at that time were largely polytheistic—people believed in all kinds of spirits. Perhaps Jesus analyzed the situation, felt that things had gone to an extreme, and attempted to provide a solution. Embracing a monotheistic concept, he proposed that people should not believe in other gods or spirits, but just worship one. Perhaps that's how the idea of a 'solitary' god got started.

Mrs. Eberle: Would such manipulation be appropriate on the part of a Bodhisattva?

Master: Things had gone to an extreme and Jesus was trying to rescue people. But in attempting to correct the situation, he overcompensated and set up another extreme. He failed to establish the Middle Way. He was not alone in doing that—that is the failing of religions in general.

Mr. Eberle: All religions require belief. Does Buddhism require belief in anything?

Master: Buddhism teaches about cause and effect. If you plant a certain cause, you will reap a certain effect. If you plant causes to become Jewish, you will reap that effect. If you plant causes to become Catholic, you will reap that effect. Buddhist causes yield Buddhist effects, and so forth.

Things are a result of causes and conditions coming together. Therefore, the Buddha does not expound a principle that tends in just one direction, but expresses infinite principles that do not hinder one another and do not hinder the principles of other religions either. Rather, the principles of Buddhism completely include and explicate the principles of other religions, which are all contained within it.

And finally, you should not believe a word of the principles I have been expressing! Are you tired?

Answers: Not tired, but cold.

Master: The reason you are cold is that my explanations have not been warm.

One of the listeners: They have been heart-warming, but not foot-warming.

Master: Then dispense with your feet and just retain your heart.

] 弁

FEBRUARY 24, 1973 | SATURDAY

On Being Clear Before Becoming Involved

[Editor's note: The Master is addressing a disciple who is considering getting involved in a Buddhist dictionary project sponsored by another organization headed by a layperson.] You can get involved in projects for the sake of Buddhism. However, you must have a clear understanding of the issues before you get involved.

First, we are not the servants of a certain layman, and so we do not have to obey his orders when we visit his place.

Second, if we become involved in a project, it has to be of value to Buddhism and make a contribution to Buddhism. However, if people want to do away with the Sangha altogether, insisting that everyone in Buddhism is a scholar, then will there be monastic scholars or only lay scholars?

Third, that conference was held to investigate a multi-lingual dictionary project. Well, who will hold the copyright? Does it belong to Buddhism, or to a private individual? If the copyright belongs to Buddhism, then who will be funding the project? You have to be clear about those issues.

Fourth, after the dictionary is completed, will it be given away free or sold? What are the details involved in that aspect?

Many related questions must be made clear. If you do not make the issues clear, even if you get your own name on the back of the book, of what use is it? If people who do the most work on

TIMELY TEACHINGS

the project get their names printed in the book, then will they be doing it for the sake of fame?

You indicated that you want to become involved in this project, but would you be jumping into it all confused? The plan was that one of you was to have been chairperson at that conference, but what did you gain by having served as chair? ᚦ

MARCH 3, 1973 | SATURDAY

On Publishing a Monthly Buddhist Journal

Today we received a copy of a Buddhist journal published in Taiwan. The feature story highlights a commencement exercise held at a Buddhist Academy. This journal is quite fine; it is first-rate among Buddhist journals. It is well organized and nicely laid out. Those of you who read Chinese can take a look at it; there is only one English article in the publication.

Also in this issue of the journal, each of the graduates is introduced briefly—about two hundred words per article. The introductions describe where each graduate is from, and describe his or her personality, cultivation, and talents. The articles are eloquent and clear. We can write to the journal's editor and ask permission to reprint these biographical sketches in our monthly journal *Vajra Bodhi Sea*, which will help promote young people in Buddhism.

From the contents of this journal, we can assess what the Dharma Master who heads that Academy is doing in Taiwan. It's a pity the rules are a little lax; if they can step up and be more vigorous, then they will do even better. Their Buddhist Studies programs are coming along nicely, however.

In publishing a journal, we should make progress instead of pro-crastinating. You should definitely keep ahead of the schedule. Do not wait till the end of the month to send the journal to our subscribers. Publishing a journal is part of the Buddhadharma, part of turning the Dharma wheel. We should ask ourselves: "When this journal gets into the hands of the readers, what benefit will it bring to them? What kind of resolve will it inspire in the reader?" We should focus on that. ◖

NOVEMBER 23, 1973 | FRIDAY EVENING

On the Importance of the
Dharma Flower Sutra

[Historical note: In November, 1973, the first volume of an English translation of the *Dharma Flower Sutra* (*Lotus Sutra*) was published. The translator was Bhikshu Heng Qian.]

Master: The *Dharma Flower Sutra* contains wonderful and inter-penetrating principles. It is recognized as the sutra that describes how to become a Buddha. Only when someone who investigates the Buddhadharma has understood this sutra can he or she be said to understand Buddhism. Therefore, if you truly wish to study Buddhism, or if you want to become a Buddha in the future, you should own a copy of this sutra. When you aren't reading it yourself, you can give it to your friends or relatives. It makes a most valuable gift. This is an opportunity no one should miss. ⊣

DECEMBER 2, 1973 | SUNDAY EVENING

On Finding Ways to Help Buddhism Flourish

Every Friday we are going to hold a meeting to investigate and discuss true principles. Everyone is welcome to take part and bring up questions for people to investigate. You should not regard this as an ordinary event. In the future if this is done on a large scale, people of all religions can get together to investigate how to help the world, how to spread Buddhism throughout the world, and various other questions.

So, from now on, every Friday we will hold this meeting from 12:30-2:30. During the meeting, everyone should express his or her opinions so we can look into them together. You shouldn't wait for one certain individual to bring up questions for discussion. Everyone has a share in this. It will be an excellent opportunity for you to express your wisdom. Each one of us should reflect, "How can I be a true Bodhisattva and a vigorous cultivator?" We shouldn't let the days pass in vain, eating our one meal a day, sleeping every night, and translating sutras or listening to explanations of the sutras every day as part of the daily routine. There's not much point in passing our lives that way. We must make new progress. "Since I'm a Buddhist disciple, I must do something to help Buddhism expand and grow. Otherwise, how can I face the Buddhas of the ten directions and the three periods of time?" We should constantly be thinking about how we can propagate Buddhism and make it flourish.

XII. Propagating the Dharma

Also, we should all make vows. Guo Mo made a vow not to talk. We should all make vows not to let it rain or snow within a ten-mile radius of the monks doing Three Steps One Bow. They cover a distance of five miles each day, so a ten-mile radius should be sufficient. Everyone should make this vow because that's the way it must be; it cannot be any other way. It is similar to how earthquakes are not permitted to occur. When we bow to the Buddhas or recite the Buddha's name, we can dedicate the merit so that the gods, dragons, and the rest of the eightfold pantheon of ghosts and spirits will not allow it to rain or snow within ten miles of the bowing monks, because they are already undergoing too much suffering. ⊣

JANUARY 29, 1974 | TUESDAY EVENING

On Not Permitting a Third Person to Join the Two Bowing Monks

After those two monks began their Three Steps One Bow pilgrimage, Guo Yi also wanted to make a resolve to follow in their footsteps, literally. It's a good thing I didn't let her go. Otherwise, the two monks would surely have failed in their pilgrimage. Why is this? They would be bowing on the one hand and worrying about how to help this nun on the other. If there were a nun bowing behind them, both sides would have had false thoughts about helping each other, which would have detracted from the sincerity of their resolve. That's why I didn't okay this. I didn't give my permission for this.

Later, another monk, Guo Hui, wanted to go bow with the two. Although this wish was not bad, it's easier to take care of the matters of food and shelter when there are only two people. There is just enough room for two in the tent. There is not enough room for three people, even if they sit up, and the tent would be very stuffy and suffocating. Therefore, I didn't allow Guo Hui to join them, either.

If two people bow, they have a certain amount of merit. If three people bow, the world will not say, "Oh, look, there's one more!" and have more faith as a result. Such a bowing pilgrimage influences people to make a commitment to realize *bodhi*. Two people are sufficient to make this influence felt; there is no need for a third person. ⏹

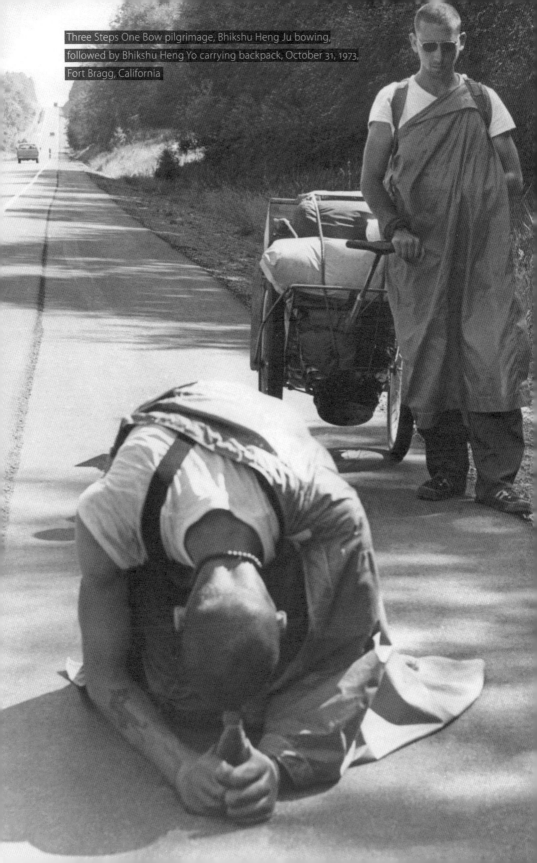

Three Steps One Bow pilgrimage, Bhikshu Heng Ju bowing, followed by Bhikshu Heng Yo carrying backpack, October 31, 1973, Fort Bragg, California

GLOSSARY

A **Amitābha**

"Limitless Light," name of the Buddha of the Land of Ultimate Bliss.

Amitābha Sutra

a sutra explains the causes and circumstances for rebirth in the Western Land of Ultimate Bliss of Amitābha Buddha. It is the only sutra that Śākyamuni Buddha spoke spontaneously without waiting to be requested.

annihilationism

the non-Buddhist view that existence ends with death and there is no rebirth.

ascetic practices

particularly difficult practices, especially the twelve ascetic (*dhūta*) practices recommended by Śākyamuni Buddha, involving frugality with regard to clothing, food and drink, and shelter.

asura

a "being who likes to fight," one of the meightfold pantheon of ghosts and spirits, found among heavenly beings, human beings, animals, and ghosts.

Avataṃsaka Syllabary

a dharma practiced and taught to the Youth Sudhana (Good Wealth) by the Youth Who Well Knows the Multitude of Skills and found in Chapter 39 of the *Avataṃsaka (Flower Adornment) Sutra*. The syllabary consists of 42 special Sanskrit syllables, whose power and functions are inconceivable and endless. The syllables are recited in a complex ceremony that accompanies recitation of the *Avataṃsaka Sutra*.

B **Bhikshu (*bhikṣu*)**

a fully ordained Buddhist monk, one who leads a pure and celibate life and upholds 250 precepts.

Bhikshuni (*bhikṣuṇī*)

a fully ordained Buddhist nun, one who leads a pure and celibate life and upholds 348 precepts.

birth & death

the state of common, unenlightened beings, who perceive themselves as being born and dying, transmigrating endlessly in the six paths of rebirth.

blessings

the Sixth Patriarch describes blessings:

> A confused person will foster blessings,
>> but not cultivate the Path
> And say, "To practice for the blessings
>> is practice the Path."
> While giving and making offerings
>> brings blessings without limit,
> It is in the mind that the three evils
>> have their origin.
> By seeking blessings you may wish
>> to obliterate offenses
> But in the future, though you are blessed,
>> offenses still remain.

bodhi

awakening, enlightenment, the Way.

bodhi **resolve (*bodhicitta*)**

the resolve to achieve *bodhi* through practice of the Bodhisattva Path. Also translated as *bodhi* mind.

bodhimaṇḍa

"site of enlightenment," any place of Buddhist practice—a temple, a monastery, a hermitage—regardless of its size.

Bodhisattva

an enlightened being who does not enter nirvana but chooses instead to remain in the world and save living beings.

Bodhisattva Path

the path of benefiting, rescuing, and enlightening both oneself and others through cultivating the ‣ Six Perfections and the myriad practices; the foundation of the Great Vehicle (Mahayana) teaching.

Bodhisattva Precepts

Ten Major and Forty-eight Minor Bodhisattva Precepts set forth in the *Brahma Net Sutra* for those who wish to practice the Bodhisattva Path.

Buddha

one who has achieved the ultimate, perfect enlightenment.

Buddhadharma

methods of cultivation taught by the Buddha that lead beings to enlightenment. It is just worldly dharmas; it is also the mind dharmas of all living beings.

Buddhahood

the state of perfect enlightenment of a Buddha.

C   ***chan* session**

a period of time devoted entirely to meditation.

cultivation

the practical application of the methods taught by the Buddha that lead to enlightenment, likened to the process of cultivating a field, starting from plowing and planting and resulting in fruition, harvest, and storage.

D   **Dharma (Buddhadharma)**

the teachings of the Buddhas; the Truth.

dharma door

an entrance to the Dharma, a method of practice leading to enlightenment.

Devadatta

Śākyamuni Buddha's cousin and his rival in life after life.

Dharma-ending Age

the last of the three ages of Dharma. After the Buddha speaks the Dharma, there follows the Proper Dharma Age, which lasts 1000 years. It is followed by the Dharma Image Age, which also lasts 1000 years. The last period is the Dharma-ending Age, the age strong in fighting, which lasts for 10,000 years. During this age, the understanding and practice of the Buddha's teachings gradually decline and disappear.

Dharma Flower Sutra (Lotus Sutra)

a major Mahayana sutra spoken in the last period of the Buddha's teaching, in which the Buddha proclaims the ultimate principles of the Dharma, uniting all previous teachings.

Dharma Master

a teacher of Dharma, a respectful term of address for members of the Sangha. Dharma protector (1) a layperson who provides necessities and assistance to monks and nuns, enabling them to devote themselves to spiritual practice; (2) ghosts and other spiritual beings that protect the Triple Jewel. ▸ eightfold pantheon.

Dharma Realm

the enlightened world, the totality of the realm of the Buddhas

Dharma-selecting eye

the ability to discriminate between what is proper Dharma and what is not.

dhyāna

a Sanskrit word that translates as "stilling one's thoughts" and refers to meditation. ▸ *chan* in Chinese, zen in Japanese.

E **Earth Store Bodhisattva**

one of the Four Great Bodhisattvas, known for his filial piety and for his great vows to rescue beings from the hells.

Earth Store Sutra (Sutra of the Past Vows of Earth Store Bodhisattva)

the sutra of filial piety, spoken by the Buddha for his mother, Lady Māyā, in the Heaven of the Thirty-three.

eightfold pantheon

eight kinds of spiritual beings who protect the Dharma, namely gods, dragons, *yakṣas* (speedy ghosts), *gandharvas* (incense-inhaling spirits), *asuras* (beings who like to fight), *garuḍas* (great eagle-like birds), *kinnaras* (musical spirits), and *mahoragas* (huge snake-spirits).

enlightenment

it means enlightening to one's own mind, that is "understanding the mind and seeing the nature."

eon

usually the translation of the Sanskrit word ▸ *kalpa*.

F   **false thoughts**

idle, confused thoughts of the conscious mind that obstruct one's inherent wisdom.

five desires

the five desires can refer to the five defiling sense objects—forms, sounds, smells, tastes, and tangible objects—or to wealth, sex, fame, food, and sleep.

five *skandhas*

the five psycho-physical components that constitute a sentient being: form, feeling, thinking, formations, and consciousness. The Sanskrit word *skandha* means "heap" or "aggregate."

Flower Adornment (Avataṃsaka) Sutra

the king of kings of sutras spoken for Bodhisattvas upon the Buddha's enlightenment.

four assemblies

Bhikshus, Bhikshunis, *upāsakas*, and *upāsikās*.

G   *gandharva*

an incense-inhaling, music-making spirit that belongs to the ▸ eightfold pantheon.

god (*deva*)

any of the beings inhabiting various heavens and possessed of long life spans and supernatural powers, though not immortal, omnipotent, or enlightened. Those who generate appropriate good karma are reborn in the heavens; however, gods eventually die and are reborn in lower realms according to their karma.

good roots

accumulated good deeds done within the Buddhadharma. "Planting" good roots leads to the reaping of good rewards in the future. Good roots planted in the past bring rewards now or in the future.

Great Compassion Mantra

one of the most widely used and most efficacious of all Buddhist mantras, the Great Compassion Mantra is a Dharma taught by Guanyin Bodhisattva, and teachings on it are found in the *Dhāraṇī Sutra*.

Great Compassion Repentance

a ceremony associated with Guanshiyin Bodhisattva that involves bowing, repentance for negative karma created since time without beginning, recitation of the Great Compassion Mantra, and the making of vows. This ceremony is held daily at the monasteries of Dharma Realm Buddhist Association.

Guanyin (Guanshiyin) Bodhisattva

the Bodhisattva of Great Compassion, whose name means "Observer of the Sounds of the World" (Sanskrit: Avalokiteśvara)

H ***Heart Sutra***

this brief sutra spoken by the Buddha, whose full title is the Heart of the *Prajñā-Pāramitā-Sūtra*, discusses emptiness and expresses the perfection of wisdom.

J **Jade Emperor**

a deity revered in Daoism and popular Chinese religion, known as God in Christianity and as Śakra or Indra in the Hindu pantheon, lord of the Heaven of the Thirty-three.

K ***kalpa***

the Sanskrit word *kalpa* means "a long span of time" and is often translated as "eon".

$$1 \ kalpa = 139{,}000 \ \text{years}$$
$$1{,}000 \ kalpas = 1 \ \text{small} \ kalpa$$
$$20 \ \text{small} \ kalpas = 1 \ \text{middle-sized} \ kalpa$$
$$4 \ \text{medium} \ kalpas = 1 \ \text{great} \ kalpa$$

karmic obstacles

obstructions or hindrances from past deeds which obstruct one from attaining enlightenment

King Yama

the ruler and judge of the underworld who passes judgment on all the dead. King Yama has a stern appearance and an uncompromising attitude, but the heart of a Bodhisattva.

kumbhāṇḍa ghost

a barrel-shaped ghost that gives people nightmares and may paralyze them by sitting on top of them.

L **Land of Ultimate Bliss (Sukhāvatī)**

the Western Paradise or Pure Land created by Amitābha Buddha's forty-eight vows. Beings who sincerely recite his name may be reborn there.

Lotus Sutra (Dharma Flower Sutra)

a major Mahayana sutra spoken in the last period of the Buddha's teaching, in which the Buddha proclaims the ultimate principles of the Dharma, uniting all previous teachings.

M **mantra**

phrases of sound whose primary meanings are not cognitive, but on a spiritual level that transcends ordinary linguistic understanding.

merit and virtue

inner humility is merit and outer practice of reverence is virtue. Not being separate from one's own pure nature is merit and correct use of one's own pure nature is virtue.

Mencius (Mengzi)

a Chinese philosopher and sage (c. 371 - 289 B.C.E.), who transmitted and further developed the philosophy of Confucius.

Middle Way

the Buddhist concept of moderation, which advocates avoiding extremes by balancing oneself in the midst of dualities.

Mount Sumeru

the Sanskrit word Sumeru means "Wonderfully High." It is the central mountain of every world-system.

N *nirvana*

a state of ultimate tranquility realized by enlightened sages.

O **Om Mani Padme Hum (*oṃ maṇi padme hūṃ*)**

the six syllabled mantra of the Bodhisattva of compassion, Guanshiyin or Avalokiteśvara.

P   **Path**

the spiritual path of cultivation; the ultimate truth realized through following that path (Chinese: *dao*).

prajñā

transcendental wisdom. There are three kinds of *prajñā*: literary, contemplative, and ultimate.

prajñā pāramitā

the perfection of transcendental wisdom.

precepts

rules of ethical conduct set forth by the Buddha to help cultivators regulate their bodies, mouths, and minds. In Buddhism, there are 5 precepts for laypeople, 10 precepts for novices, 250 precepts for fully ordained monks and 348 precepts for fully ordained nuns, and 10 major and 48 minor Bodhisattva precepts for those who bring forth the Bodhisattva resolve.

Precept Platform

the area where the precepts are transmitted; the site of ordination.

Proper Dharma

the Teachings of the Buddhas in their pure, untainted, and uncompromised form where emphasis is on individual morality, group harmony, and actual practice to reach certifiable attainment of sagehood.

R   **recitation session**

a period, usually seven days long, devoted to intensive and continuous recitation the name of a Buddha or a Bodhisattva and sometimes a sutra associated with that Buddha or Bodhisattva.

S   **Sahā**

"endurance," the name of the our world, where beings endure suffering and even regard it as bliss.

samādhi

a state of concentration attained through meditation and other practices. There are many types and levels of *samādhi*.

Śākyamuni (Buddha)

the historical Buddha of this world who was born in India as Prince Siddhārtha Gautama over 2,500 years ago.

Sangha

the order of Buddhist monks and nuns.

Esoteric School

the study and practice of mantras and other esoteric methods.

Six Perfections

the practices of Bodhisattvas, also called the Six Pāramitās, they are: giving, holding precepts, patience, vigor, *samādhi*, and wisdom.

Sixth Patriarch

Great Master Huineng (Tang dynasty, 628-713 C.E.), the Sixth Buddhist Patriarch in China, whose teachings are recorded in the *Sixth Patriarch's Dharma Jewel Platform Sutra*.

Sudden Teaching

the teaching of sudden and instantaneous enlightenment taught by the Sixth Patriarch.

Śūraṅgama Sutra

one of the most important Mahayana sutras and the first sutra to disappear in the Dharma-ending Age, this sutra discusses the Śūraṅgama Samādhi, contains the Śūraṅgama Mantra, and has a cautionary section on demonic states of mind that may occur in meditation.

sutra

a Buddhist scripture that consists of discourses spoken by Buddhas, Bodhisattvas, or other enlightened disciples of the Buddhas.

T **ten directions**

north, south, east, west, northeast, northwest, southeast, southwest, above, and below. This phrase is used to denote "all directions."

Ten (Wisdom) Powers

(1) The wisdom power to distinguish principle from nonprinciple. (2) The wisdom power to know the retributions for karma created in the three periods of time. (3) The wisdom power to know all *dhyānas*, liberations, and *samādhis*. (4) The wisdom power to know the levels of the faculties of all sentient beings. (5) The wisdom power to know the various understandings. (6) The wisdom power to know the various realms. (7) The wisdom power to know where all paths lead. (8) The wisdom power of the unobstructed heavenly eye. (9) The wisdom power to know previous lives and the state of nonoutflows. (10) The wisdom power to eternally sever habits.

Tripiṭaka

the Buddhist canon, which is classified into three *piṭakas* ("baskets," "stores," "treasuries")-sutras, *vinaya* (moral code), and *śāstras* (commentaries).

Triple Jewel

the Buddhas (fully enlightened beings), the Dharma (the teachings of Buddhas), and the Sangha (the community of monks and nuns, who may be either sages or ordinary people, who have renounced the household life and cultivate the Path).

U **Universal Door Chapter**

the twenty-fifth chapter in the *Dharma Flower Sutra*. It describes the spiritual powers of Guanyin Bodhisattva and the responses gained from praying to that Bodhisattva.

V *vajra*

an indestructible substance usually represented by diamond, with the qualities of being "durable," "luminous," and "able to cut."

Vajra (Diamond) Sutra

one of the most popular Buddhist sutras, the *Vajra Prajñā Pāramitā Sutra* explains how the Bodhisattva relies on the perfection of wisdom to teach and transform beings.

Y **Yongjia, Great Master (665-713 C.E.)**

a Chan Master in Tang dynasty China who become enlightened upon reading the *Vimalakīrti Sutra*, was certified by the Sixth Patriarch, and later wrote the "Song of Enlightenment."

DHARMA REALM BUDDHIST ASSOCIATION BRANCH MONASTERIES

Dharma Realm Buddhist Association
The City of Ten Thousand Buddhas

4951 Bodhi Way, Ukiah, CA 95482 USA
Tel (707) 462-0939
Fax (707) 462-0949
cttb@jps.net
www.drba.org

Buddhist Text Translation Society

4951 Bodhi Way, Ukiah, CA 95482 USA
www.bttsonline.org

Instilling Goodness Elementary and
Developing Virtue Secondary Schools

4951 Bodhi Way, Ukiah, CA 95482 USA
Tel (707) 468-3896(girls)
Fax (707) 468-1138 (boys)
instillgood@drba.org

Dharma Realm Buddhist University

4951 Bodhi Way, Ukiah, CA 95482 USA
Tel (707) 468-9112
drbu@drba.org

The International Translation Institute

1777 Murchison Drive,
Burlingame, CA 94010-4504 USA
Tel (650) 692-5912
Fax (650) 692-5056
drbaiti@jps.net

Institute for World Religions /
Berkeley Buddhist Monastery

2304 McKinley Avenue,
Berkeley, CA 94703 USA
Tel (510) 848-3440
paramita@drba.org

The City of the Dharma Realm

1029 West Capitol Avenue,
West Sacramento, CA 95691 USA
Tel (916) 374-8268
Fax (916) 374-8234
drbacdr@jps.net

Avatamsaka Vihara

9601 Seven Locks Road,
Bethesda, MD 20817-9995 USA
Tel & Fax (301) 469-8300
hwa_yean88@msn.com

Blessings, Prosperity, and
Longevity Monastery

4140 Long Beach Boulevard,
Long Beach, CA 90807 USA
Tel (562) 595-4966

Gold Mountain Monastery

800 Sacramento Street,
San Francisco, CA 94108 USA
Tel (415) 421-6117
Fax (415) 788-6001
drbagmm@jps.net

Gold Sage Monastery

11455 Clayton Road, San Jose, CA 95127 USA
Tel (408) 923-7243
Fax (408) 923-1064
drbagsm@jps.net

Gold Summit Monastery

233 1st Avenue W., Seattle, WA 98119 USA
Tel (206) 284-6690
Fax (206) 284-6918

Gold Wheel Monastery

235 N. Avenue 58, Los Angeles,
CA 90042 USA
Tel (323) 258-6668
drbagwm@pacbell.net

Long Beach Monastery

3361 East Ocean Boulevard,
Long Beach, CA 90803 USA
Tel (562) 438-8902
drbalbsm@aol.com

Gold Buddha Monastery

248 East 11th Avenue,
Vancouver B.C., V5T 2C3 CANADA
Tel (604) 709-0248
Fax (604) 684-3754
drbagbm@mdi.ca

Avatamsaka Monastery

1009 4th Ave. S.W., Calgary,
AB T2P OK8 CANADA
Tel (403) 234-0644
ava@nucleus.com

**Dharma Realm Buddhist Books
Distribution Society**

11th Floor, 85 Chung-hsiao E. Road,
Sec. 6, Taipei TAIWAN ROC
Tel (02) 2786-3022
Fax (02) 2786-2674
drbbds@ms1.seeder.net

Amitabha Monastery

7 Su-chien-hui, Chih-nan Village,
Shou-feng, Hualien County TAIWAN ROC
Tel (03) 865-1956
Fax (03) 7980-1272

Dharma Realm Guan Yin Sagely Monastery

161 Jalan Ampang, 50450 Kuala Lumpur
MALAYSIA
Tel (03) 2164-8055
Fax (03) 2163-7118

Fa Yuan Sagely Monastery

1, Jalan Utama, Taman Serdang Raya,
43300 Seri Kembangan, Selangor MALAYSIA
Tel (03) 8948-5688

Lotus Vihara

136, Jalan Sekolah, 45600 Batang Berjuntai,
Selangor MALAYSIA
Tel (03) 3271-9439

**Malaysia Dharma Realm Buddhist
Association Penang Branch**

32-32C, Jalan Tan Sri Teh Ewe Lim,
11600 Jelutong, Penang MALAYSIA
Tel (04) 281-7728
Fax (04) 281-7798

Prajna Guanyin Sagely Monastery

Batu 5-1/2 Jalan Sungai Besi,
Salak Selatan, 57100 Kuala Lumpur MALAYSIA
Tel (03) 7982-6560
Fax (03) 7980-1272
pgysm1@gmail.com